iWork for Seniors

A RIDICULOUSLY SIMPLE GUIDE TO PRODUCTIVITY ON YOUR MAC

Scott La Counte

RIDICULOUSLY SIMPLE BOOKS
ANAHEIM, CALIFORNIA
www.RidiculouslySimpleBooks.com

Table of Contents

***Disclaimer**: Please note, while every effort has been made to ensure accuracy, this book is not endorsed by Apple, Inc. and should be considered unofficial.*

Pages for Mac

INTRODUCTION

Pages is powerful software, and if you get a Mac, it's free. But let's face it: you've probably spent most of your life using Word—or if you were a renegade, WordPerfect.

For a Mac user, Pages can make your documents really shine...but first you need to know how to use it. This guide will help!

Instead of spending hundreds of pages on functions you probably will never use, it shows you what you really want to know: the basics.

In no time, you'll be creating visually stunning documents!

It will show you the ropes—including how to do all those things you are used to doing in Microsoft Word- and help you with some of the features you may not even know about.

Ready to get started? Let's go!

Note: This guide is based off of the bestselling series The Ridiculously Simple Guide to Pages For Mac. It has an added section on accessibility

[1]

The Basics

This chapter will cover:

- How to get Pages
- Opening your first document
- Pages crash course
- Formatting text
- Layouts and styles

How To Get Pages

Depending on how you acquired your Mac, you may or may not have Pages already. Getting it is easy. And even better: getting it is free! (you can see if you have it by going into the Launchpad from the dock and searching for Pages).

There's one catch: not all Macs are supported. But most are. MacOS 10.14 is required to run Pages, which means you must have one of the following computers:

- MacBook: Early 2015 or newer
- MacBook Air: Mid 2012 or newer
- MacBook Pro: Mid 2012 or newer
- Mac Mini: Late 2012 or newer
- iMac: Late 2012 or newer
- iMac Pro
- Mac Pro: Late 2013 or newer; Mid 2010 or Mid 2012 models require a Metal-capable GPU

As long as you have one of those, then you can go to the App Store (it's in your Launchpad). Pages is a digital download only—you cannot obtain a physical copy of it. The download is a few hundred MB.

From there, type in Pages in the search, and hit the return key.

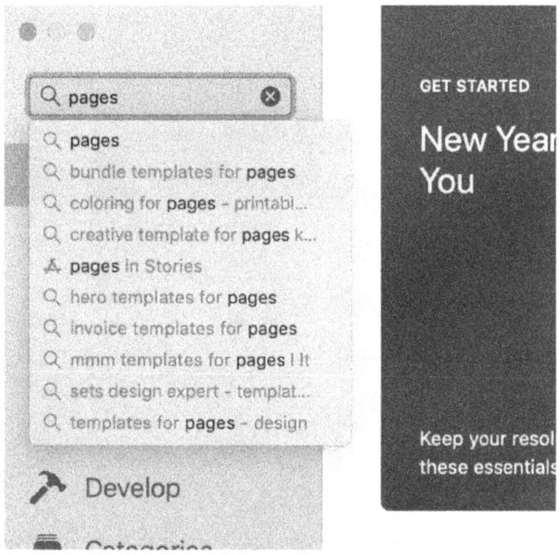

If you have it, the return result will have an Open button; if you don't have it, the result will show a Get button. When you click Get, you'll be prompted to put in your Apple ID and password; if you don't have an Apple ID, then follow the onscreen instructions to get one (this is free).

Running Pages for the First Time

When you first open Pages, you'll be asked if you want to use iCloud. I recommend you do; this makes it easy to save and open documents across all devices—if you are writing a document on your phone, for instance, you can open that document and continue working on it from your tablet—it's all very seamless and doesn't require anything extra on your part once it's set up.

If you set up iCloud, you can even access and type documents right in your browser—there's nothing else to install on your computer, which means "technically" you could use Pages on a Windows computer or even a Chromebook or Android device—I'll show you how at the end of this chapter.

The Pages Crash Course

The first time you use Pages, you'll get a brief tutorial. You can either watch it or skip it.

Each time you open Pages, you'll be greeted with a directory box that asks you if you want to open a document or if you want to create a new one. We'll be working off a new document in this chapter, so click "New Document" in the lower left corner.

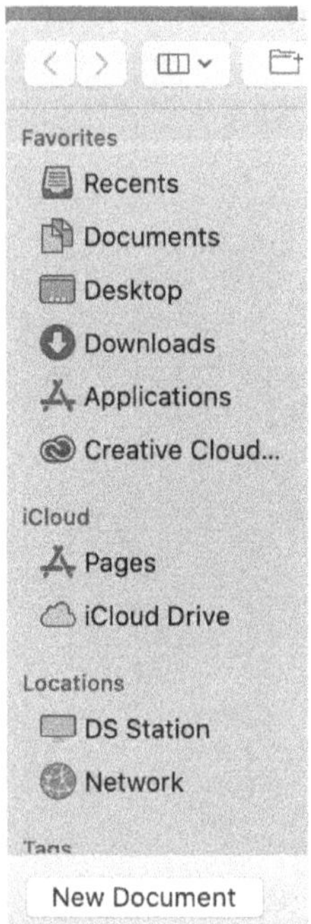

The next box you'll see is all the available templates you can use. A template is a premade document that you can add text into. For example, if you want to write a resume, you can use the resume Template, and you would just keep the formatting but type over the text that's there with the text that matches you. Templates are listed under categories.

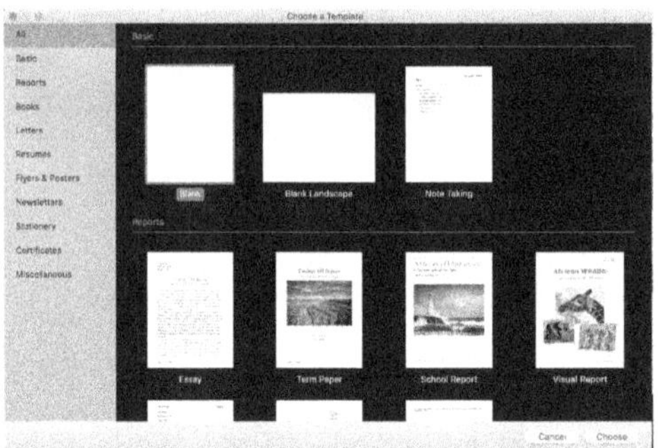

If you don't want to start with a template, then click on the first option (which says Blank).

First time users of Pages are often a little disappointed the first time they use Pages; if you've Word, then you have ribbons and menus and options everywhere! Pages looks pretty bare next to that.

Don't worry—looks can be deceiving; there are plenty of options when you know how to find them, and I'll show you each of them in this book.

If you feel overwhelmed already because there are options, you can hide that side panel by clicking on the Format button in the upper right corner.

Now that you have a blank screen, let's go over the very basics of Pages.

SELECT

To select a single word, move your mouse over it and click twice.

SELECT PARAGRAPH

To select all words in the paragraph, click three times over any word in the paragraph you want to select.

SELECT ALL

Select All selects everything in your document. It's a very powerful command! It brings up the same options as Select, but any changes you make will be applied to the entire document.

To Select All, use Command + A on your keyboard.

SELECT OPTIONS

Now that you have the text selected, what do you do? If you click with two fingers on your trackpad or mouse, then the options box comes up. We'll go over what these options are as we continue in the book.

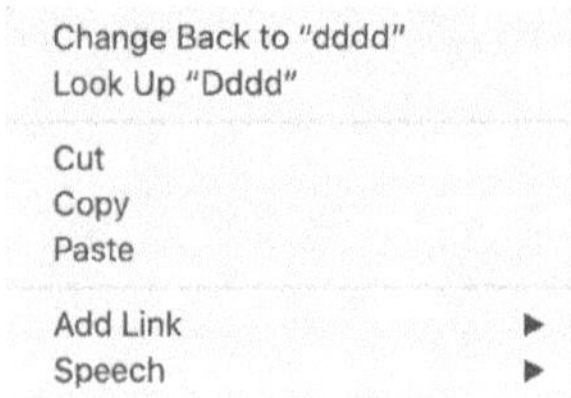

Cut, Copy and Paste

To copy and paste words (and images, tables and charts) quicker, you can use keyboard shortcuts.
Selecting content and hitting COMMAND + C will copy it.
Selecting content and hitting COMMAND + X will cut it.
And hitting COMMAND + V will copy the content anywhere you want it in the document.

Find and Replace

Find and Replace is a handy little feature in Pages that allows you to replace your selection with alternatives.

Let's say you just wrote the opening chapter to your first book. But once you are done, you realize you want your character to be a 'her' instead of a 'him,' and you want to replace all of the "he said" with "she said." It can be done in seconds!

Go to edit from your menu bar, and select Find > Find.

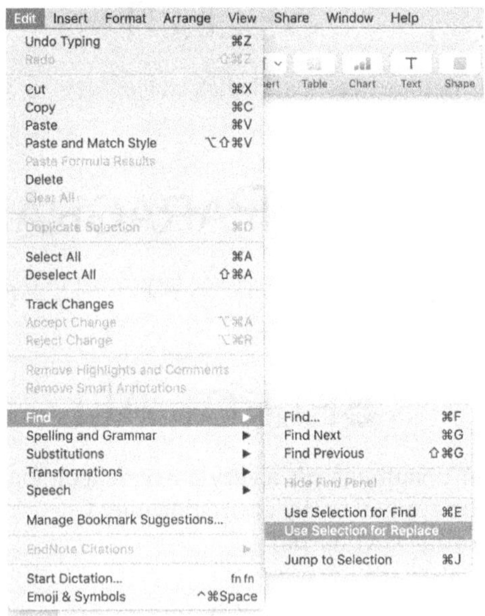

From here you can find all the uses of the word you want to find, but you can also click the down arrow on the left side and select Find & Replace. This lets you search for a word (top line) and replace the word once it finds it (bottom line). When you have both the find and replace word added, then you can click Replace & Find.

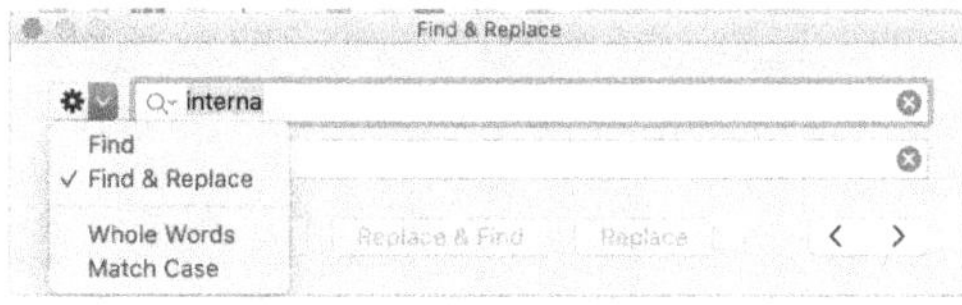

DEFINE

Pages has a handy little dictionary built in. You can select any word, tap the trackpad twice to bring up the options menu, and tap Look Up to see the definition of any word.

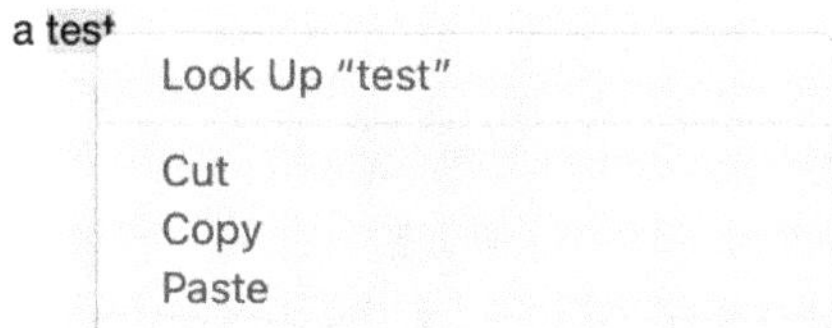

The dictionary will give you multiple definitions (and a thesaurus); even more, you can select options at the bottom to see movies related to the word, Siri Knowledge (which is encyclopedic information), apps related to it, and more!

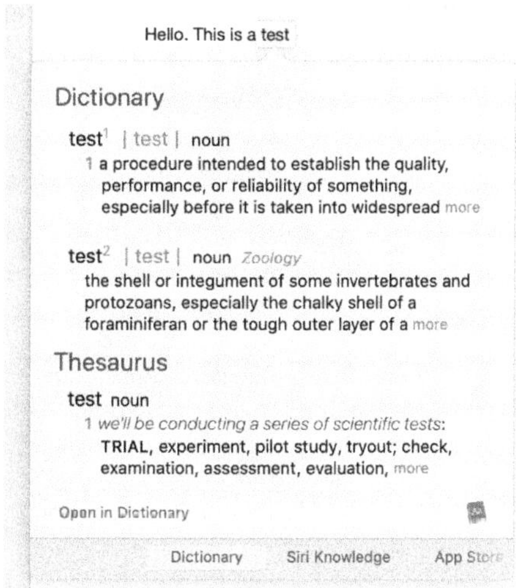

COPY STYLE

The Style command lets you copy and paste styles, like the Microsoft Word format painter feature. If you ever want to make a piece of text look like another, just select the text with the format you'd like to copy, click Format > Copy Style; then select the text you want to alter and click Format > Paste Style. This can be a major time saver!

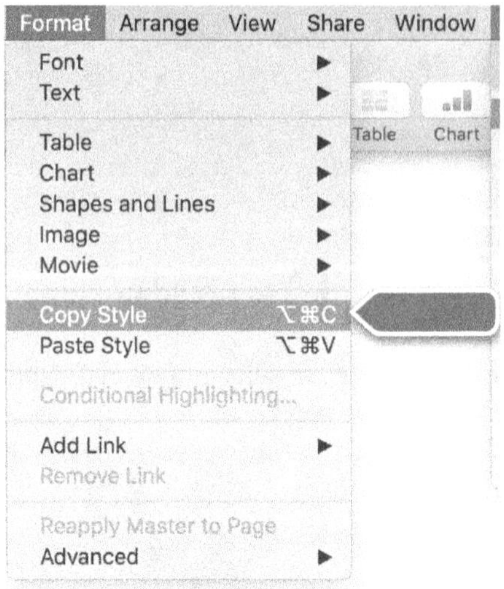

INSERTING HYPERLINKS

If you want to insert a hyperlink to an internet resource, just type out the link. Pages automatically detects hyperlinks and will insert the link for you. To edit the link or to change the displayed text, just click the link and then tap Link Settings. Here you can edit the link itself, change the text displayed, or remove the link altogether.

If you aren't typing a web address, but want to link it to a web address (for example, you are typing: "I go to UCLA" and you want to provide a hyperlink to UCLA), then select the word you want to hyperlink and click with two fingers to bring up the options. From here, just click Add Link and select the kind of link you want to add. You can edit and remove it the same way as in the previous paragraph.

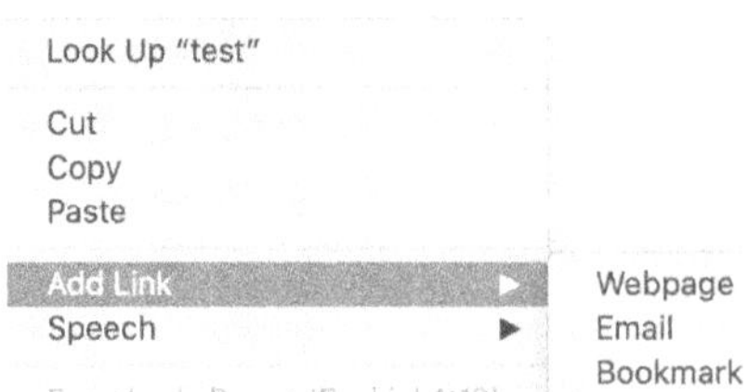

UNDO/REDO

If you mess up (for example you delete a paragraph that you shouldn't have) you can Undo it by going to Edit > Undo; you can also redo it under the same menu.

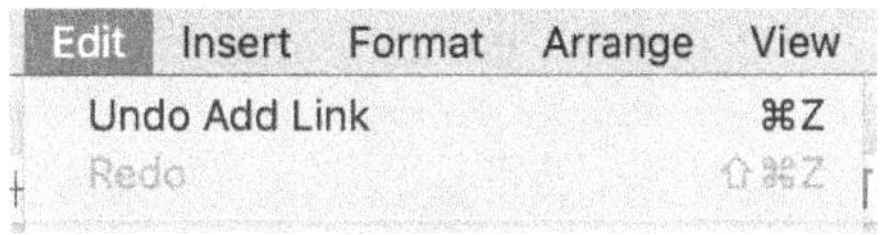

HANDS-ON EXERCISE

This exercise will help you familiarize yourself with the commands we've covered in this section. Just follow the steps below, referring to the above if needed.

Open a blank document.

Type the sentence "The quick brown fox jumps over the lazy dog."

Select the entire sentence.

Copy the sentence.

Tap Enter to start a new line.

Paste the sentence.

In the second sentence, select the word "brown" and replace it with your favorite iPad suggestion.

In the second sentence, add a Phonetics guide to the entire sentence for English learners in the language of your choice (use the guide of your choice). Hint: this sentence can be selected with a triple tap!

Your document should now look like this:

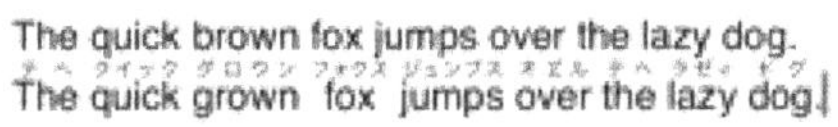

THE FORMATTING TOOLBAR

There are a few menu options to work with in Pages, but in this section, we will be covering the Formatting Toolbar, which is on the right side of your document.

Under Text, it will say "Body" by default. When you click it, you'll see several options. "Body" is normal text in a document—the text you are reading right here would be considered Body Text. Documents have several types of paragraph text; for example, each section of this chapter has a "Heading"—you could just change the font size and make it "look" like a heading, but using a Paragraph Style tells Pages what kind of text it is so it can put together a table of contents later.

Some of the styles will not be very common, "Label Dark" for example.

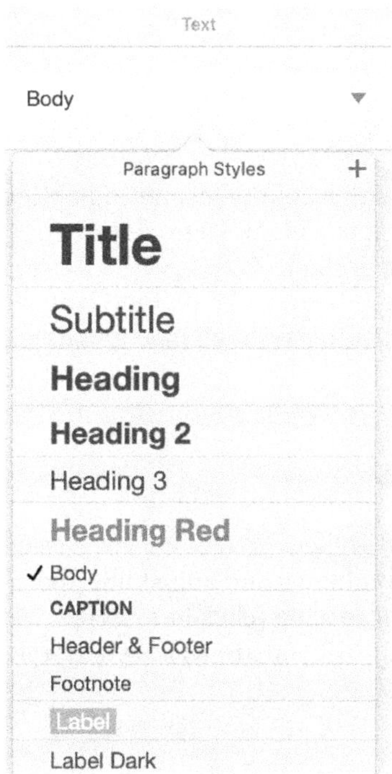

Under this is options for Style, Layout, and More. Let's stay on Style for now, so the next option is Font.

It says 11pt Helvetica; this is the font. If you tap on it, you'll be able to select a new font and adjust the size. Pages offers a healthy font selection, including perennial favorites like Arial, Times New Roman, and Helvetica. Some notable absences include Comic Sans (and yet Papyrus still made the cut), Calibri, and Cambria.

The "regular" dropdown shows you all the style choices for that font (some fonts have different options).

The next three buttons are fairly standard. If you're not familiar with computerized word processing, though, remember B for Bold, I for Italic, and U for underline. The S with a line through it puts a strike across any text you type.

Below this are your alignment buttons. Tap them for options to align your text left, center or right, or justify it. Justified text is text that fills one line exactly. Try it out to see how it works.

The next two buttons are indent buttons. Use them to indent, or to move backwards through indents.

Finally, below this is where you can add bulleted lists and line spacing (if you want to double space, for example).

HANDS-ON EXERCISE

This is exercise will help you practice with all of the formatting options available to you in the formatting toolbar.

Type up a heading and a few lines of text in a blank Pages document (you can also use your "quick brown fox" document from the previous exercise if you prefer).

Change your heading so that it appears in Georgia, 20 pt. font, bold, and underlined. Center the heading.

Change the text under the heading so that it is right aligned and italicized.

More Formatting Options in Styles

LAYOUT

The Layout menu lets you put text into columns and adjust line spacing. Yes, you can use Pages to draft that paper for your picky professor who insists on 1.25 spacing (click indents)!

You can also use layout to create columns (if you are writing a newsletter, for example).

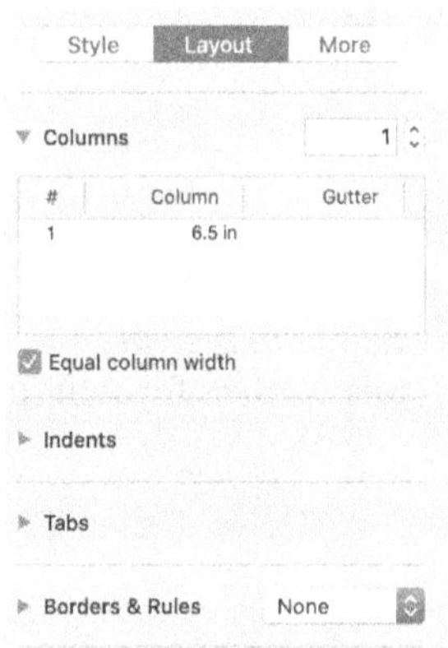

MORE

The More option is what you will use for pagination and hyphenation.

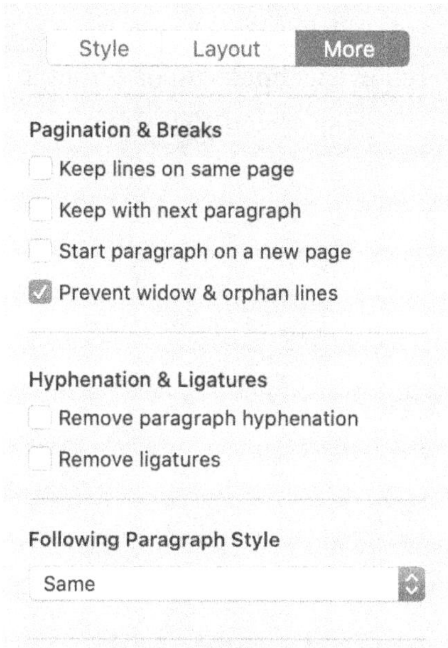

Opening Pages From iCloud

Pages can be run right from your browser; it's great for editing, but for intensive design work, the best solution will be your computer.

To access it from your browser, head to iCloud.com and sign in with your Apple ID.

The first screen you'll see will show you all the things you can do from the cloud; one of them is using Pages. Click it once to open it.

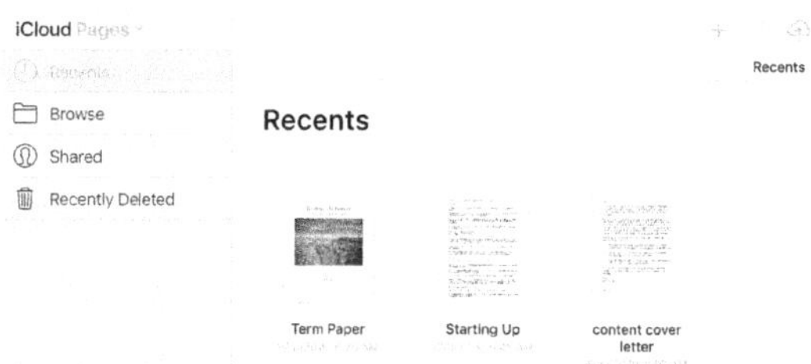

As long as you've been saving your work to the cloud, then any recent docs will show up here, and you can click on their thumbnail once to open them.

You can additionally start a new Doc by clicking on the + button in the upper right corner. This will open up Pages for iCloud. All the features covered in this book can be found in Pages for iCloud as well.

Managing Documents

Saving in Pages is pretty straightforward—especially if you've used Windows before. It's under File > Save.

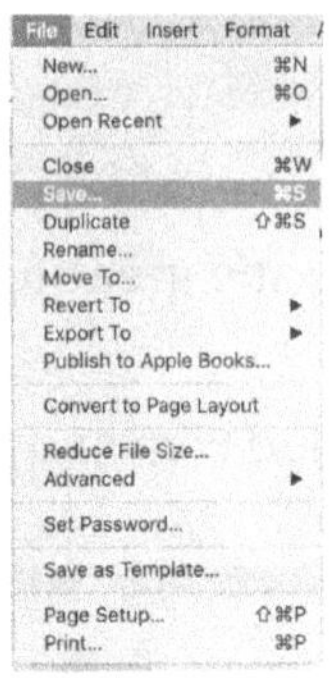

Before we move forward with using other features in Pages, I want to go over the less straightforward ways to manage documents.

Renaming Documents

Renaming documents is very easy. Like with many things in Pages, there's more than one way to do it. The easiest way is when your document is open; just click on the name in the top center of the document.

The next way is File > Rename.

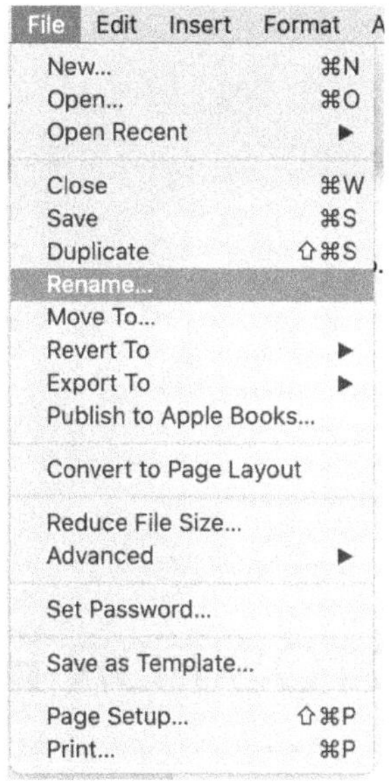

The third way is to find it in Finder, click with two fingers, and select Rename.

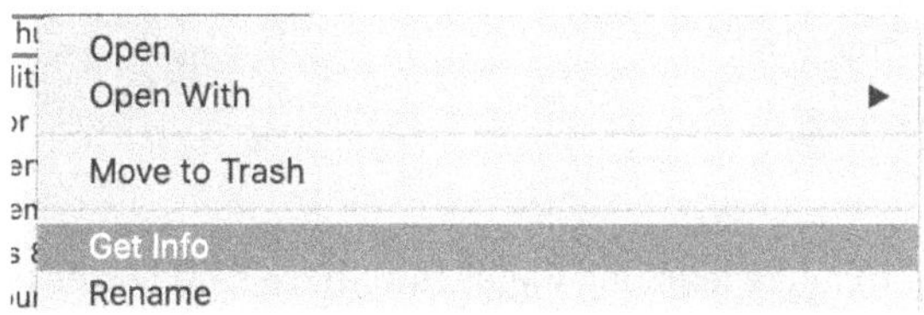

Hands-On Exercise

These exercises are going to get progressively more challenging! Ready to try your hand at some serious formatting?

Open up a blank Pages document.

Copy and paste a chunk of text from somewhere else (I used the Lorem Ipsum generator at lipsum.org to get five paragraphs of filler text).

Hint: you can visit a webpage and copy text the same way you would in Pages. Then, go back to Pages and paste.

Format it so that it displays as 14 pt., justified, bold, double-spaced red Arial.

Format your text so that it is displayed in three columns. (Remember Columns is under layout.)

[2]

PHOTOS FOR PAGES

This chapter will cover:

- Insert image
- Arrange / Rotate / Wrap image
- Edit Mask / Alpha
- Image Styling

As much as possible, I'm trying to make learning Pages fun; there's no better way to make something fun than with photos!

As we go, we'll be learning more about styling tips, but before we get there, we are going to learn about photos—not just about inserting them into the document, but about how to apply more advanced techniques to them.

INSERTING AN IMAGE

Inserting an image can be done several ways. You can copy and paste an image into the document, you can drag a photo into the document, or you can pick it manually.

To pick it manually, you can go to Insert > Choose, and then find the file location.

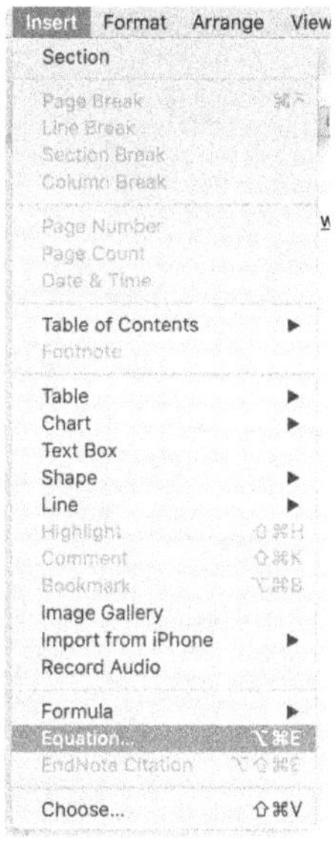

The quicker way to add a photo, however, is from the menu. Click the image button, which shows you all the different media types you can add. Why would it show movies and music? You can't exactly print those out, right? It shows these options because Pages lets you create interactive electronic documents. This section will focus on photos, however. You can get photos by clicking on Photos or Image Gallery (if the photos are in your gallery) or by clicking "Choose" to pick where the photo is located.

If you pick photos, it's not going to show you all of your photos—just the photos in that photos area of your Mac. You could, for example, have a photo on your USB drive. If that's the case, then you'd want to pick "Choose" from the previous menu instead of photos.

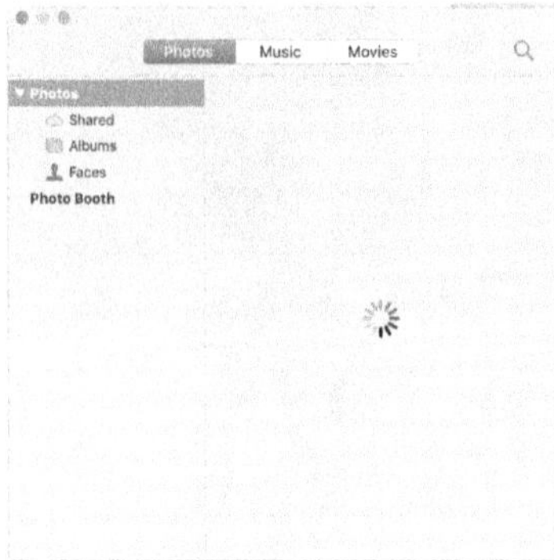

Arranging Images

Resize and Rotate

Once your image is inserted, you can use your mouse to move it, resize it, and rotate it. Resizing is pretty straightforward. Click the image, then move to the corner or side of the image and move the little squares on the edges in and out. To rotate the image you'll do the same thing, but when you get to the corner of the image, press the Command key on your keyboard. This will show you a curved line and also show you the percentage of the rotation as you move the image.

Hint: Looking for images? I often use a website named pexels.com to find public domain (or free to use images).

There's one more way to rotate an image. When you click on the image, you'll notice that the side panel that you used to format text has changed. It's now a new menu with controls to format an image.

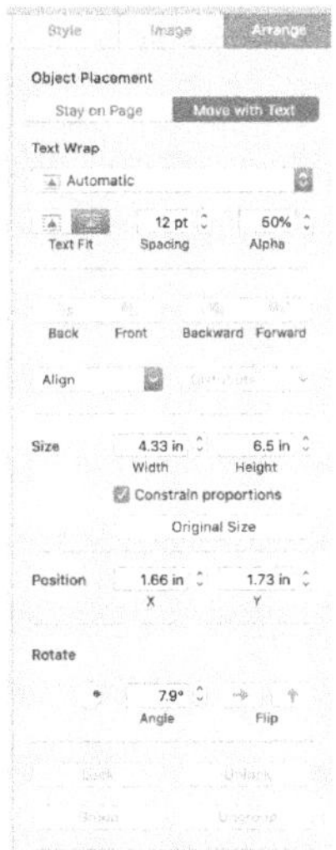

There are three buttons on top of this menu (Style, Image, Arrange); we'll go over the first button in the next section, but for this section, go to Arrange.

On the bottom of this menu, there's a section called Rotate; angle is what you want to use. The mouse is a quick and easy way to rotate your image, but if you want precision, then this is the best method. Next to the Angle button, you can also vertically and horizontally flip the image using the arrows.

Text Wrap and Placement

Let's go back up to the top of the image arrange menu; the first thing you see is Object Placement. The default is Move with Text; this means as you add text above the image, the image moves down. Stay on page means you want it locked into place on the page and it won't move—this is commonly used for watermarks.

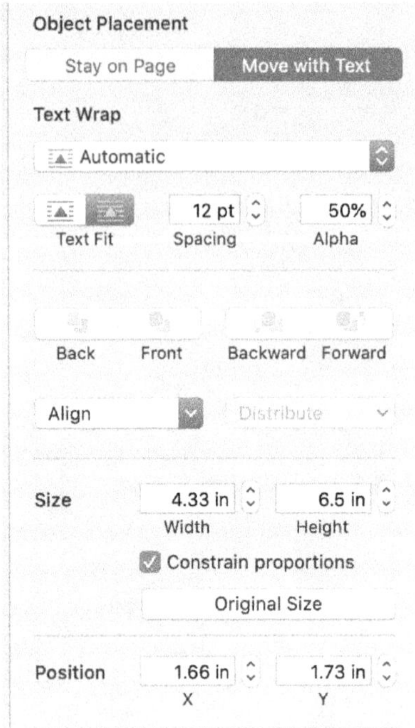

Below this is the Text Wrap. Automatic is the default setting, but if you click on it, you'll notice several other options.

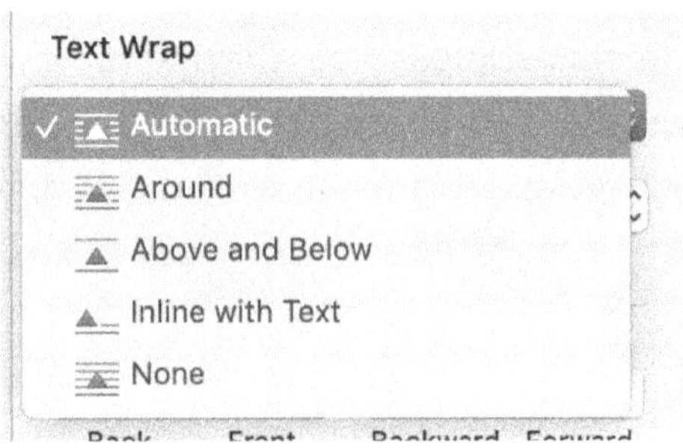

The default option has text above or below the object.

If you want text to wrap around the image, then just click Around.

Notice the white space around the image is kind of tight? If you want it more squared off, then go below the text wrap to Text Fit and you can make it more even with the toggle.

The example below uses the first option under fit.

The next set of options let you pick the size of the image; again, you can do this manually with your mouse, but this lets you be a little more precise.

Finally, the last option lets you pick the placement of the image—if you want it in the middle of the page, for example.

Earlier, I said you could make an image a watermark; great! But you'll notice the options that let you move the image back / forward are greyed out. So how do you make a watermark if you can't move the object behind the text?

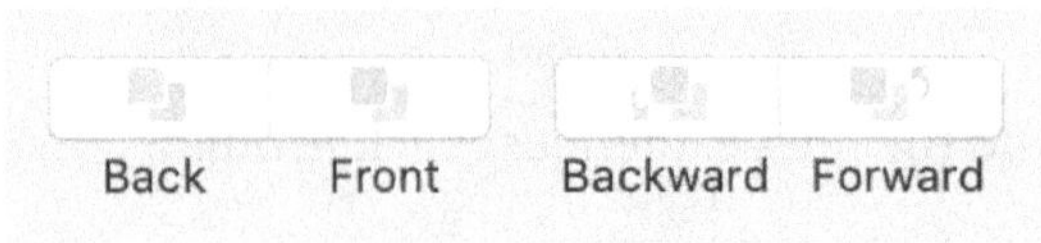

It's tricky. The current mode we are using is Word Processing mode. It's much easier to edit and get everything to align right, but options like these will be missing. To make a watermark, we need it to be in Page Layout mode. We can convert it, but we'll lose all of our text, unfortunately.

To convert it, go to File > Convert to Page Layout.

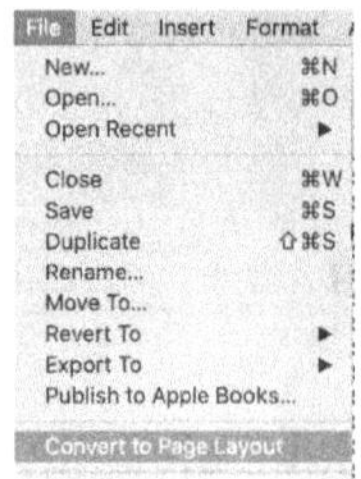

The image can now be moved to the back, but here's the big drawback. Text is now in a text box (see below). That makes dealing with margins and new pages a lot harder. This mode is great for things like fliers; not so good for lengthy documents. So you're out of luck? Not exactly. I'll show you how to add watermarks in a better way later in this chapter.

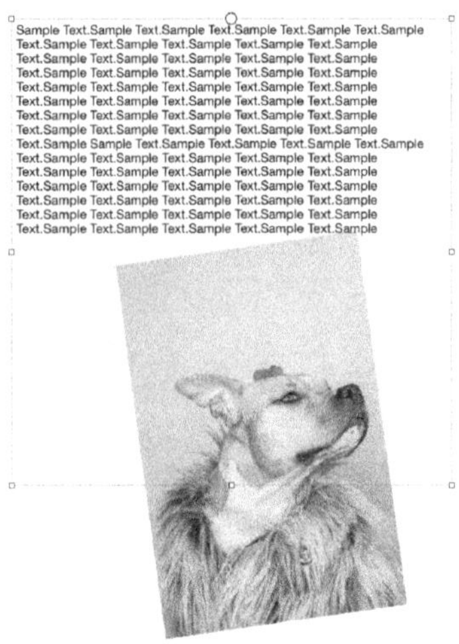

IMAGE GROUPING

There's one last section that's greyed out. Grouping. Grouping is greyed out because you need two images to use it.

Add a second image, then click the image, press command on your keyboard and select the second image; the Group option is no longer greyed out. What grouping does is put two images together, so that when you edit the size, rotation, etc., you are treating the two photos as one image.

If you want to edit just one image, you don't have to ungroup it. You can double click the image to tell Pages that you want to keep them grouped, but you want to make changes to one photo while they are grouped.

WATERMARKS

Earlier, we saw how you couldn't send an object to the background to create a watermark without converting it to Page Layout mode. So that means a word processing document can't have a watermark, right? Nope!

You can create a watermark with something called Section Masters. Once you make all the changes you want to the image and have it where you want it to go, go to Arrange > Section Masters > Move Object to Section Master. It's now a watermark and every new page will show the image.

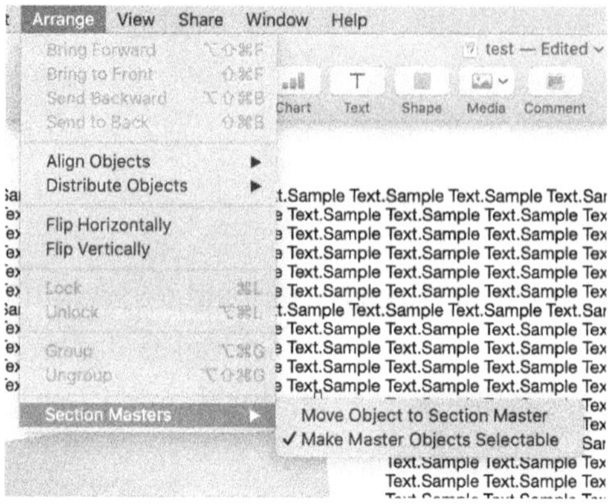

Edit Mask and Alpha

With your image selected (note: if the images are grouped, you need to double click the image you want to edit—you can't edit both images at the same time), select the Image button.

This brings up options for image enhancements. At the bottom is the Adjustments section; this section is pretty self-explanatory - the Exposure and Saturation sliders will change the amount of exposure / saturation in the image. The Enhance button will do an auto enhancement based on what the computer thinks the image should look like (the reset button will undo it).

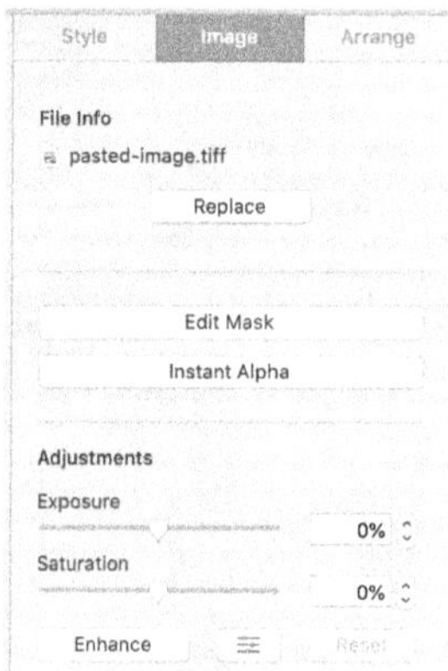

Next to the Enhance button is a control button; this will bring up more adjustment controls.

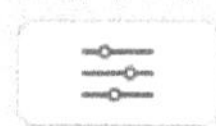

Most people probably won't need this many controls, but it's helpful to know it's there.

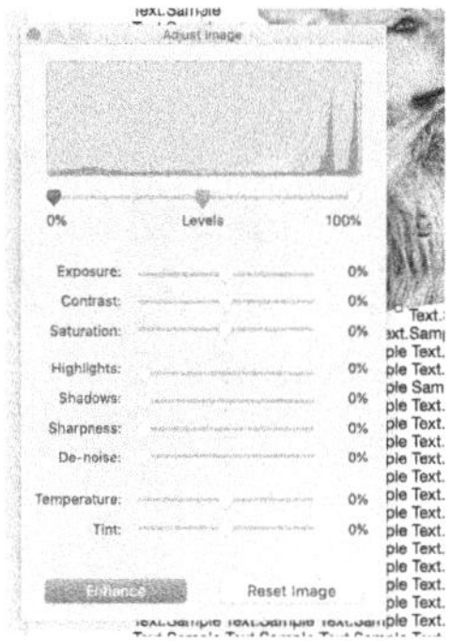

The section that may not be as easy to understand is the top section: Edit Mask and Instant Alpha.

Edit Mask is essentially an image crop. You can use this to cut off parts of the image without resizing it.

Instant Alpha is one of my personal favorite image editing tools. It removes the background of the image. It's great when your image has a very solid background (you're standing against a solid color wall, for example).

One you click on it, the cursor turns to a square box and you click and drag over the areas you want to take out.

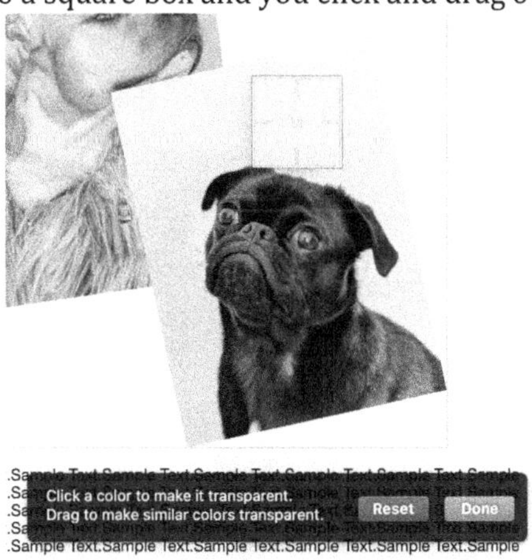

As you click, the sections that are removed will turn a different color to indicate what has been removed. When you're done, let go of the mouse and click the done button.

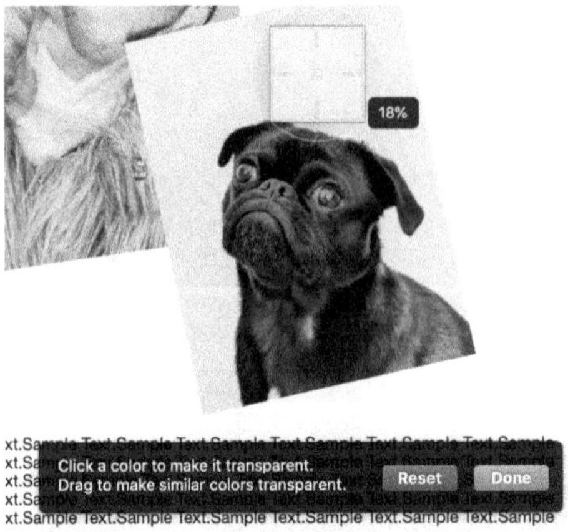

As you remove the background, it is also autocropping; so if you've removed the background from the top, the image has automatically been cropped to accommodate for it.

Styling Your Image

Now that we know how to move an image around, let's add some style to it.
To style your image, tap the image. Style is the first button on the image edit menu.

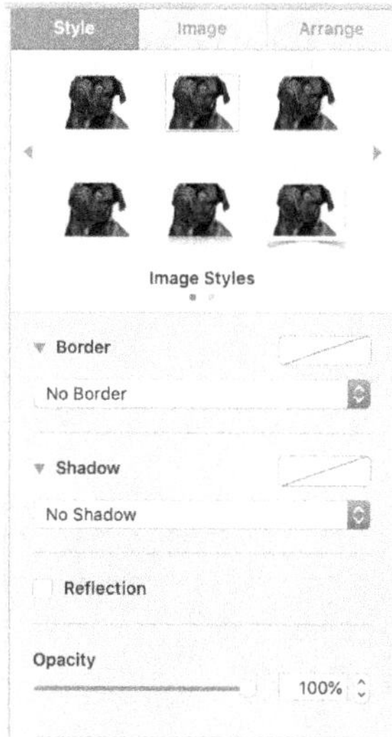

BASIC STYLES

The top box lets you add quick, pre-defined image styles to your image. For example, if you want your image to have a box around it.

Most people will probably want to do manual editing to the photo, but if you use the arrow in this section, you'll notice a + button. Once you manually make changes to the image (add your transparency, borders, etc.), you can use this button to save these changes, so you can apply them to another photo that you want to have a similar look and feel.

BORDER

The next section is the Border; there is no border on the image by default. If you click the box with the red diagonal line, it will show a drop down of all the different styles available.

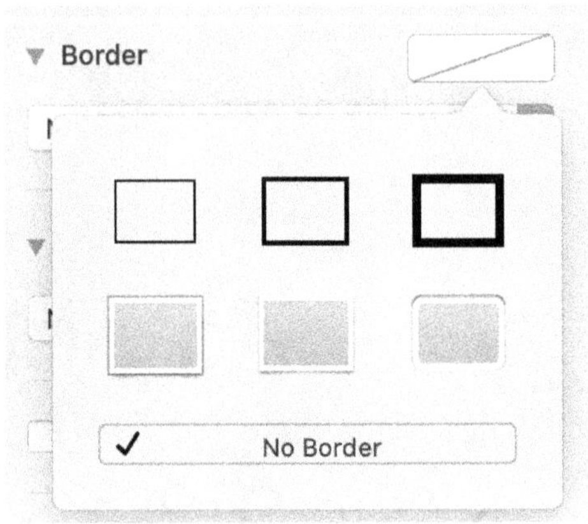

Once you pick your border style, you be able to adjust the weight of the border using the slider.

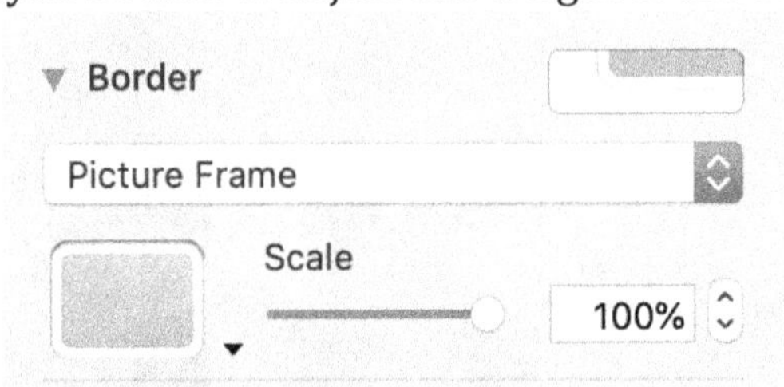

If you click the preview of the border, you will also see all the different border styles for the style that you have picked. Styles vary depending on the style you are using.

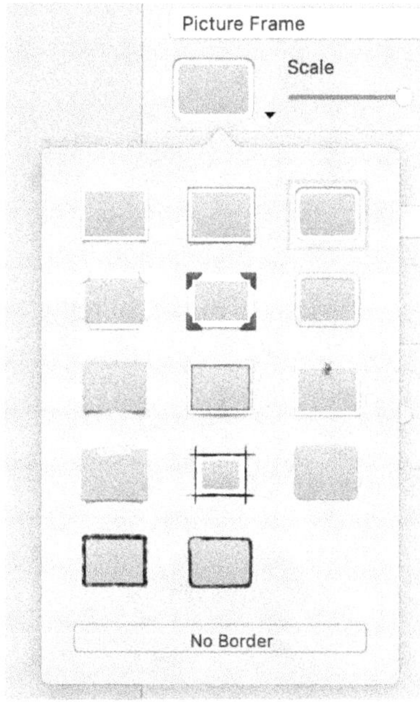

Shadow

Shadows can add a little more dimension to your photo and help it pop off the page more. It works very similar to Borders; click the thumbnail with the red line through it, then pick the shadow style.

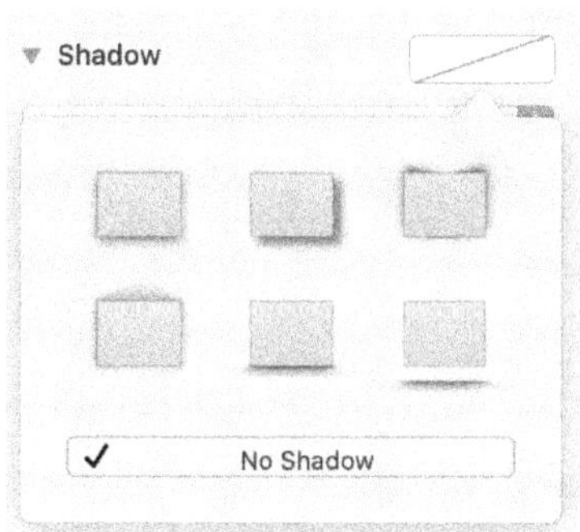

Once you pick the style, you'll get several shadow options to increase or decrease the amount of shadowing used.

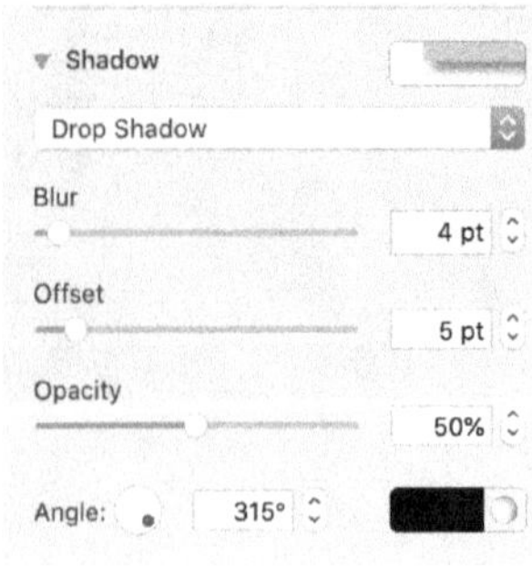

As you make changes, the image will change in real-time, so you immediately see the effects. Notice in the image below how the image has a more 3D look?

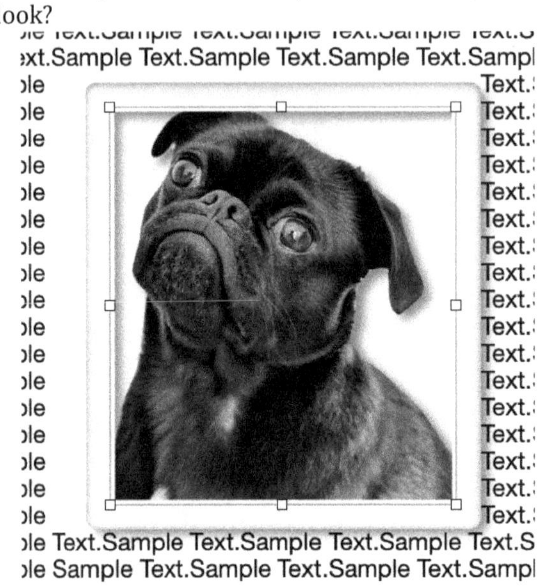

Reflection

Reflection is a simple check / uncheck box; you can use the slider to adjust the amount of reflection used, but that's the only edit available.

You can see in the example below how the reflection gave the image the appearance of an image reflecting on the page (the reflection is the darker area on the bottom of the image).

Transparency

The final style change is transparency. Transparency makes an image more see-through (see the example below). This is great for something like a watermark, but doesn't help a lot if you don't have something below the image.

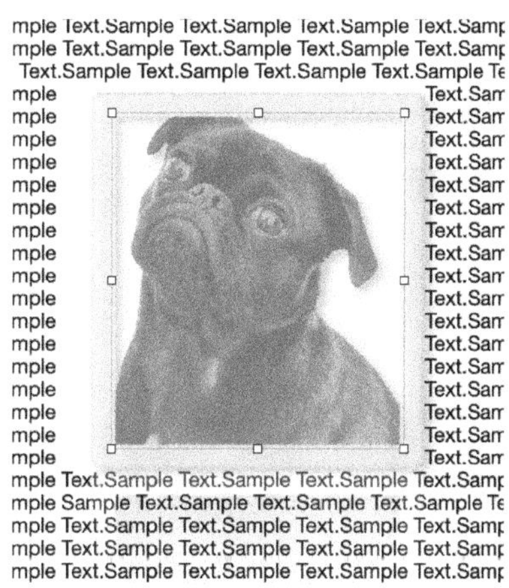

In the below example, I put the transparent image above another photo to illustrate how you can use it on top of another image.

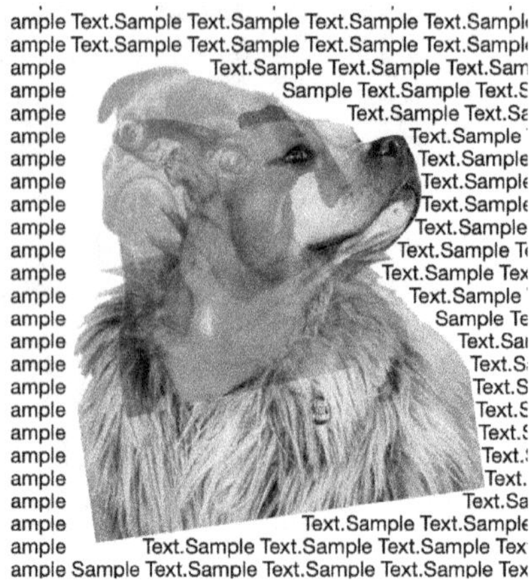

HANDS-ON EXERCISE

1. Insert an image into a blank document (or copy and paste the image from the Internet using Command C and Command V).
2. Give the image a special Photo Corners border (or a border of your choosing).
3. Give the image a large, fuzzy shadow.
4. Give the image a 76% reflection.
5. Set the image opacity to 68%.
6. Resize the image so that you can see the full image and its reflection without scrolling.

Your screen should now look something like this:

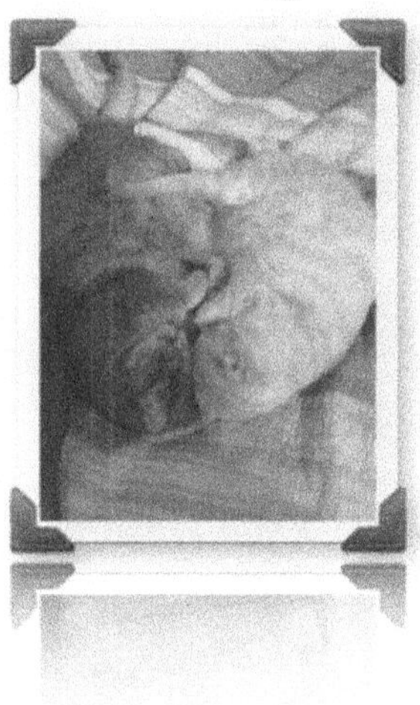

[3]

Tables

This chapter will cover:

- Inserting a table
- Styling a table
- Deleting a table
- Importing a table

Pages works seamlessly with other iWork apps like Numbers and Keynote; this is especially true with tables. You can insert tables into your document manually, but you can also import tables from Numbers into it. This section will show you how and will also serve as a brief introduction to Numbers for the iPad.

Inserting a Table

If you have ever added a table in Word, then you may be used to picking the size and width before adding the table; in Pages, you add the table and then adjust it accordingly.

To add a table, tap the Table button from the top menu bar (you can also use Insert > Table from the menu options at the top of MacOS). You'll have several styles to pick from, but again, this is different from Word where you drag to the number of rows and columns that you want.

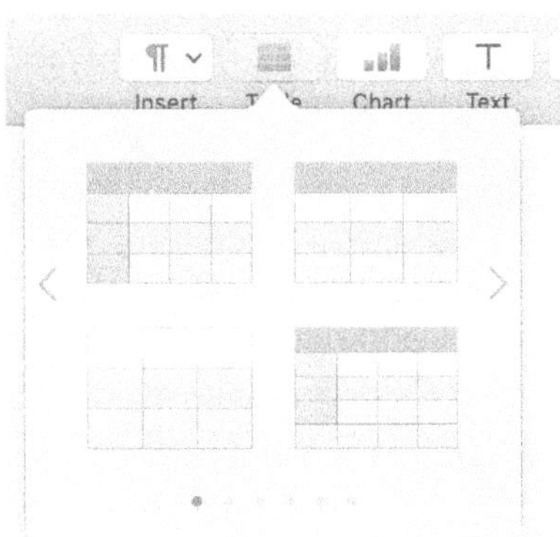

Adding Columns and Rows

Your table is now inserted, but chances are it's not the right size.

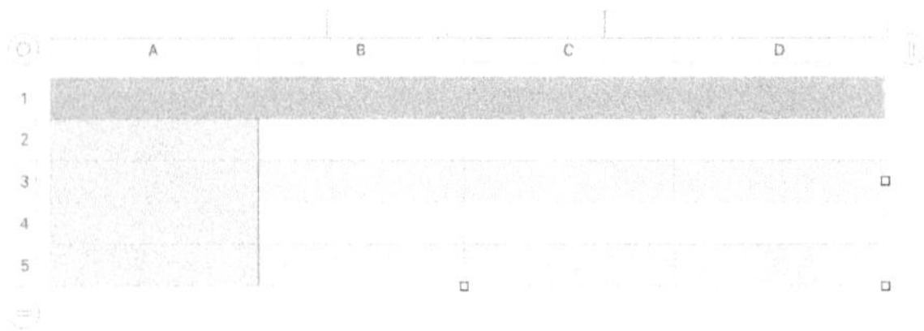

At the bottom of the last row (or the side of the last column) there's a circle with two lines. Click on either of those to adjust the number of columns / rows. You can either use the up / down arrows to pick, or you can click the number and then type the amount you want.

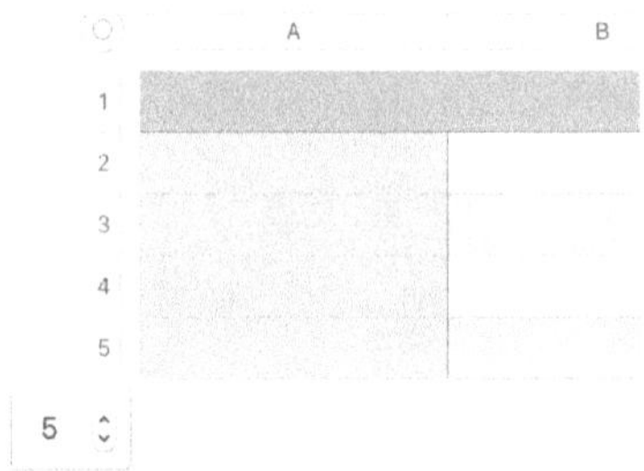

Interacting with Tables

It can be a little tricky to work with a table in Pages at first. Double clicking a cell will bring up the keyboard, but single clicking it will select the entire cell (Microsoft Excel users should have an easier time with this concept).

If there's no text, you can single click and start typing, but if you want to edit the text that's already there, then you need to double click.

Row / Column Options

If you want to delete or add a row / column, then go to the row or column you want to make changes to, and then click the drop-down arrow. Several options will come up.

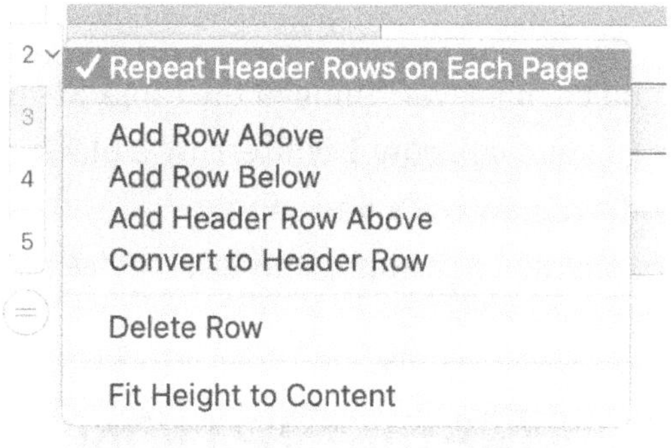

You can also click the number associated with the row / column to select all. This is helpful if you want to copy / paste a row or column.

Styling Tables

Apple's predefined tables look great, but if you've got a specific color scheme or style in mind, it's easy to customize your tables to match that. Just select your table (or certain cells in your table) and look to the right side menu, which has changed to a table style menu.

Table Options

The first set of options are for the entire table.

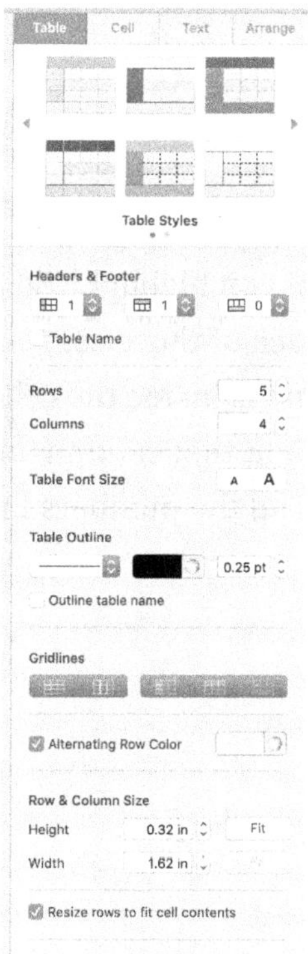

These are all options that would change everything in the table. Such as the table outline; if you can see grids and alternating row colors (if you want row 1 white, row 2 black, row 3 white, row 4 black, etc.). You can also increase the font size and add new rows and columns.

The Table Styles at the top are similar to the image styles; they're predefined styles.

CELL OPTIONS

The table options are great if you want to change everything about the table. But what if you just want to change a cell, column, or row? That's where the Cell Option tab comes into play.

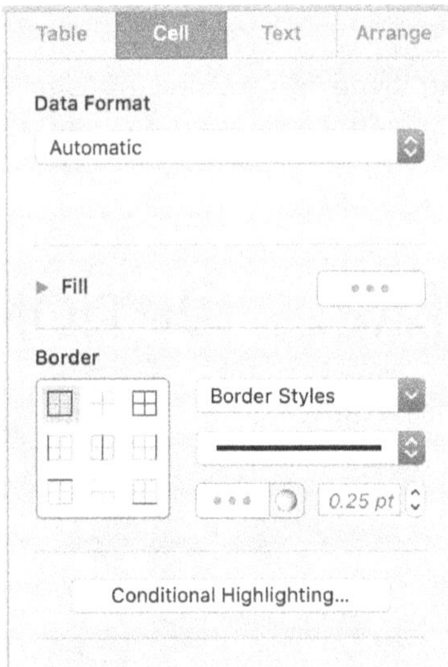

It says "Cell" but Cell here is anything that you highlight. So if you highlight one cell, then it's just that cell; but if you highlight multiple cells, then it's each of those cells.

Data Format is where you can change what is inside the cell; what does that mean? Let's say one of your columns had only currency; you could highlight that column and then say that everything in those cells were currency; so a dollar sign would be added to all the numbers in the cells.

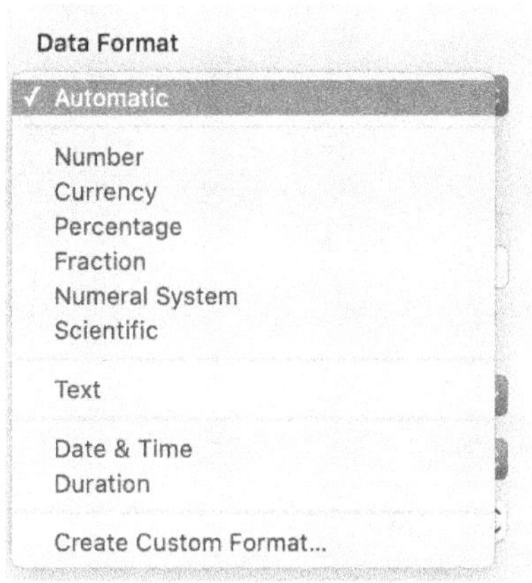

You can change the color of the cell under Fill; you can change the border style, border color, and border weight under Border.

Conditional Highlighting is a little less obvious than those first couple of options.

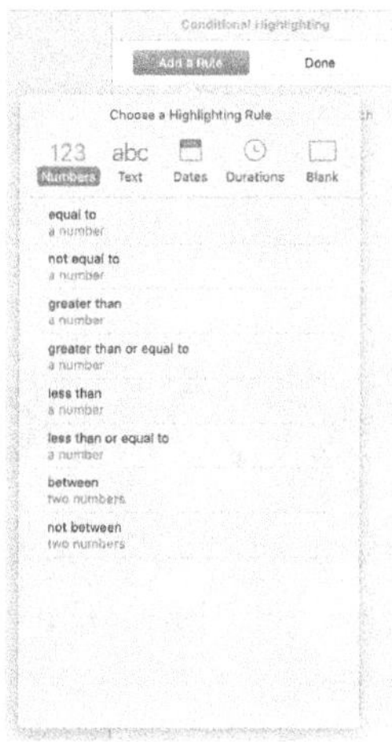

This lets you create rules; for example anytime you have a cell with the number 2, the cell text turns Bold.

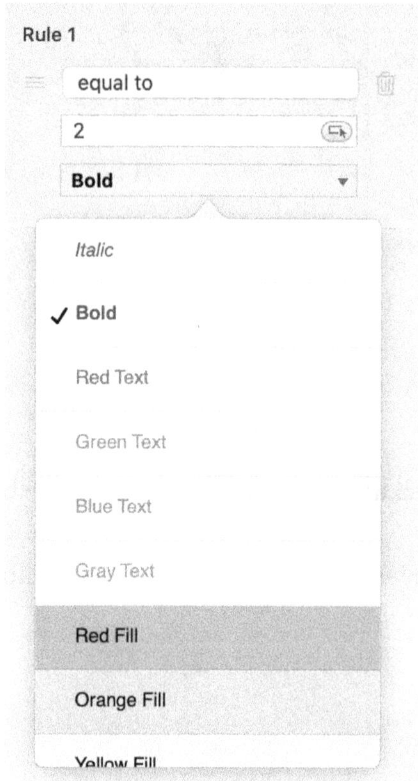

TEXT OPTIONS

By now you should understand how to format text. It's no different when you are doing a table. The same rules as before apply—any cell you highlight will have the text changed—so if you have the entire row highlighted, then all the text in those cells changes.

There is one box worth noting: Wrap text in cell. It's just a check / uncheck box, but it's important because if you have a long string of text and you want it to fit within a cell without going into the next cell, then you need it to wrap.

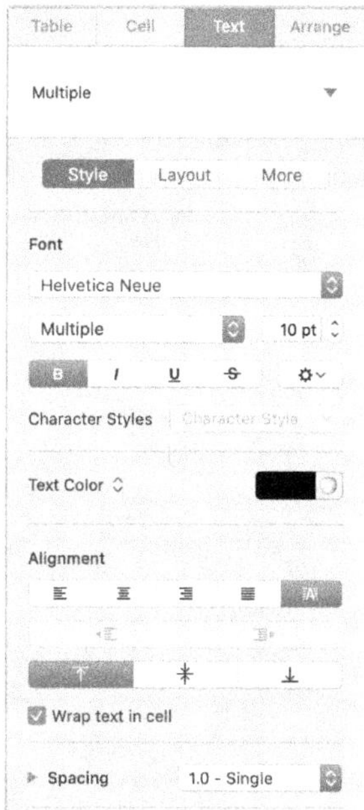

Here's an example of wrapping off.

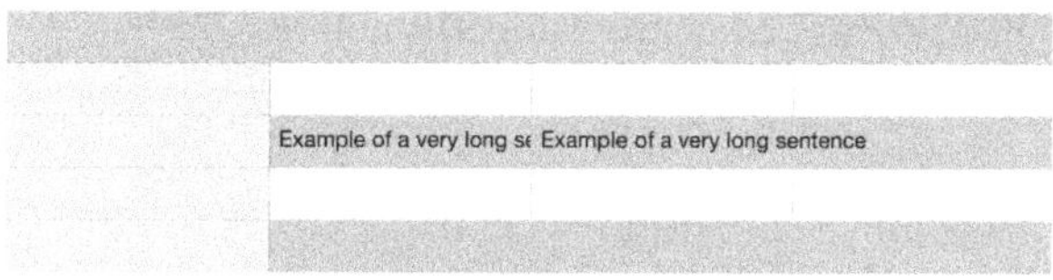

And here's what it looks like on.

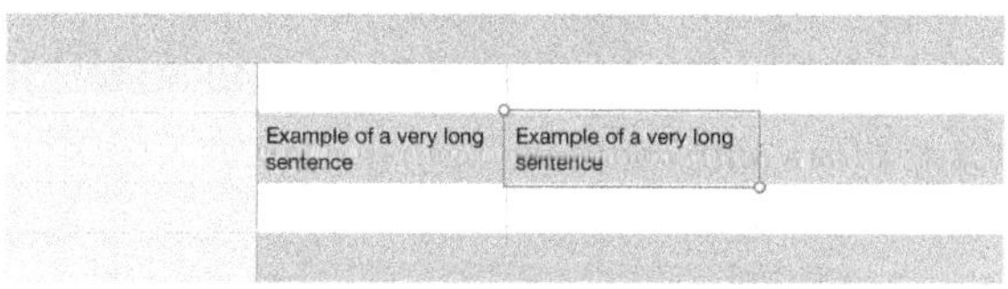

ARRANGE OPTIONS

Just like text options are the same as formatting options outside of the table, Arrange Options are almost identical to the options covered in Photo Arrangement options.

Deleting Tables

Deleting an entire table is a quick process. Click the table. Hit delete.

Importing Tables

Importing a table from somewhere else can be done a few different ways.

The first, and quickest, way is to copy and paste the table. Command V is obviously the easiest way to do this, but go to the Edit menu. Notice there are a Paste and Paste and Match Styles options? If you aren't getting the paste results that you want, try this Paste instead.

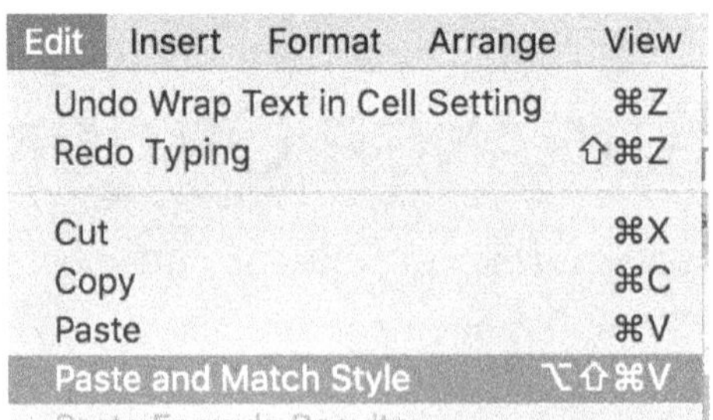

If you don't need to make changes to the table, what a lot of people prefer to do is just make a screenshot of the spreadsheet: Command + Shift + 3 (or Command + Shift + 4 if you want to do only select areas of the screen).

HANDS-ON EXERCISE

This one's a little more of a challenge!

1. Insert a table with the style of your choice.
2. Adjust the table so that it contains three rows and three columns (including headers)
3. Enter labels for each row and column and numerical data in each cell.
4. Select your bottom row and copy it.
5. Add an additional row.
6. Paste your copied row into the new row.
7. Select the whole table and turn alternating rows on.
8. Turn on Header Row Lines.
9. Change the Table Font to Arial.
10. Select your column headers. Change them to a green fill with blue bold underlined text centered in the middle of the cell and right aligned.

Now your screen should look something like this:

	Column 1	Column 2
Row 1	1	2
Row 2	3	4
Row 2	3	4

[4]

CHARTS

This chapter will cover:

- Inserting a Chart
- Editing Chart Data
- Styling a Chart

Charts can add color and interest to your documents, as well as help you present data more clearly. Pages includes a powerful Charts feature that allows you to quickly create beautiful, customizable charts that really pop out of the page.

Now that you know how to use Tables, using Charts will be a breeze.

INSERTING A CHART

To insert a chart in Pages, tap the Insert button, then tap Charts. From here, you'll choose the type of chart (bar, area, line, pie), as well as the style you want. Choose from several different color schemes in 2D, 3D, and interactive. If you change your mind about your chart choice, you can always change it later, without losing any data you've entered. Just tap on your favorite chart to insert it into your document.

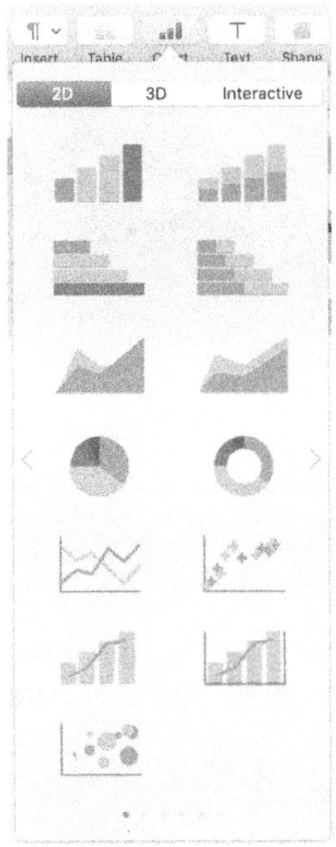

As with almost everything in Pages, you can also add Charts from the top menu (Insert > Chart).

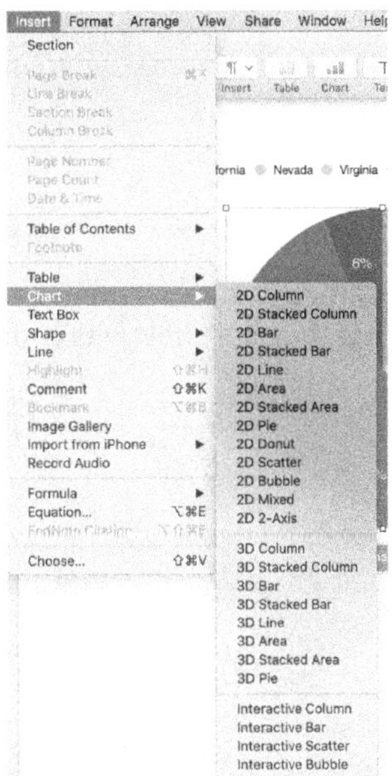

Once you have your chart picked, a chart that's already filled out will be added to your document (I'm using a Pie chart in this chapter, but the same features apply to almost all of the charts—they just look a little different).

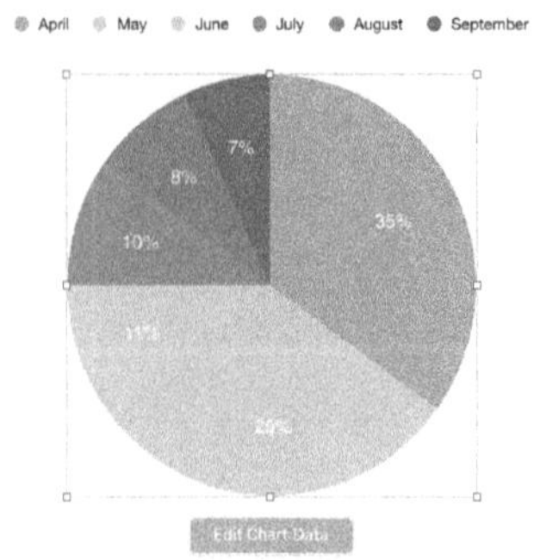

EDITING CHART DATA

It's so nice for Pages to put a pretty chart that's all filled out into our document, right? Sure! But wouldn't it be nicer if it had meaningful data? To add your own data, click Edit Chart Data. This brings up a mini table that you can edit with whatever information you want.

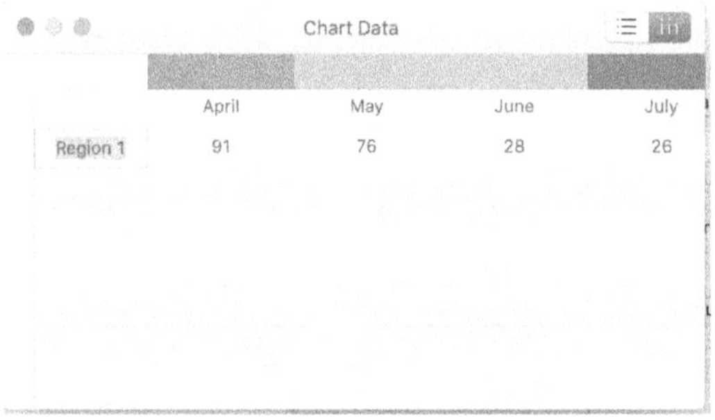

I'm going to replace the months with the names of states, and use an entirely different data range. The chart changes with each change I make in the table. Notice that the chart below is completely different from the one above?

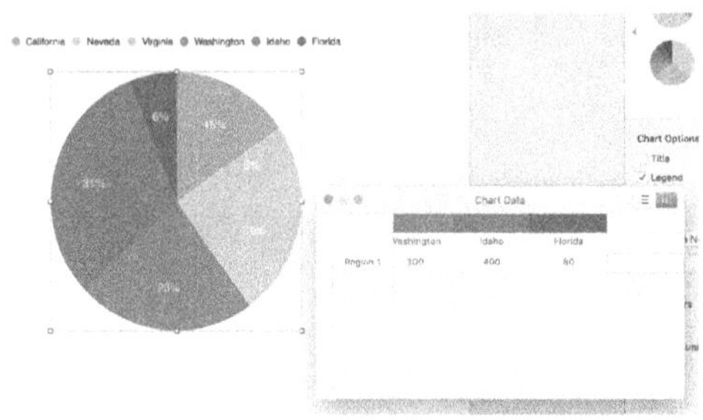

You can enter additional rows if you need to—but this won't work on all charts (like the pie chart).

STYLING YOUR PIE CHART

Now that you have the data you want, it's time to style it.

If you did a pie chart, then you'll see three options on the side (Chart, Wedges, Arrange).

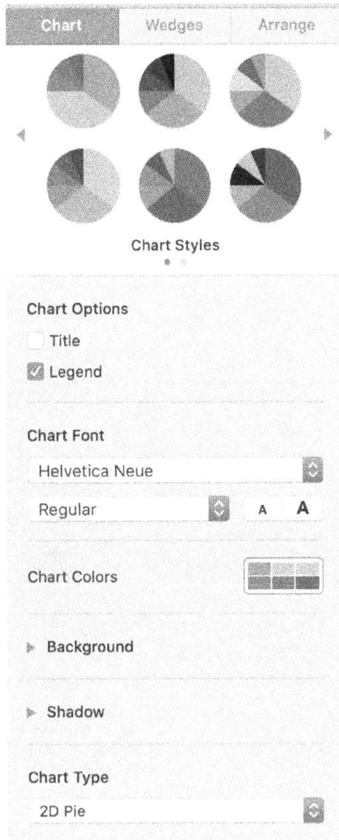

Other charts (like bar charts) have four (Chart, Axis, Series, Arrange).

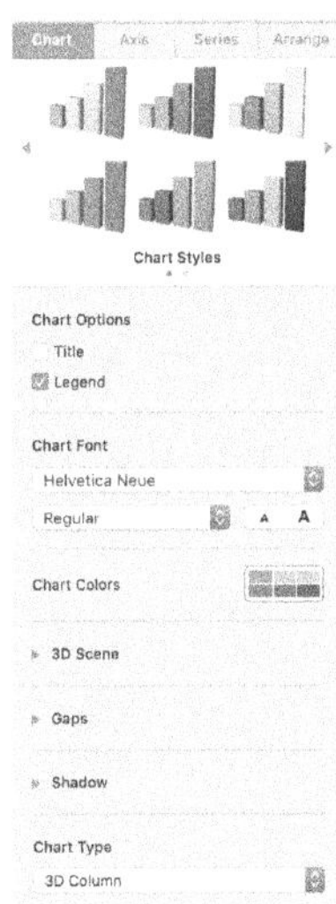

I'll go over the two extra options for a bar chart in the next section.

In the Chart section you can make changes to the entire chart. By default the chart has no title, but if you check off the box, a title (cleverly named "Title") is added to your chart; you'll probably want to name it something else. To do that (and this also applies to renaming pretty much anything in your chart) double click on it and start typing.

Below the title is where you can change the font, and under that, the chart colors. When you click on the chart colors, it gives you a whole host of pre-defined colors. But what if you want to pick your own?

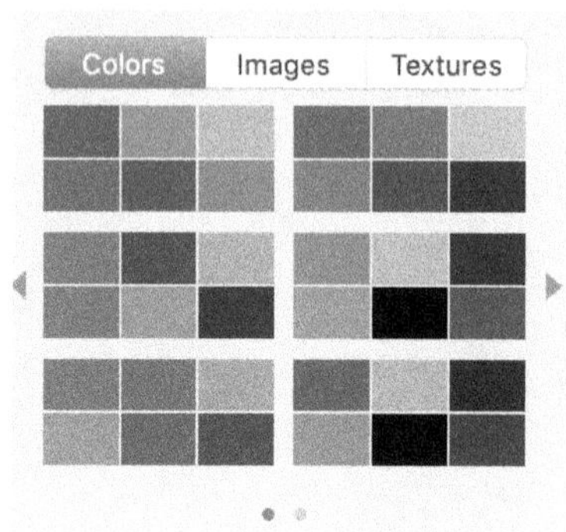

There's one extra small step to picking your own colors. You have to double click on the wedge that you want to change the color of, and then over on the menu options to the right of it, click Style (Style is a new option that's only there if you double click the wedge). From here, you can pick a color under "Fill."

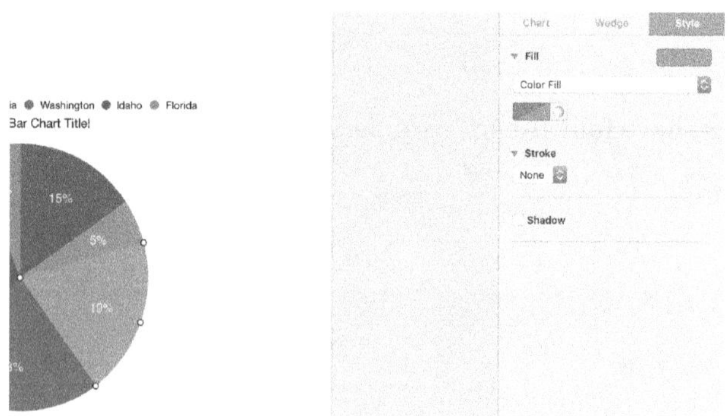

While we are in this section, let's go just under it to Stroke and Shadow. Both of these options help a wedge stand out a little. This is useful if you want to illustrate one area of the chart over others. See in the example below how I added a dotted line (and increased the line weight to 4) and also added a shadow.

If you really want that wedge to stand out, try pulling it apart from the chart. You can do that by clicking on the Wedge option, and then changing the Wedge Position. Look at the example below; the wedge is now separated in the chart.

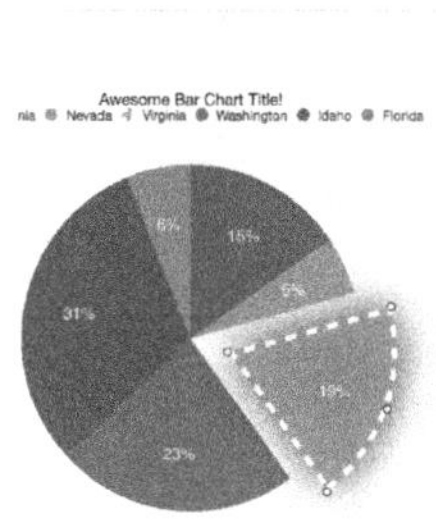 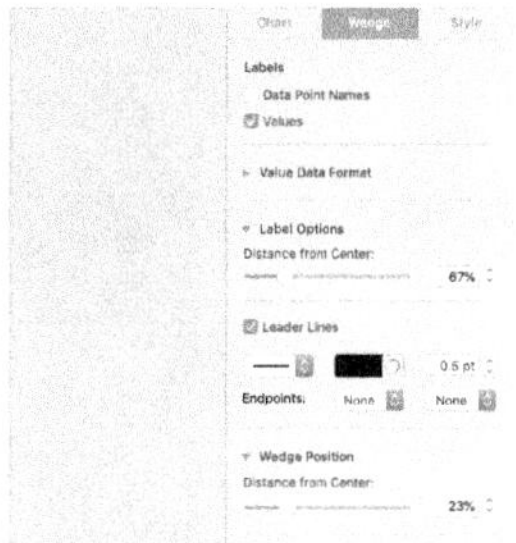

Now let's go back to the chart section and look at the other options we can apply to the entire chart. You can give it a background, add a shadow to it, and finally, change the Chart Type. You can make it a different Pie chart or turn it into a line chart (note: this will probably interfere with your data and you may have to redo some of it).

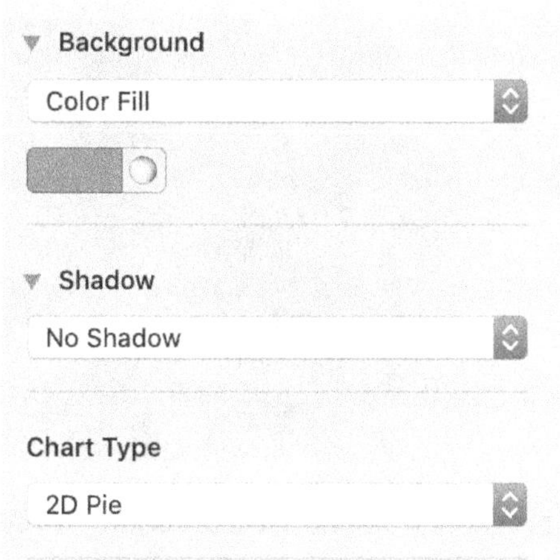

We saw how going to the Wedge section could separate your single wedge from the rest. If you don't double click the wedge and change it, below is what happens.

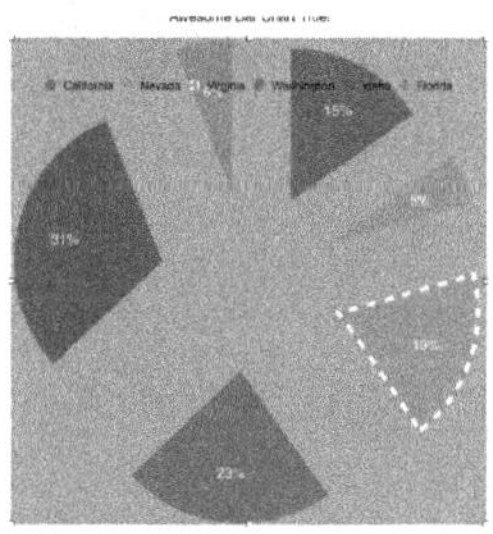

All the wedges separate. If that's what you want, then perfect! If that's not what you want, undo and then double click the wedge you want to separate.

Checking off Data Point Names will put the names of the value in chart (you can also keep it in the Legend).

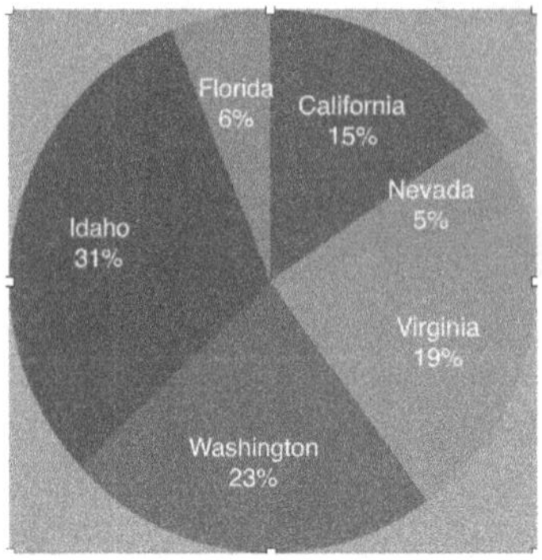

The values on the chart are currently shown as percentages; if you prefer showing them as numbers (or another value type), you can change this under Value Format.

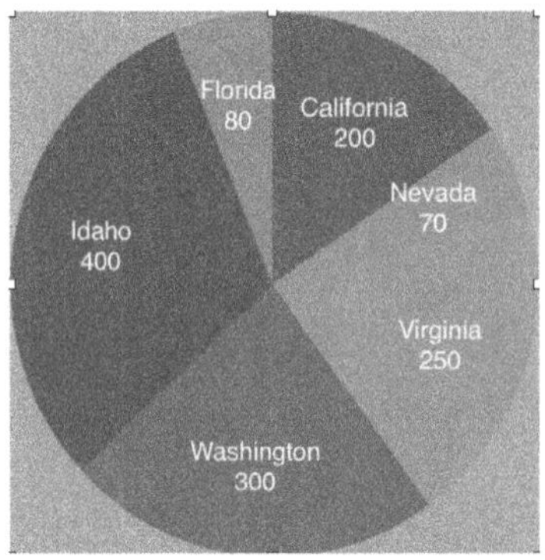

If you check off Lender Lines, you probably won't notice a difference; to see what the lines are, click the Straight drop-down and change it to Angled.

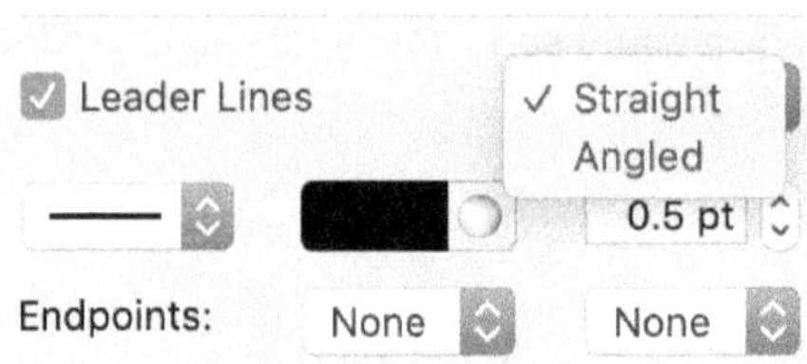

You should now see lines to the sides of the chart.

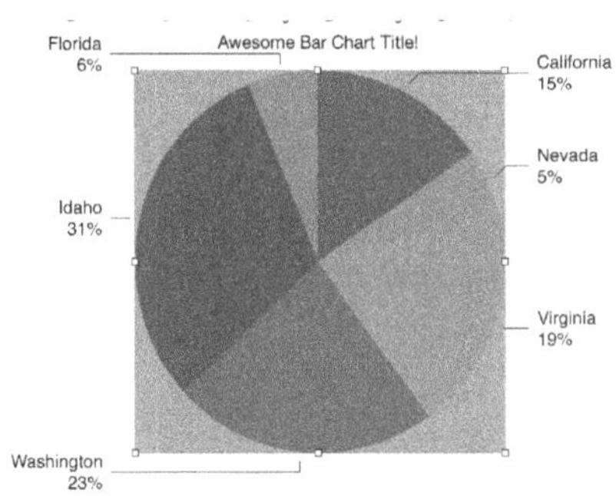

The arrange option should look familiar to you. You've seen it in the Tables section and the Photos section; it's the same features.

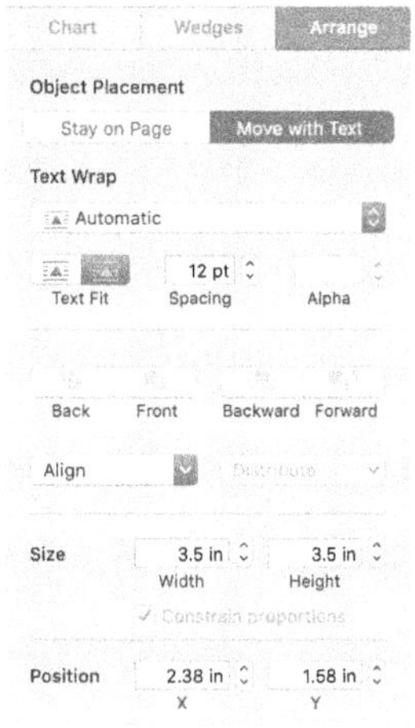

STYLING YOUR BAR CHART

Now that you know how to style a Pie Chart, you'll have no problem with the Bar Chart; it's basically the same, but with more options for labels.

In the axis sub-tab, you can turn category labels, series names, gridlines, and titles on and off. Similarly, in the Y-axis or X-axis sub-tab, you can turn value labels, gridlines, and titles on and off. Here you can also specify the number format you'd like to use and adjust the value scale settings. Number formatting includes the option to add prefixes and suffixes, like currency symbols or suffixes like %, millions, etc.

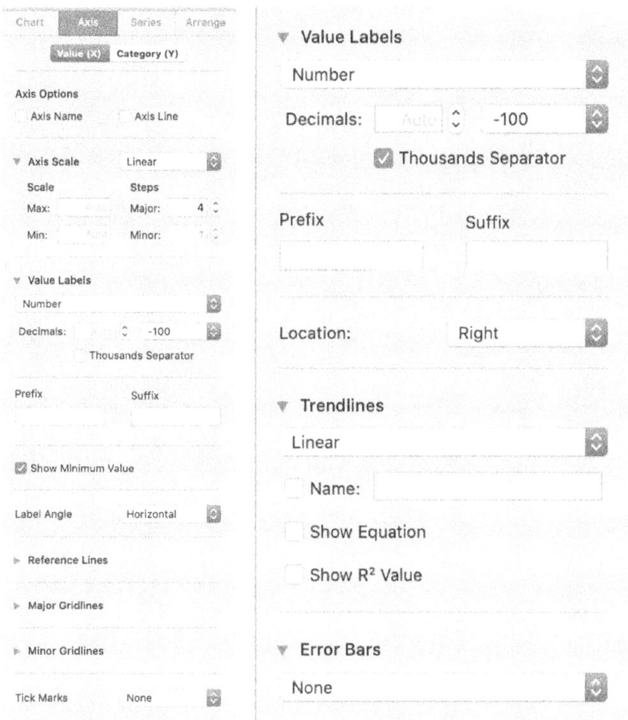

Note: the contents of the sub-tabs change depending on the orientation of your chart. The number formatting option may appear under either the x- or y-axis, depending on the type of chart you've inserted.

HANDS-ON EXERCISE

Let's create a chart! Create a chart with the following specifications:

1. Insert a 3D bar chart.
2. Edit the data so that it shows how much money Company A and Company B made in the years 2010, 2011, and 2012 (amounts are up to you!).
3. Show gridlines on the chart for both the x and y-axis.
4. Give the chart the title "Profits of Company A and Company B."
5. Give the category axis the title "Year" and the value axis the title "Profits."
6. Remember that the x and y axes depend on what orientation your bar chart is in.
7. Give the value axis value labels a dollar sign prefix and a K suffix.
8. Change the shape of the bars to cylinders.

Your screen should now look something like this:

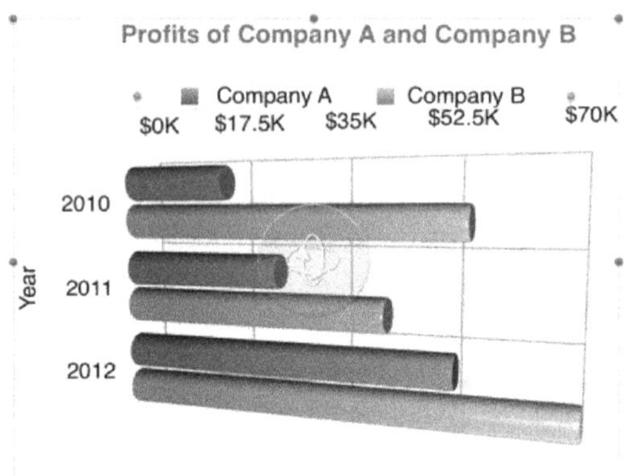

[5]

SHAPES

This chapter will cover:

- Inserting a Shape
- Resizing Shapes
- Creating Text Boxes

Pictures are great! They really help your document look snazzy. But there's one more type of graphical illustration you should consider: shapes. Shapes can be great additions to a document – they can be used to draw attention to an area of a document or to illustrate your points graphically. Pages offers a number of handy pre-made shapes for you to use, and I'll show you how to get the most out of them.

INSERTING A SHAPE

To insert a shape into a document, click the shape button or go to Insert > Shape from the top menu. This will bring up all the shapes available for you. Find the one you like and click it to insert it.

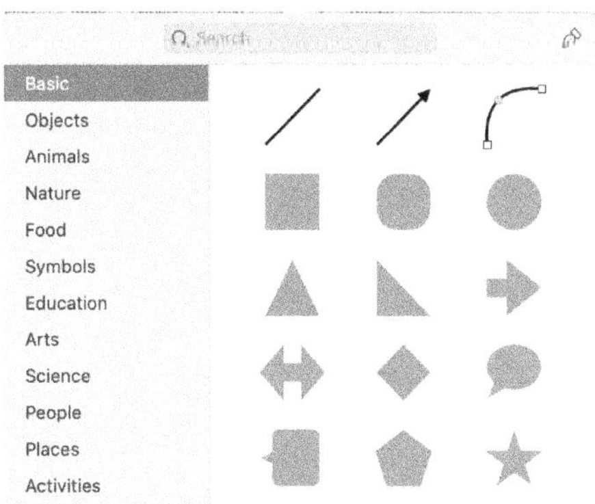

Remember that you can change the color, border and shadow/reflection effects later!

Shapes sounds a little misleading. If you're like me, you're probably thinking square, circle, etc. But shapes in Pages are kind of like clipart. Yes, basic shapes are there, but so are other things. In the example below I searched for "Dog" and got five results!

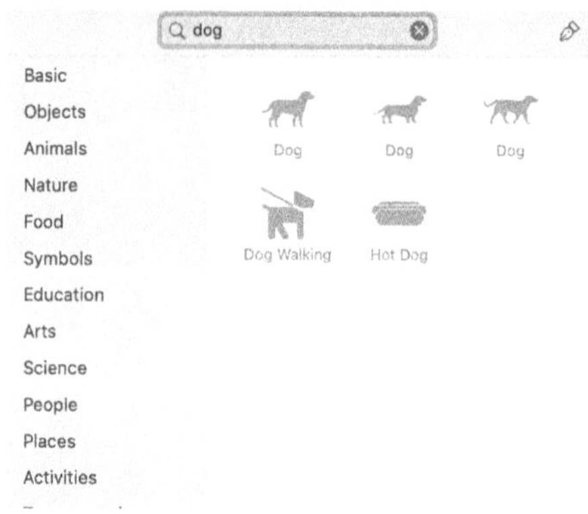

Resizing Shapes and Adjusting Proportions

Shape resizing is just like resizing photos: tap on a corner and drag it to the desired size. However, with Shapes, you can also adjust proportions. What does that mean? It's better shown than explained. Double tap your trackpad on the shape to bring up the shape options. Now click "Make Editable."

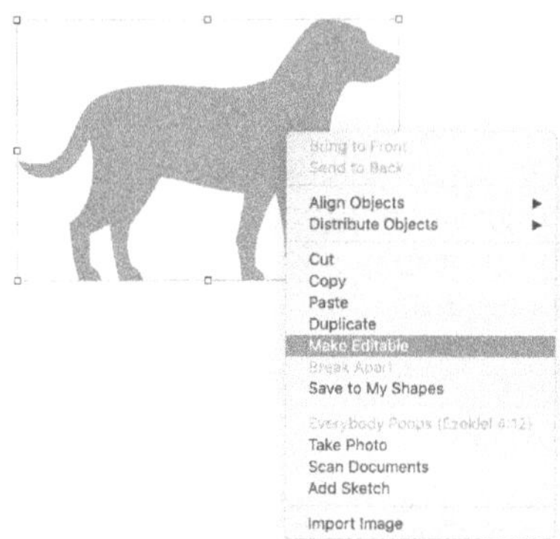

There's now a bunch of dots on the shape. These represent points that you can adjust.

As an example, I moved the point inward from the dog's stomach and look what happened.

By default you make these changes with a curved point, but you can change this by bringing the options up again. Notice the three different points?

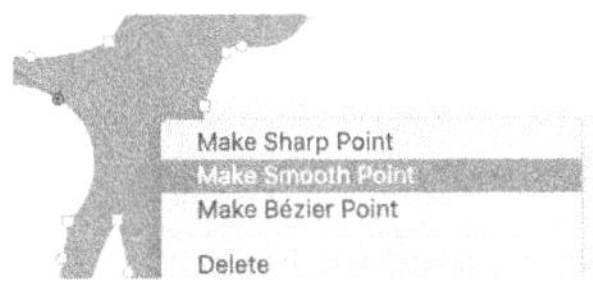

Moving and Rotating Shapes

To move a shape, simply tap on it and drag it to a new location. To rotate a shape, click the image then press the command button—just like you would an image.

Adding Text to a Shape

To add text on top of a shape, double-tap on it to activate its text field. Then just type your text!

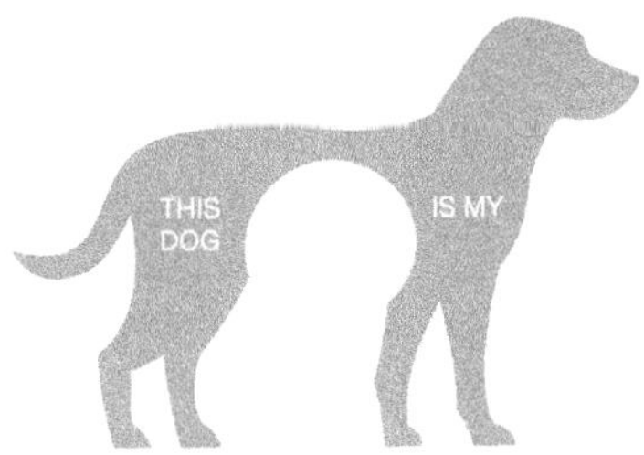

Creating Text Boxes

There's one more type of shape, but it's not under shape. It's a Text Box. Text Boxes are exactly what they sound like—floating boxes that have text.

Why use a Text Box instead of typing out the text? Ideally, you want to use them when you are making something like a title—not when you are typing out your epic novel. It's for short text that you want to stand out.

Unlike standard text, Text Boxes are treated in the same way images are, so you can easily move them around and have other things wrap around them.

To get started, click the T in the menu.

You can also do Insert > Text Box.

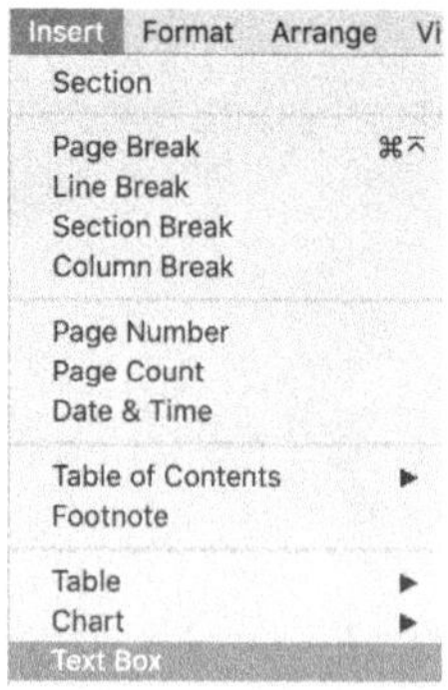

This puts a floating box with generic text in your document.

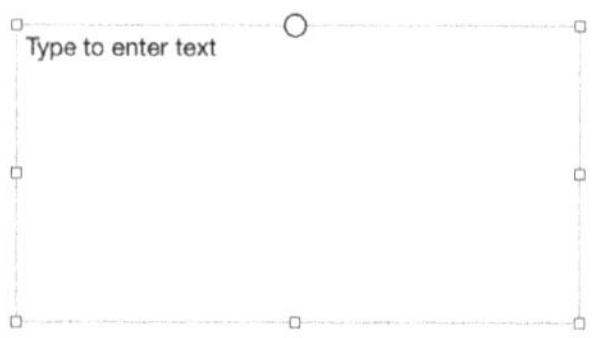

You can change the color of the box and more by clicking on Style; it has all the same types of options that you'd find in the Image or Shape options.

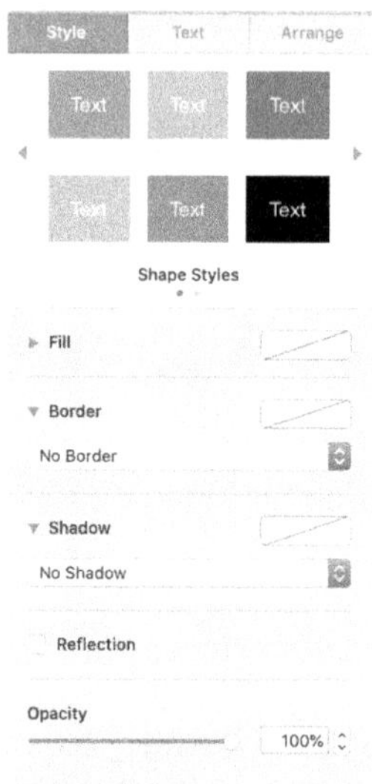

Because it's a Shape, you are able to edit it like you would a shape. In the below example, I curved out the bottom portion of the box.

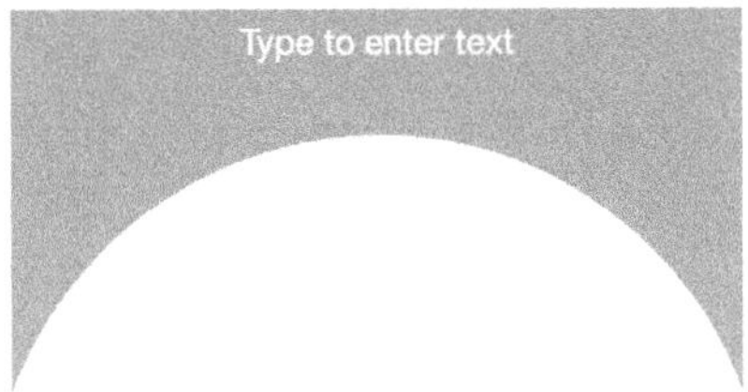

Styling Shapes and Text Boxes

Styling Shapes and Text boxes is the same as styling an image, so I won't repeat myself here. If you are confused about styling, referred to the section in the Photos chapter.

Hands-On Exercise

Let's practice using shapes and text boxes. Follow the directions below.

1. Insert two shapes of your choice.
2. Make one shape blue with a gradient and texture. Give it a solid 1 px black border. Add a shadow effect and reduce its opacity to 50%.
3. Make the other shape red with a gradient. Add a shadow effect.
4. Add text to each shape - make one read "Blue" and the other "Red."
5. Make the text white, underlined, and in Marker Felt typeface. Hint: don't forget about copying and pasting styles!

Now your screen should look something like this.

[6]

Document Setup

This chapter will cover:

- Change margins
- Custom paper size
- Headers / Footers
- Bookmarks
- Table of contents
- Track changes

For most documents, using the preset template will do the job; for those who need a bit more customization, there is Document Setup (for Word users, this is kind of like Page Setup); here you will be able to adjust margins, headers and footers).

Entering Document Setup Mode

To use Document Setup, you can go to View > Inspector > Document Setup.

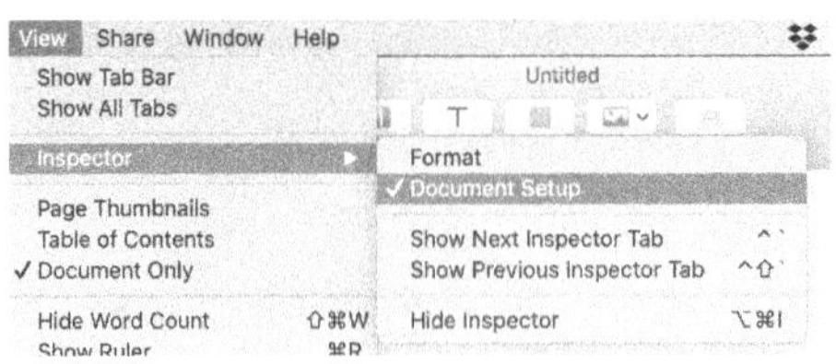

You can also use the Format / Document toggle icons in the menu bar to switch between them.

This brings up your main document editor with three tab options: Document, Section, Bookmarks.

CHANGING DOCUMENT MARGINS AND SIZE

In Document Setup, the settings that pertain to margins and paper size are all found in the first tab: Document.

At the top of the settings, under Printer and Paper Size, you can see all the different paper sizes available. Keep in mind that changing to a different printer may give you more (or less) sizes.

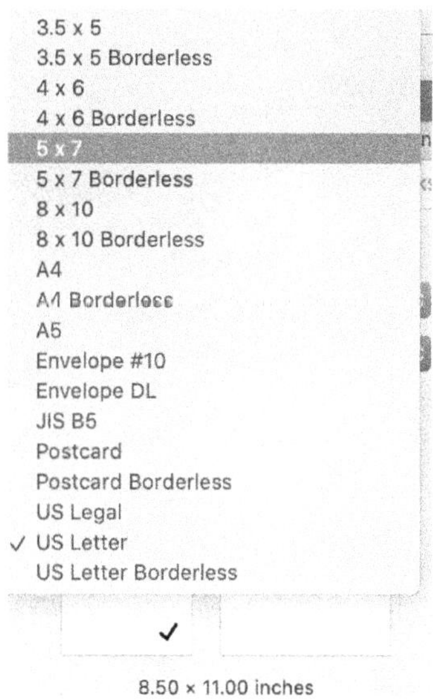

Below this, you can change the orientation of the paper from portrait to landscape.

Finally, you can change the margins under Document Margins. One inch all around is the default setting.

To change the margins, go to Document Setup, then drag the margins to where you would like them to go. Tap "Done" when you are finished.

CREATING CUSTOM PAPER SIZE

What about if you don't see your size? You can create a custom size, but keep in mind if you are printing the document, it may not print correctly.

To create a custom size, go to File > Page Setup.

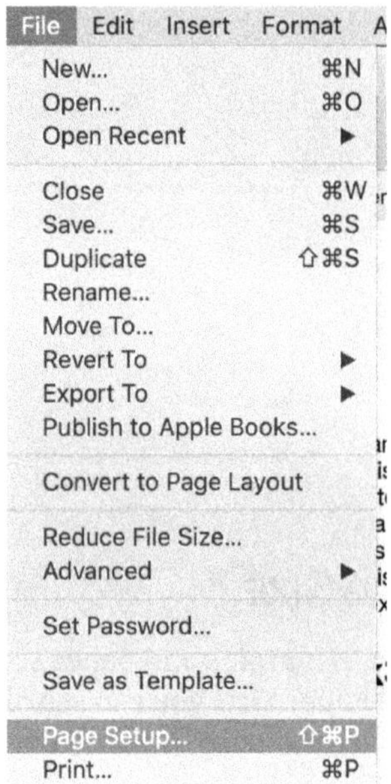

Next, click the drop down under Paper Size.

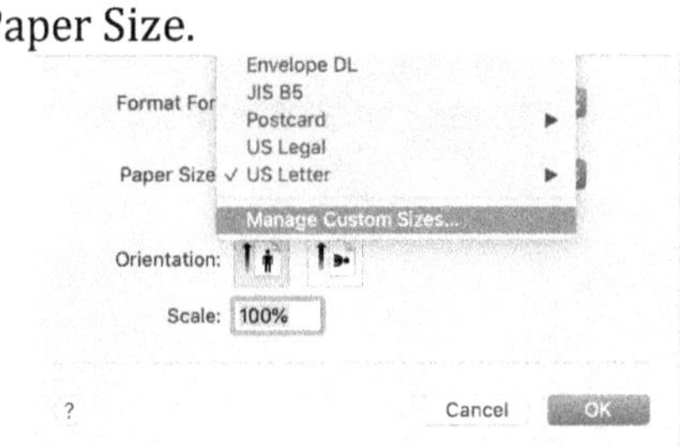

Finally, add your custom size.

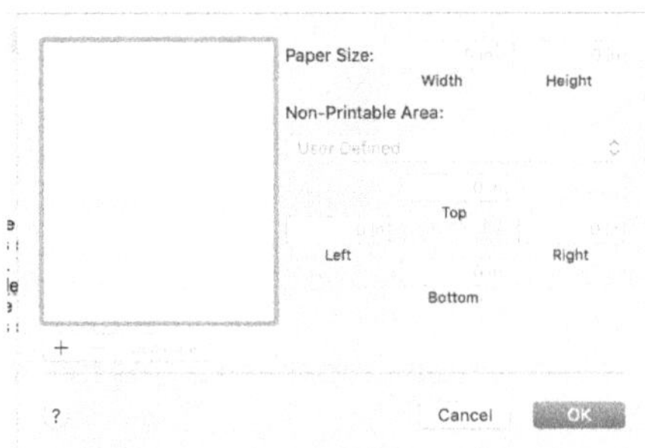

Hyphenations and Ligatures

At the bottoms of Document Setup are two checkboxes: Hyphenations and Ligatures. Checking them turns them on and off.

Hyphenation puts a dash next to long words at the end of the page margin—the idea is to make the document look more even by breaking up a word and continuing it on the next line.

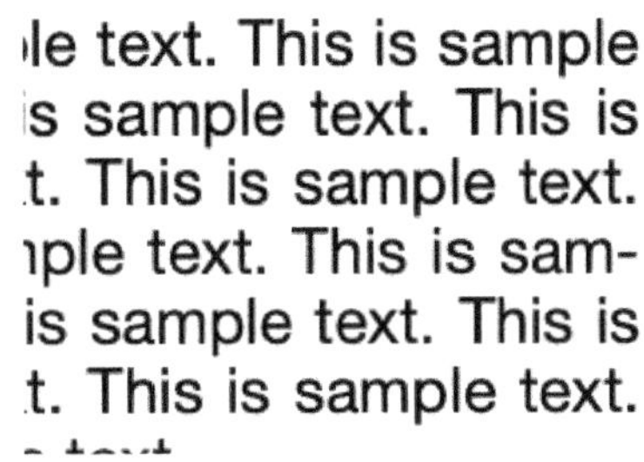

Ligatures are two letters that are combined together to create one character. See some examples below.

AE → *Æ*
ae → *æ*
OE → *Œ*
oe → *œ*
ff → *ﬀ*
fi → *ﬁ*

Headers and Page Numbers

One of the most useful features of Document Setup Mode is its header and footer options. These document elements will appear on every page of your document. You'll also be able to add page numbers from here.

You can control the size of the Header / Footer in the Document section of Setup.

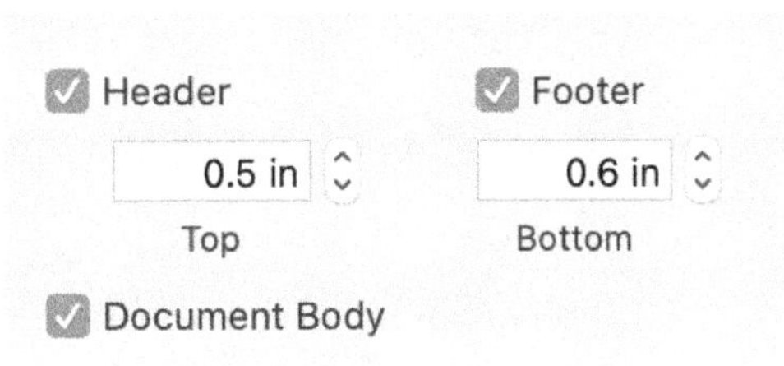

The placement of the Header / Footer is controlled in Section.

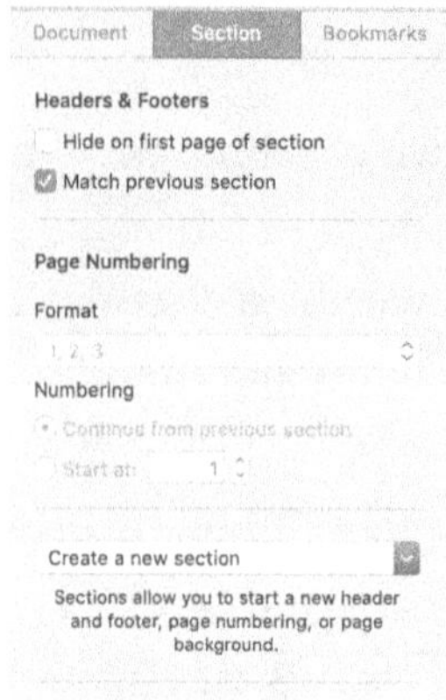

Section lets you tell Pages not to put your Header / Footer on your title page, for example, or to have your numbering start at a certain page.

To insert your Header / Footer, just move your cursor to the top of the page; you'll see a table of sorts with three cells—these represent left, right and center align. You'll also have the option to add the page number to any of these cells.

Bookmarks

Bookmarks are perfect for electronic works. When you add a bookmark it indexes it, and then you can later hyperlink to that bookmark. So you could be on page 2 of a 500 page document, and have it reference a bookmark on page 87; when the user clicks it, it jumps to the section bookmarked.

To create one, highlight the text you want to bookmark, go to the Bookmark tab of Document Setup, and click the Add Bookmark button.

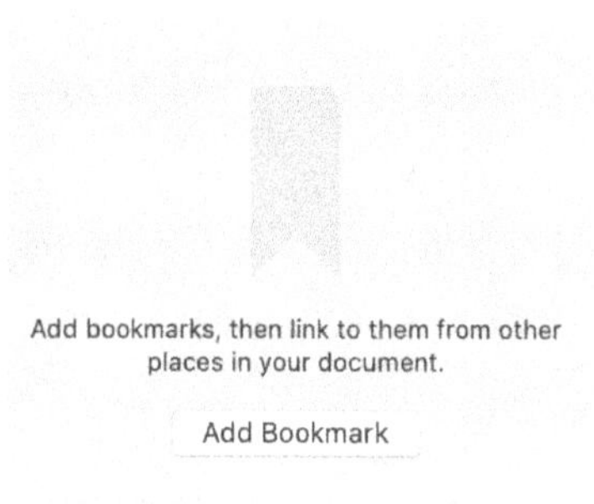

The bookmark is automatically named whatever text you highlighted. So if the text you highlighted says "This is a bookmark" then the bookmark is called "This is a bookmark".

You can single click the name and rename it. This will only change the name of the bookmark and not the text itself.

Table of Contents

If you are working with a document that needs a table of contents, then you first need to make sure you are using the correct headings. Headings tell Pages what will go into the table of contents.

To create a heading, highlight the text you want to be the heading (a chapter title, for example), then go to the format side bar.

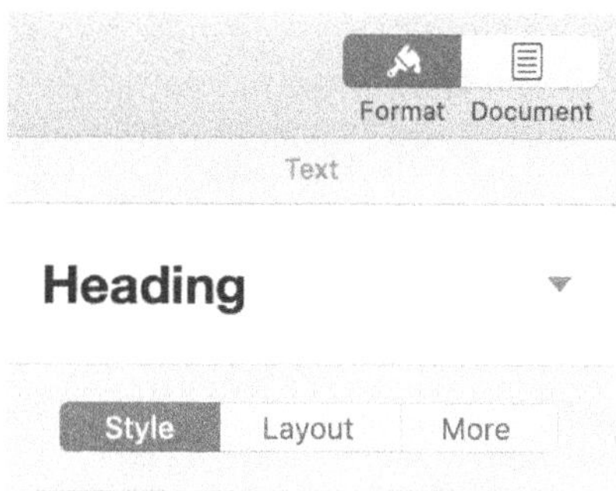

Click the drop down next to Heading and select the type of heading. Heading is usually chapter titles; heading 2 is usually sections; and heading 3 is sections within sections.

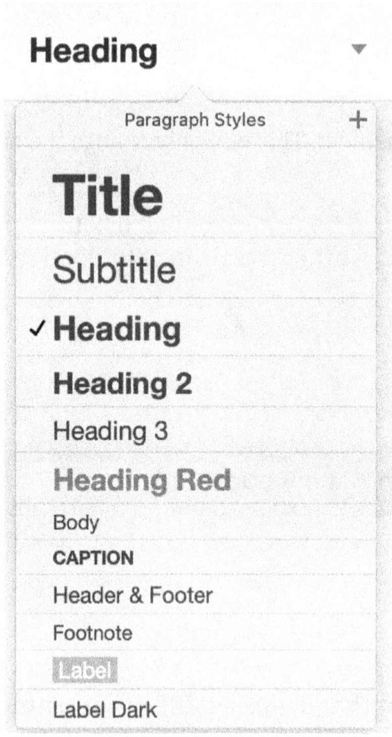

Clicking the arrow next to the heading lets you change how it's formatted; for example, if you want your heading to match the formatting you have, then just click Redefine from Selection.

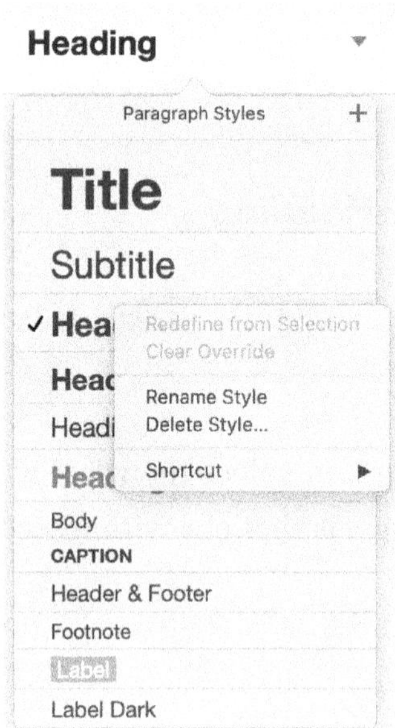

Once you have all the headings in the document, then go to Insert > Table of Contents and select the kind you want. Document is the most common.

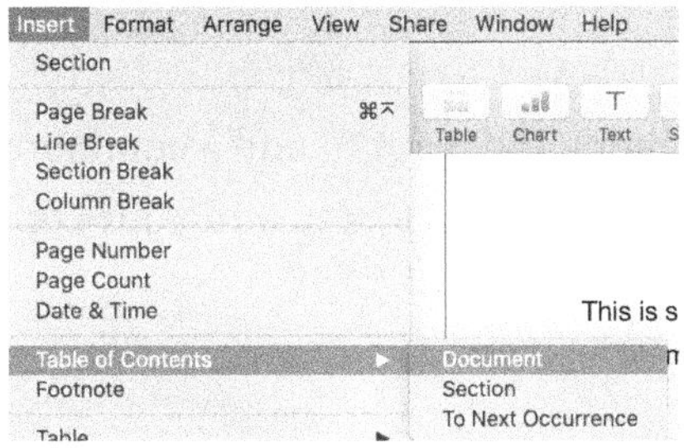

If you click on the inserted table of contents, there will be a table of contents formatter in the format options in the right pane of Pages; you can select what you want to appear in your table of contents here. For example, if you only want Heading 1 to appear, then uncheck everything else.

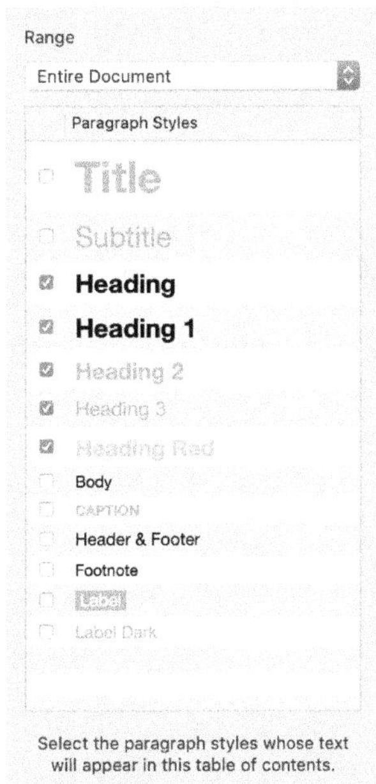

INSERT FOOTNOTES

To insert a footnote into your document, highlight the text you want to add a footnote to, then select Insert > Footnote.

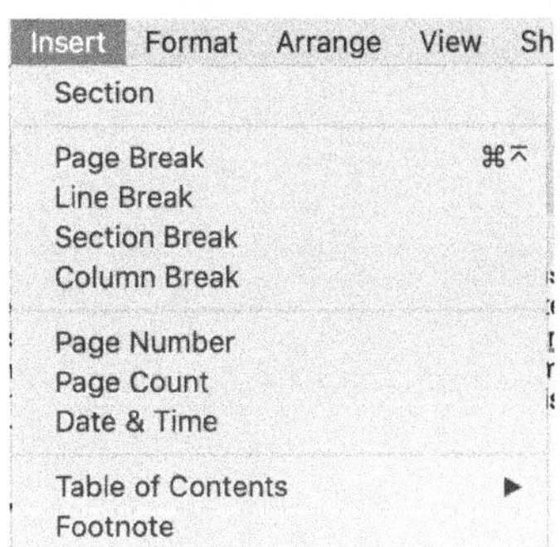

INSERT COMMENT

If you are editing someone's document and want to add a comment, highlight the sentence you want to add a comment to, right click (or click with two fingers) and add your comment, then click done.

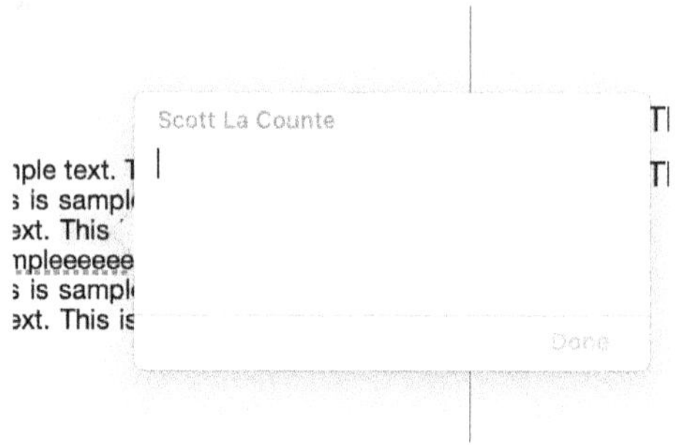

TRACK CHANGES

If you are editing a document, it's also a good idea to turn on Track Changes; this lets the other person see what you have changed.

Track changes is turned on under Edit > Track Changes (it's turned off in the same place).

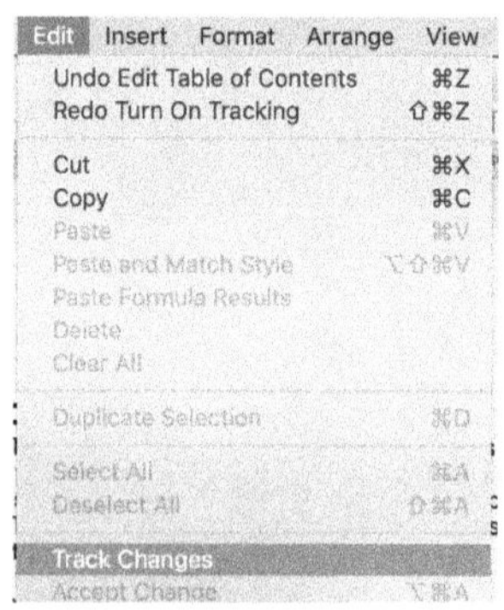

When it's turned on, a new bar appears at the top of the document, and the color of the changed text is also different. The user now has to accept or reject changes in the document; if they reject them, then the changes go away.

[7]

TEMPLATES

This chapter will cover:

- Using third-party Pages Templates
- Creating your own Templates

Pages for iPad comes with over 50 templates in ten categories - some for letters, some for reports and professional use, and others for personal correspondence and announcements.

What exactly is a Template? A Template is a document that's already formatted—complete with text and images. Why would you want that? The idea is you delete the text (and replace the images) to make it your own, but save time on the sometimes complicated formatting aspect of it.

If you are looking for a standard business letter, try "Classic Letter" or "Formal Letter." For a more unusual, offbeat look, you can also try the Personal Photo letter and Modern Photo letters.

Some templates contain multiple pages — for example, a "splashy" front page with enough space for a large photo, followed by more subdued pages for delivering details.

Most of the academic and business-related style templates fall under this category. "Project Proposal," "Term Paper," and "Visual Report" would all be excellent bases with which to start for a highly graphical educational or proposal project.

Pages also includes a party invite, thank you cards, and recipe formats.

Now that you understand most of the formatting options available in Pages, you can use any of these templates as a starting off point. You can change the images, colors, and layout of each template to suit the needs of your project.

USING THIRD-PARTY PAGES TEMPLATES

50+ templates is a lot, but if you use it long enough, you probably will want a few more; if you get to that place then there are websites (and even apps), which sell Pages templates (sometimes they are free). A basic web search for "Pages templates" or even "free Pages templates" will show you what I mean.

Word of caution: like anything you download, use at your own risk. If a website looks sketchy, be wary of downloading a template.

To use a template like this, just go to the website, find a template you like, follow the site's instructions to download it to your computer's hard drive, and then sync it with your iPad as if it were any other Pages document using the iTunes File Sharing syncing process discussed in "Basic Features."

After that, Pages can open the template and you can begin to edit it. It is strongly recommended to make a duplicate of your template document before you begin working on it, so that you will continue to have a blank one for later if you need it.

These third party templates are great for more variety—for example, if you are looking to give your resume a little more creativity.

Creating Your Own "Templates"

Unfortunately, Pages currently does not allow you to save templates in the Create New Document screen. However, you can work around this sorely missed feature by setting up your "template" as a regular Pages document.

Personally, I make a duplicate of the document (i.e. File > Duplicate) and name it something like "Resume Template."

Creating Master

If you've created new styles (for example, your headings are X font, size) you can save that as the new default style for all your documents by going to Format > Advanced > Create Master from Current Page.

[8]

SHARING AND EXPORTING DOCUMENTS

This chapter will cover:

- Sharing documents
- Exporting documents

In spite of the popularity of iPhones and iPads, Apple users still often find themselves marooned in a Windows-based world. Pages is a wonderful program, but it's incomprehensible to Microsoft Word. Fortunately, Pages offers several methods for sharing and exporting Pages documents in multiple formats. Pages also makes moving documents across Apple devices absolutely effortless, thanks to iCloud.

SYNCING DOCUMENTS WITH ICLOUD

If you've enabled iCloud in your Pages app, your documents will be synced across your devices automatically, with absolutely no work required on your part. You can even access your documents online from any internet connection at www.icloud.com.

EMAILING A DOCUMENT FROM PAGES

E-mailing documents is one of the most straightforward methods of sharing your document. Go to Share > Send a Copy.

COLLABORATING

You can also collaborate on a document by going to Share > Collaborate With Others.

This brings up an option that asks how you would like the share the document.

I recommend clicking on the Share Options drop down to make sure the right permissions are enabled. For example, you can make the document readable to anyone you share it with or anyone who gets the document; you can also give the user permission to make changes.

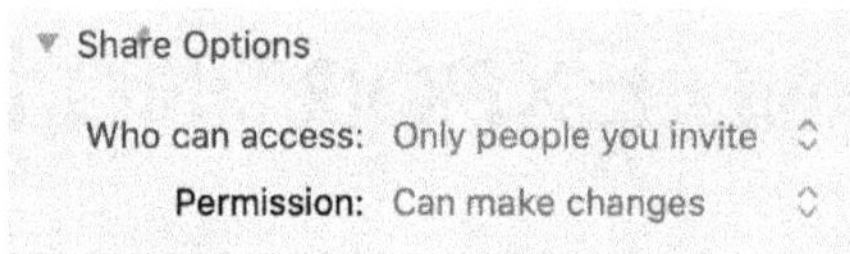

EXPORT A PAGES DOCUMENT

By default, you'll be saving your file as a .Pages document. That's great if you have Pages, but if you're sharing it with (or opening it on) a computer that doesn't have pages, or you want to create a universal PDF that anyone can see, then you'll need to export it.

This is pretty straightforward. Go to File > Export.

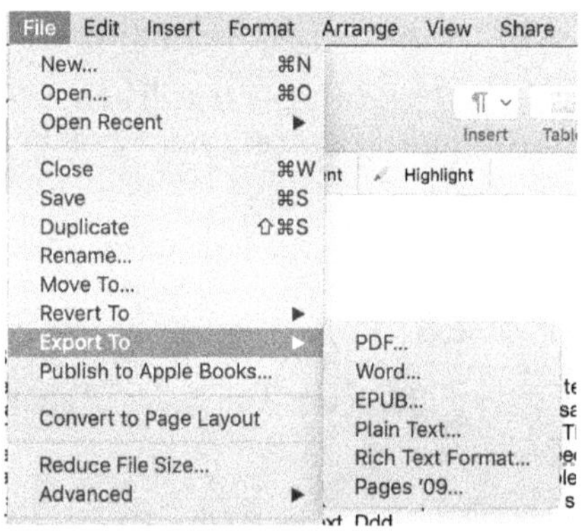

There are six different file types:

- PDF
- Word
- EPUB
- Plain Text
- Rich Text Format
- Pages '09

PDF is the best option if you want to preserve all the formatting in the document and make it look exactly as it appears in Pages. Plain Text will take out all the formatting but be readable on pretty much any editor. ePub is what you would use if you want to create an eBook of your document that can be opened on something like iBooks. Some eReaders don't open ePubs natively and will convert them—so formatting might not be retained.

PRINTING

To print a document, go to File > Print.

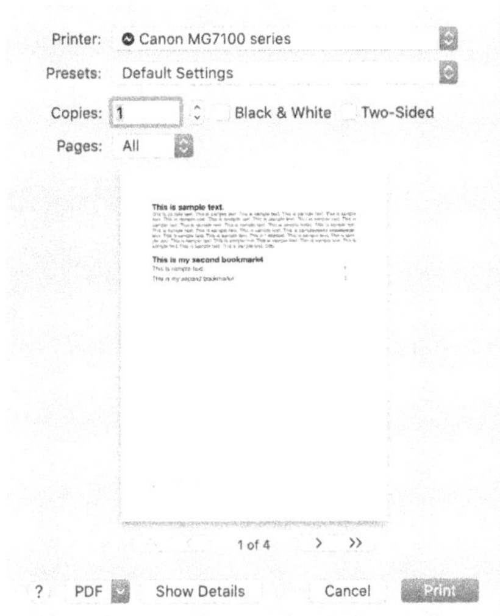

At the bottom of the print menu, there's also an option to save as a PDF. It's Pages' version of Print to File.

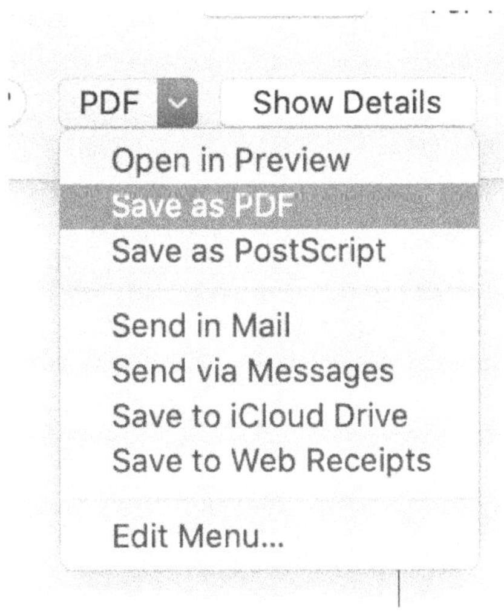

Appendix: Keyboard Shortcuts

General Keyboard Shortcuts

Action	Shortcut
Close a window	Command-W
Close all windows	Option-Command-W
Duplicate a document	Shift-Command-S
Enter full-screen view	Control-Command-F
Hide or show sidebars on the right side of the Pages window	Option-Command-I
Hide or show the toolbar	Option-Command-T
Hide Pages	Command-H
Hide windows of other applications	Option-Command-H
Minimize a window	Command-M
Minimize all windows	Option-Command-M
Open a new document	Command-N
Open an existing document	Command-O
Open the Page Setup window	Shift-Command-P
Print a document	Command-P
Quit Pages	Command-Q
Quit Pages and keep windows open	Option-Command-Q
Rearrange an item in the toolbar	Command-drag
Redo the last action	Shift-Command-Z
Remove an item from the toolbar	Command-drag away from the toolbar
Return to actual size	Command-0

Save a document	Command-S
Save As	Option-Shift-Command-S
Show or hide layout boundaries	Shift-Command-L
Show or hide the ruler	Command-R
Show or hide the tab bar	Shift-Command-T
Show page thumbnails	Option-Command-P
Show the Colors window	Shift-Command-C
Start dictation	Press Fn twice
Undo the last action	Command-Z
Zoom in	Command-Right Angle Bracket (>)
Zoom out	Command-Left Angle Bracket (<)
Zoom to selection	Shift-Command-0

Formatting Keyboard Shortcuts

Action	Shortcut
Show the Fonts window	Command-T
Show the Colors window	Shift-Command-C
Apply boldface to selected text	Command-B
Apply italic to selected text	Command-I
Apply underline to selected text	Command-U
Make the font size bigger	Command-Plus Sign (+)
Make the font size smaller	Command-Minus Sign (-)
Make the text superscript	Control-Shift-Command-Plus Sign (+)
Make the text subscript	Control-Command-Minus Sign (-)
Insert an equation	Option-Command-E

Decrease the indent level of a list item	Shift-Tab
Increase the indent level of a list item	Tab
Turn text into a link	Command-K
Add a bookmark	Option-Command-B
Cut the selection	Command-X
Copy the selection	Command-C
Copy the paragraph style	Option-Command-C
Paste the selection	Command-V
Paste the paragraph style	Option-Command-V
Paste and match the style of the destination text	Option-Shift-Command-V
Copy the graphic style of text	Option-Command-C
Paste the graphic style of text	Option-Command-V
Add a range to (or remove it from) the selection	Shift-drag
Insert a nonbreaking space	Option-Space bar
Insert a line break (soft return)	Shift-Return
Insert a paragraph break	Return
Insert a new line after the insertion point	Control-O
Insert a page break	Fn-Command-Return
Enter special characters	Control-Command-Space bar
Transpose the characters on either side of the insertion point	Control-T
Add an EndNote bibliography	Shift-Option-Command-E

NUMBERS FOR MAC

INTRODUCTION

Microsoft Excel *used* to rule them all. It didn't matter what computer or operating system you had—if you needed to create a spreadsheet, you used Excel.

Times have changed! Today, there are many spreadsheet solutions out there. Some, like Google Sheets, are pretty barebones; and others, like Excel, feel at times feature creep—there are just so many options, it's easy to get lost. If you use a Mac, iPad, or iPhone, then you have a third option that's growing in popularity: Numbers.

In addition to being simple, yet visually stunning, Numbers comes free with Apple devices. What's even better is it's pretty easy to get started, even with limited knowledge of the software.

If you really want to get the most out of it, then this guide will help. It will show you the ropes—including how to do all those things you are used to doing in Microsoft Excel - and help you with some of the features you may not even know about.

Ready to get started? Let's go!

[1]

The Basics

This chapter will cover:

- How to get Numbers
- Opening your first document
- Numbers crash course
- Formatting text
- Layouts and styles

How To Get Numbers

Depending on how you acquired your Mac, you may or may not have Numbers already. Getting it is easy. And even better: getting it is free! (You can see if you have it by going into the Launchpad from the dock and searching for Numbers).

There's one catch: not all Macs are supported. But most are. MacOS 10.14 is required to run Numbers, which means you must have one of the following computers:

- MacBook: Early 2015 or newer
- MacBook Air: Mid 2012 or newer
- MacBook Pro: Mid 2012 or newer
- Mac Mini: Late 2012 or newer
- iMac: Late 2012 or newer
- iMac Pro
- Mac Pro: Late 2013 or newer; Mid 2010 or Mid 2012 models require a Metal-capable GPU

As long as you have one of those, then you can go to the App Store (it's in your Launchpad). Numbers is a digital download only—you cannot obtain a physical copy of it. The download is a few hundred MB.

From there, type in Numbers in the search bar, and hit the return key.

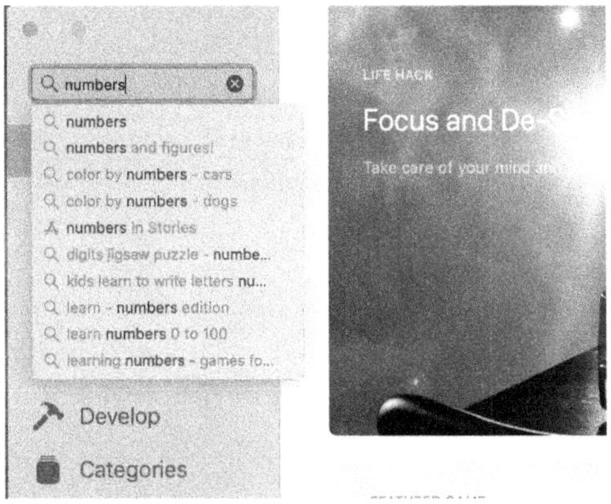

If you have it, the return result will have an Open button; if you don't have it, the result will show a Get button. When you click Get, you'll be prompted to put in your Apple ID and password; if you don't have an Apple ID, then follow the onscreen instructions to get one (this is free).

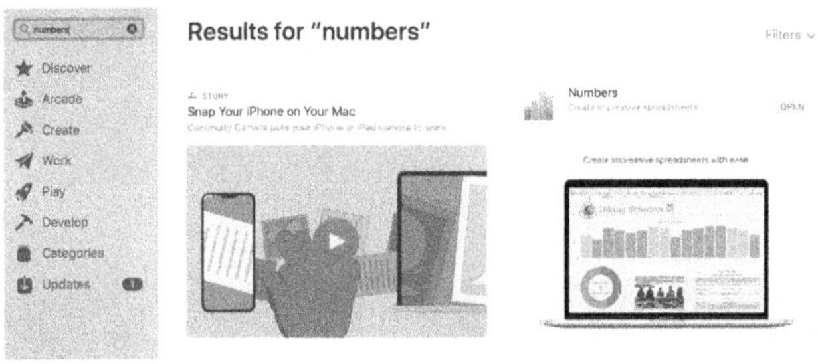

Running Numbers for the First Time

When you first open Numbers, you'll be asked if you want to use iCloud. I recommend you do; this makes it easy to save and open documents across all devices—if you are writing a document on your phone, for instance, you can open that document and continue working on it from your tablet—it's all very seamless and doesn't require anything extra on your part once it's set up.

If you set up iCloud, you can even access and type documents right in your browser—there's nothing else to install on your computer, which means "technically" you could use Numbers on a Windows computer or even a Chromebook or Android device—I'll show you how at the end of this chapter.

The Numbers Crash Course

The first time you use Numbers, you'll get a brief tutorial. You can either watch it or skip it.

Each time you open Numbers, you'll be greeted with a directory box that asks you if you want to open an existing document or if you want to create a new one. We'll be working off a new document in this chapter, so click "New Document" in the lower left corner.

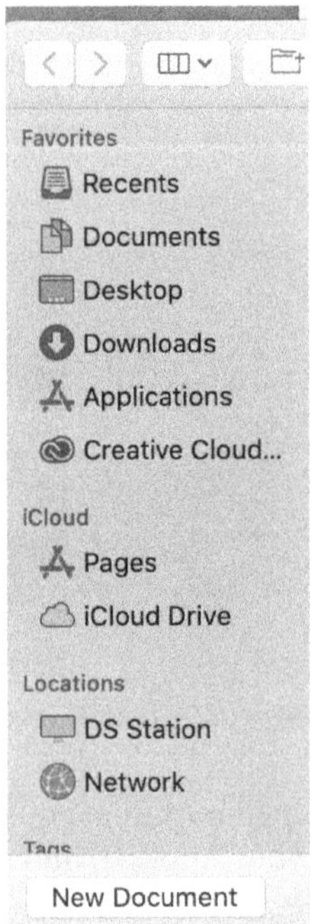

The next box you'll see is all the available templates you can use. A template is a premade document that you can add text into. For example, if you want to create a calendar, you can use the calendar Template, and you will keep the formatting but type over the text that's there with the text that matches what you want. Templates are listed under categories.

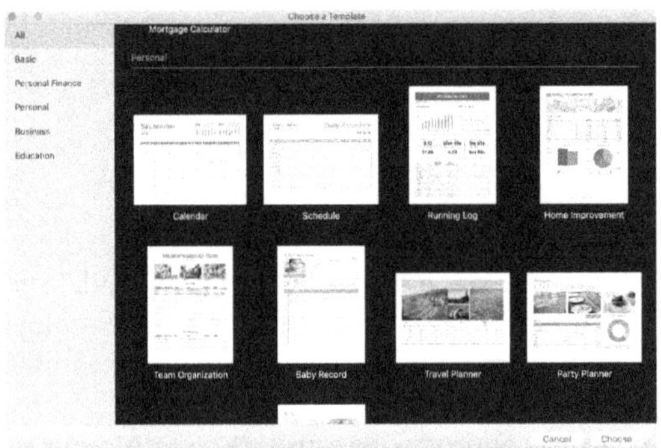

You'll probably notice something quite unique about some of these templates: they don't look like spreadsheets. Like everything Apple, they put a lot of detail into making things look beautiful. Yes you can do your old fashioned spreadsheet here, but you can do so much more.

If you don't want to start with a template, then click on the first option (which says Blank).

First time users of Numbers are often a little disappointed the first time they use Numbers; if you've Excel, then you have ribbons and menus and options everywhere! Numbers looks pretty bare next to that.

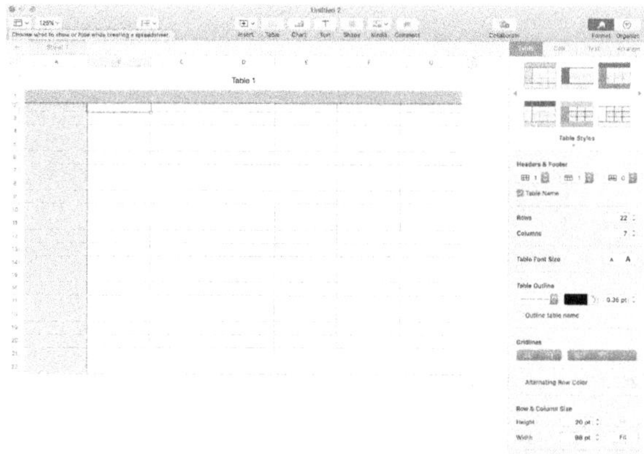

Don't worry—looks can be deceiving; there are plenty of options when you know how to find them, and I'll show you each of them in this book. If you need reassurance, look at those Templates again!

If you feel overwhelmed already because there are options, you can hide that side panel by clicking on the Format button in the upper right corner.

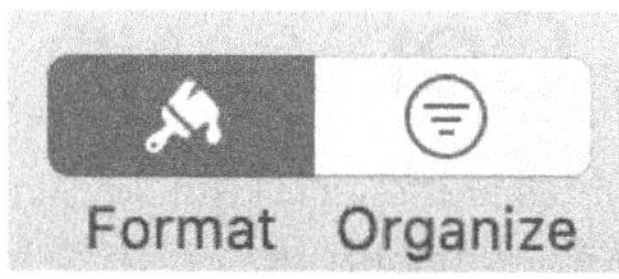

Now that you have a blank screen, let's go over the very basics of Numbers (you can click the Format button again to get the side panel back).

SELECT

To select a single a cell, move your mouse over it and click once.

SELECT INSIDE

To select inside a cell, click the cell and click twice.

SELECT OPTIONS

Now that you have the text selected, what do you do? If you click with two fingers on your trackpad or mouse, then the options box comes up. We'll go over what these options are as we continue the book.

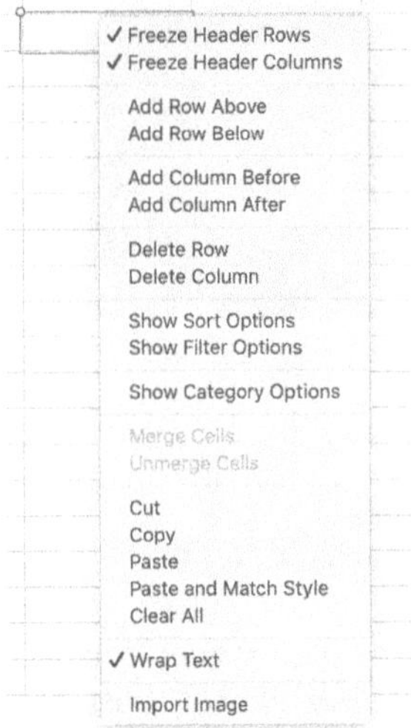

CUT, COPY AND PASTE

To copy and paste words (and images, tables and charts) quicker, you can use keyboard shortcuts.

Selecting content and hitting COMMAND + C will copy it.

Selecting content and hitting COMMAND + X will cut it.

And hitting COMMAND + V will copy the content anywhere you want it in the document.

Remember, if you click a cell and do this command, then you are copying the cell; if you only want the content in the cell (not the cell style, for example) then double click and highlight the content.

FIND AND REPLACE

Find and Replace is a handy little feature in Numbers (especially in large spreadsheets) that allows you to replace your selection with alternatives.

Let's say you just created a 1,000 line spreadsheet full of random names. But once you are done, you realize you need to spell one of the names (Sara) as Sarah. It can be done in seconds!

Go to edit from your menu bar, and select Find > Find.

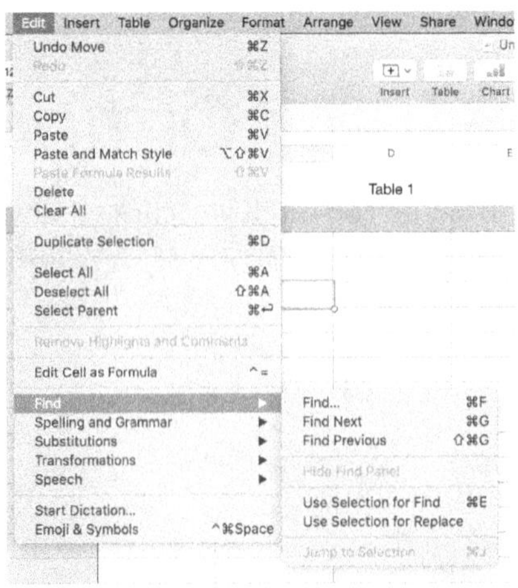

From here you can find all the uses of the word you want to find, but you can also click the down arrow on the left side and select Find & Replace. This lets you search for a word (top line) and replace the word once it finds it (bottom line). When you have both the find and replace word added, then you can click Replace & Find.

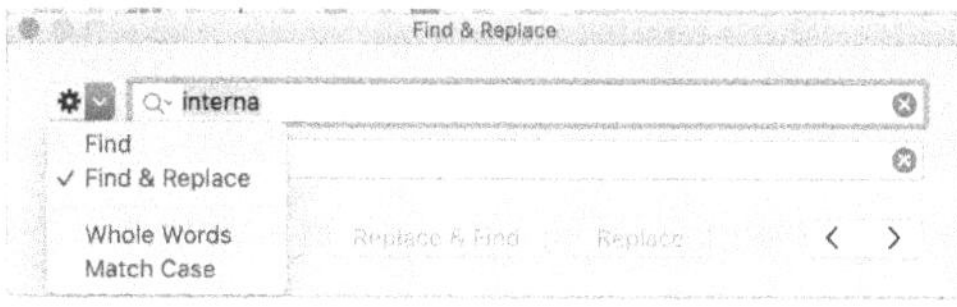

DEFINE

Numbers has a handy little dictionary built in. You can select any word, tap the trackpad twice to bring up the options menu, and tap Look Up to see the definition of any word. Remember you need to select the word and not the cell.

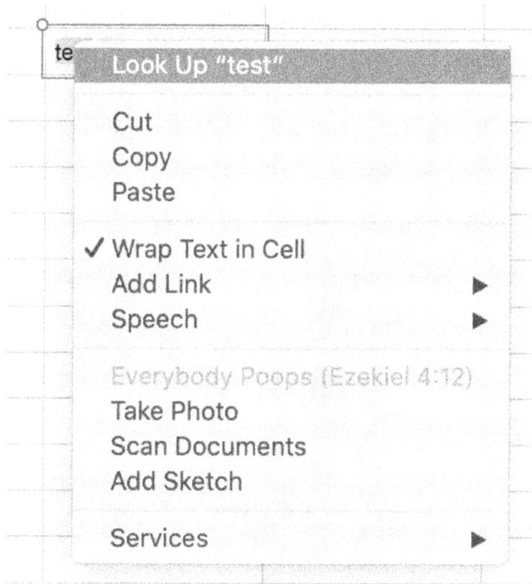

The dictionary will give you multiple definitions (and a thesaurus); even more, you can select options at the bottom to see movies related to the word, Siri Knowledge (which is encyclopedic information), apps related to it, and more!

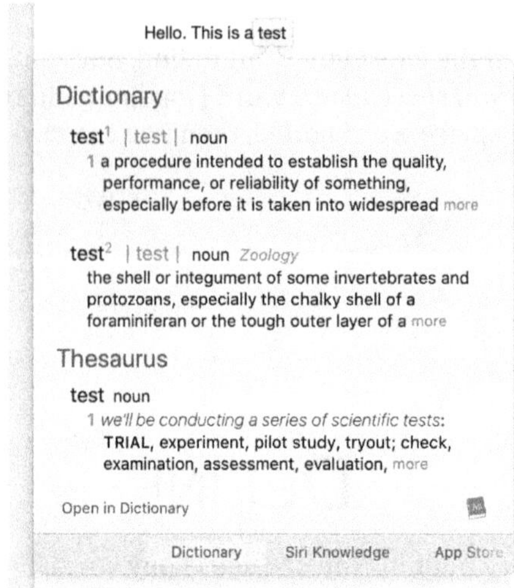

Copy Style

The Style command lets you copy and paste styles, like the Microsoft Word format painter feature. If you ever want to make a piece of text look like another, just select the text with the format you'd like to copy, click Format > Copy Style; then select the text you want to alter and click Format > Paste Style. This can be a major time saver!

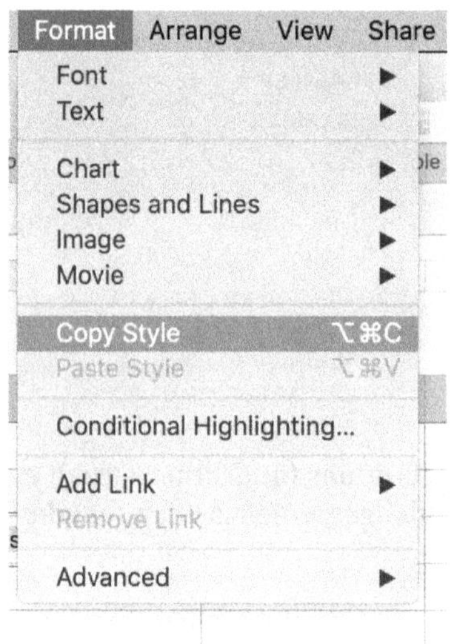

Inserting Hyperlinks

If you want to insert a hyperlink to an internet resource, just type out the link. Numbers automatically detects hyperlinks and will insert the link for you. To edit the link or to change the displayed text, just click the link and then tap Link Settings. Here you can edit the link itself, change the text displayed, or remove the link altogether.

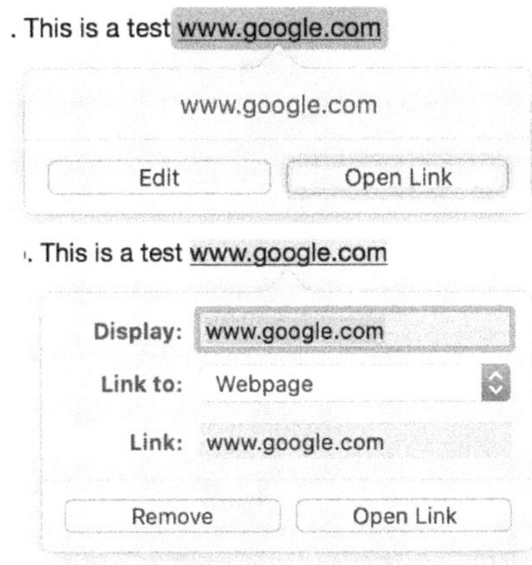

If you aren't typing a web address but want to link the text to a web address (for example, you are typing: "I go to UCLA" and you want to provide a hyperlink to UCLA), then select the word you want to hyperlink and click with two fingers to bring up the options. From here, just click Add Link and select the kind of link you want to add. You can edit and remove it the same way as in the previous paragraph.

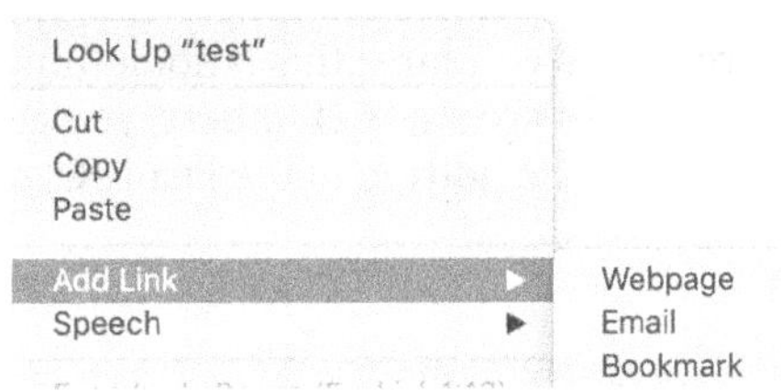

Undo/Redo

If you mess up (for example you delete a paragraph that you shouldn't have) you can Undo it by going to Edit > Undo; you can also redo it under the same menu.

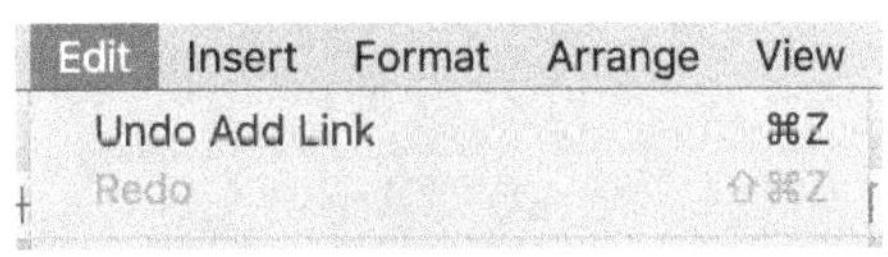

The Formatting Toolbar

There are a few menu options to work with in Numbers, but in this section, we will be covering the Formatting Toolbar, which is on the right side of your document.

The Format menu has four tabs across the top: Table, Cell, Text, Arrange.

The first tab, Table, is where you go to change the look of the overall table. For example, if you want to add a border to it. You can also set the size of the rows and columns.

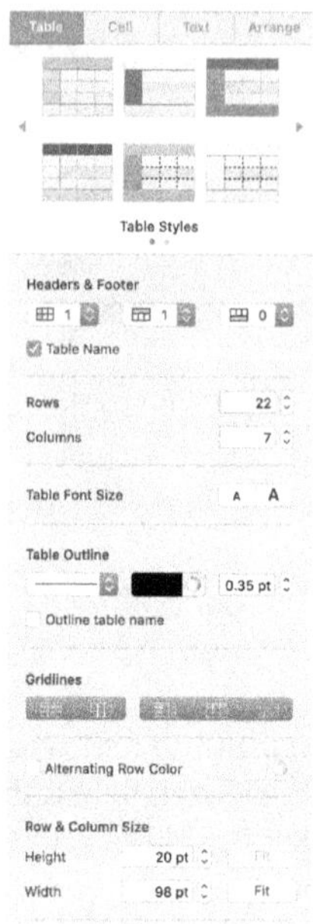

This is also where you can add more rows and columns; this is something distinctively different than Excel. In Excel, you get a spreadsheet that seems like it has endless rows; in Numbers, you get a handful, but can add more. You can do this manually by clicking once on the = button at the bottom of the last row, or to the side of the last column.

The next tab is the Cell options. Where the previous tab made changes globally to the entire table, this menu focuses on cells. You can, for example, select what kind of value the cells have (i.e., they should be formatted like dates or currency); you can also select the type of borders (if any) the cells should have.

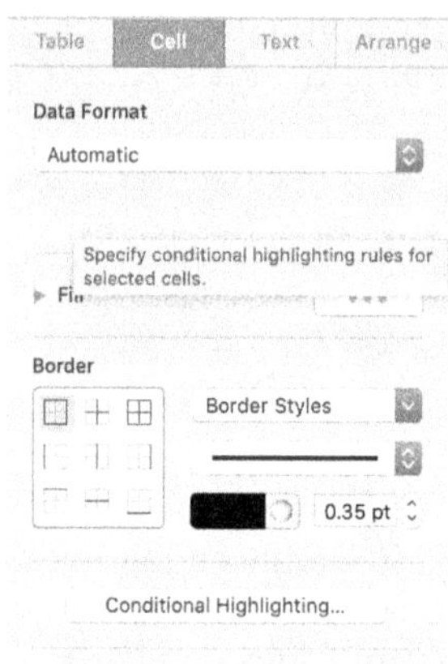

Under the Text tab, it will say "Body" by default. When you click it, you'll see several options. "Body" is normal text in a document—the text you are reading right here would be considered Body Text. Documents have several types of paragraph text; for example, each section of this chapter has a "Heading"—you could just change the font size and make it "look" like a heading, but using a Paragraph Style tells Numbers what kind of text it is so it can put together a table of contents later.

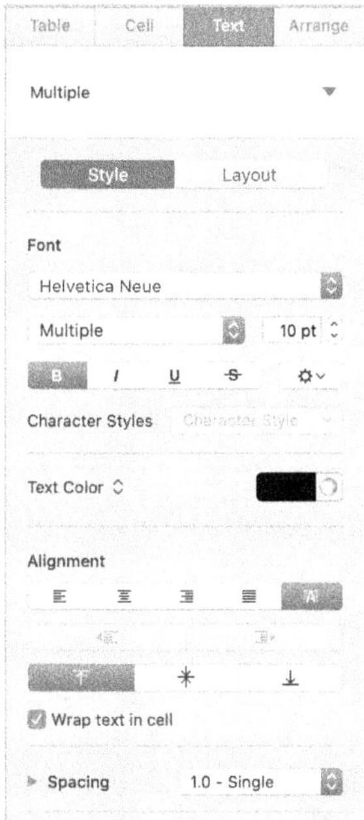

Some of the styles will not be very common, "Label Dark" for example.

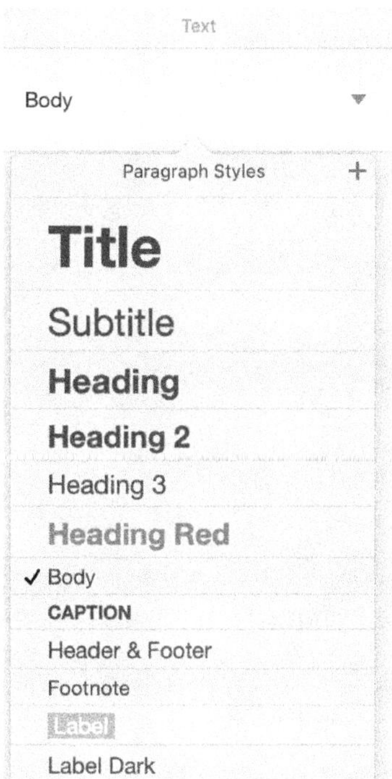

Under this are options for Style, Layout, and More. Let's stay on Style for now, so the next option is Font.

It says 11pt Helvetica; this is the font. If you tap on it, you'll be able to select a new font and adjust the size. Numbers offers a healthy font selection, including perennial favorites like Arial, Times New Roman, and Helvetica. Some notable absences include Comic Sans (and yet Papyrus still made the cut!), Calibri, and Cambria.

The "regular" dropdown shows you all the style choices for that font (some fonts have different options).

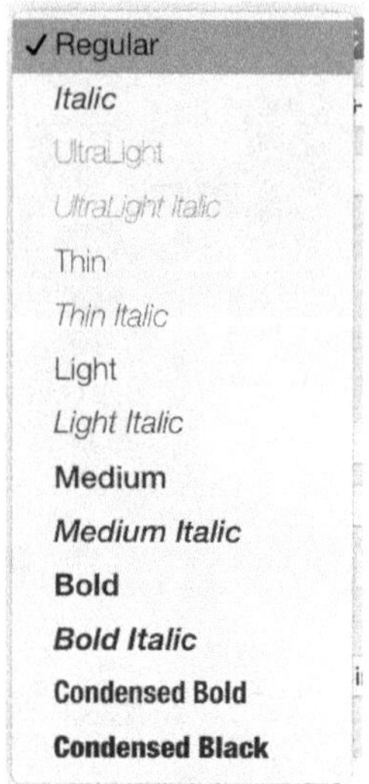

The next three buttons are fairly standard. If you're not familiar with computerized word processing, though, remember B for Bold, I for Italic, and U for underline. The S with a line through it puts a strike across any text you type.

Below this are your alignment buttons. Tap them for options to align your text left, center or right, or justify it. Justified text is text that fills one line exactly. Try it out to see how it works.

The next two buttons are indent buttons. Use them to indent, or to move backwards through indents.

Finally, below this is where you can add bulleted lists and line spacing (if you want to double space, for example).

The last tab is the Arrange menu. The Arrange menu makes a little more sense when you see how photos work in the next chapter. The thing you should know here, however, is that you should think of your spreadsheet as an object on a canvas. If you put a photo in front of it, you can go here to make the spreadsheet go in front of or behind the photo—just like you would any other object.

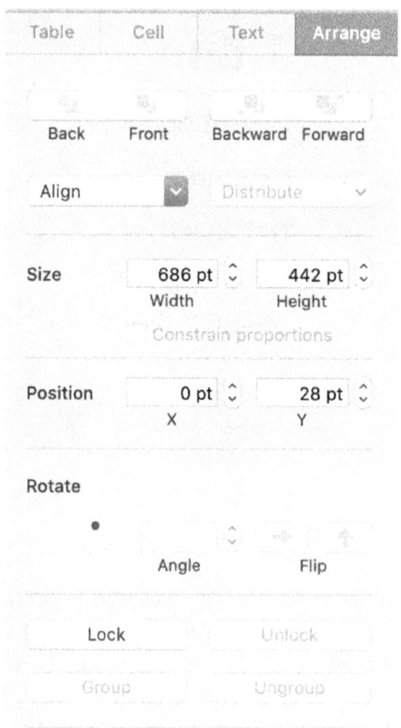

FUN WITH FUNCTIONS

Now that we've had some fun, let's get serious and learn about functions.

What is a function, exactly? Functions is basically making calculations. It lets you add up rows, see the average, and so much more.

You tell Numbers that you intend to do a Function when you hit the equals (=) key. This brings up a functions command box.

It also brings up a side menu with a list of over 250 functions!

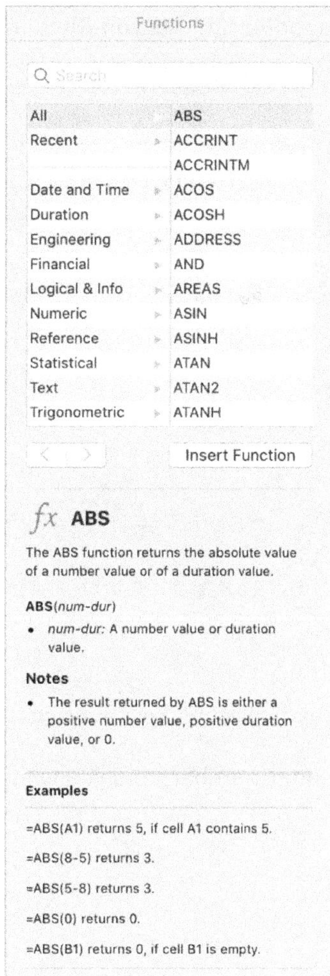

There are obviously a lot of functions! You can also see these functions on Apple's website: https://www.apple.com/mac/numbers/compatibility/functions.html

HOW DO FUNCTIONS WORK?

Functions can be quite complicated…but they can also be ridiculously easy. While there are functions that will make your head spin trying to figure them out, there are lots of functions that will be second nature to you.

You can use functions like a calculator, for example. Try it. Type "=2*3".

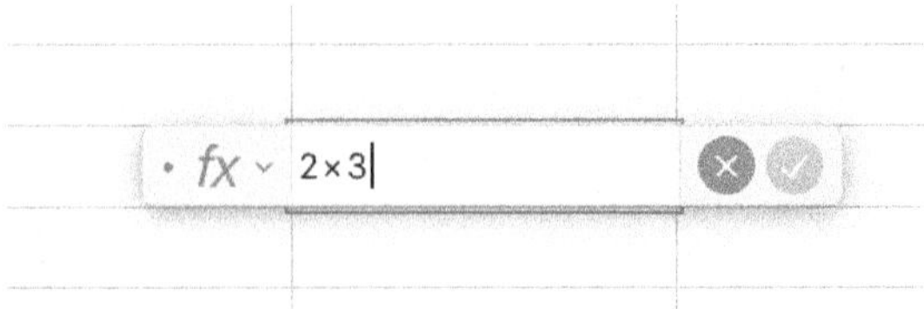

Once you hit enter on your keyboard (or click the green button), you should get 6.

The only equation that might be confusing if you've never used functions is divisions; there is no divide key on the keyboard. So if you want to divide, use the slash key "/".

You can make the equation as easy or as complicated as you want. In the example below, I am using parenthesis for a longer problem.

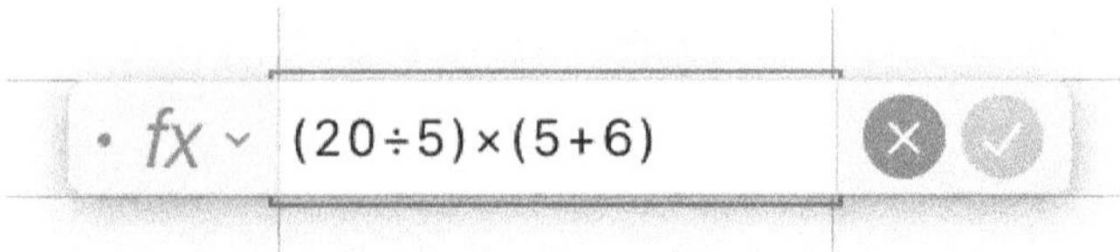

If you do something wrong, you'll get an orange triangle; you can click on the triangle and see what it doesn't like.

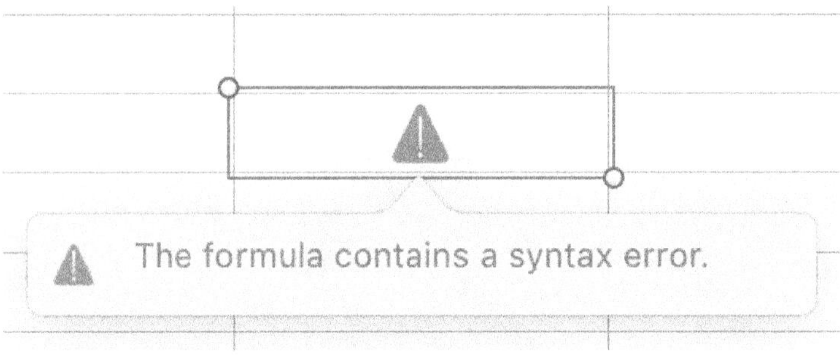

That's all nice, but couldn't you just use a calculator?! Yes! But functions really start to come in handy when you use them with the content that's in your table.

As an example, let's say you have a column of numbers and you want to add them all up.

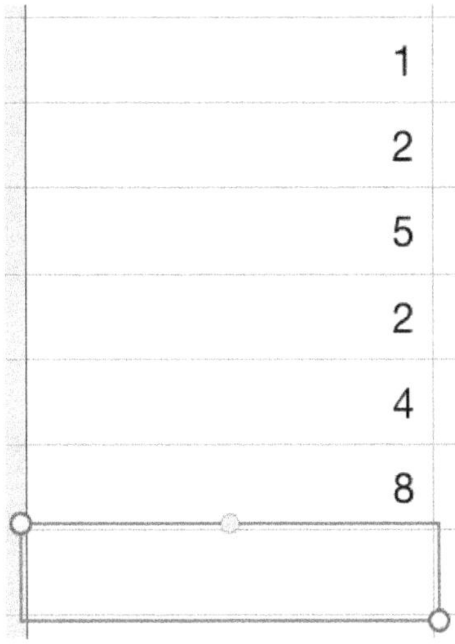

In this example, I'm going to put the sum under them, but there's no rule about this: you can do the formula wherever you want. Just hit the = key, then type "sum" and highlight what you want to add up.

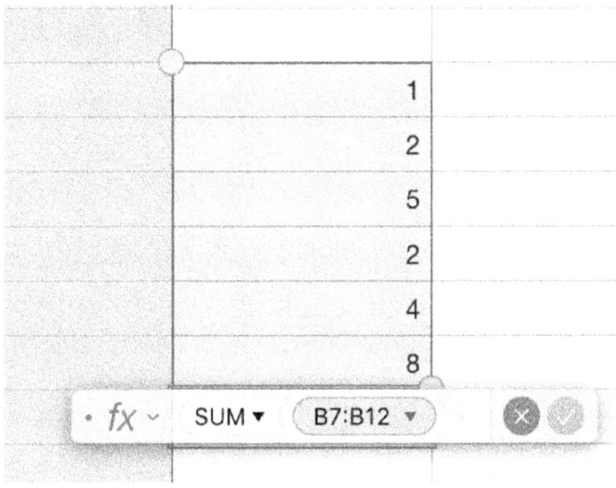

You can also hit the Command button on your keyboard and only select certain cells.

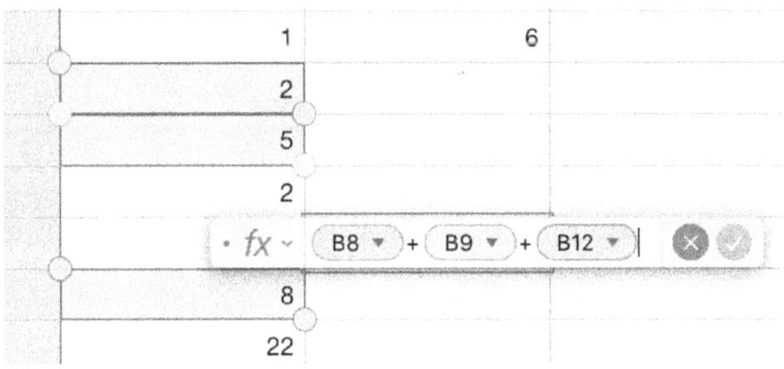

Because this is a beginner's guide, I won't cover advanced functions. Here are the basic ones that you should know:

- Average (shows the average number in a range of numbers)
- Median (shows the median number in a range of numbers)
- Min (finds the smallest number in a selected range)
- Max (finds the largest number in a selected range)
- Count (this is useful if you have numbers and text in a range; count will count all the cells with numbers for you)

- Round (if you are dealing with a lot of decimals, this can help you round to a smaller decimal point)

YOUR TABBED LIFE

Numbers borrows from most other spreadsheet applications, so it should be no surprise that you can have multiple worksheets within a document.

To add a new tab, just click the + button above the default sheet (hint: it's to the left of the tab that says "Sheet 1")

This creates a second tab (by default, it will be called "Sheet 2"). You can now toggle between two worksheets. When you start doing formulas, you can also go into another worksheet and use a figure from there (for example, you could add the cell in worksheet 1 with the cell of worksheet 2).

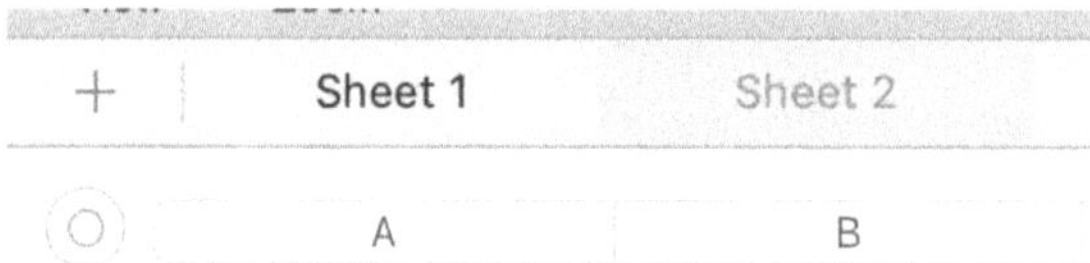

You can rename any of the worksheets by right clicking and clicking rename. In the same area, you can also delete, copy or duplicate the worksheet.

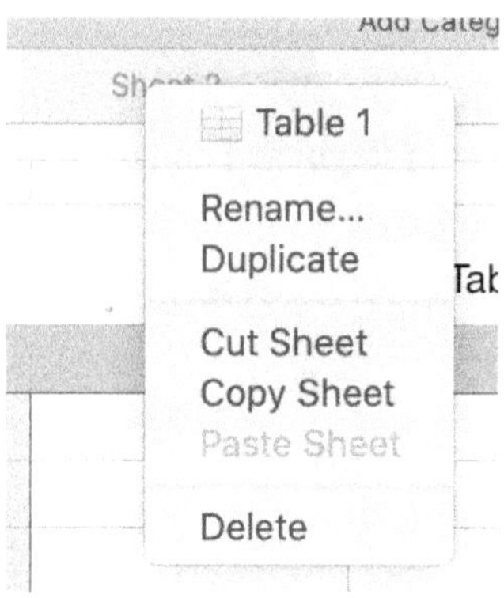

OPENING NUMBERS FROM ICLOUD

Numbers can be run right from your browser; it's great for editing, but for intensive design work, the best solution will be your computer.

To access it from your browser, head to iCloud.com and sign in with your Apple ID.

The first screen you'll see will show you all the things you can do from the cloud; one of them is using Numbers. Click it once to open it.

As long as you've been saving your work to the cloud, then any recent docs will show up here and you can click on their thumbnail once to open them.

You can additionally start a new Doc by clicking on the + button in the upper right corner. This will open up Numbers for iCloud. All the features covered in this book can be found in Numbers for iCloud as well.

Managing Documents

Saving in Numbers is pretty straightforward—especially if you've used Windows before. It's under File > Save.

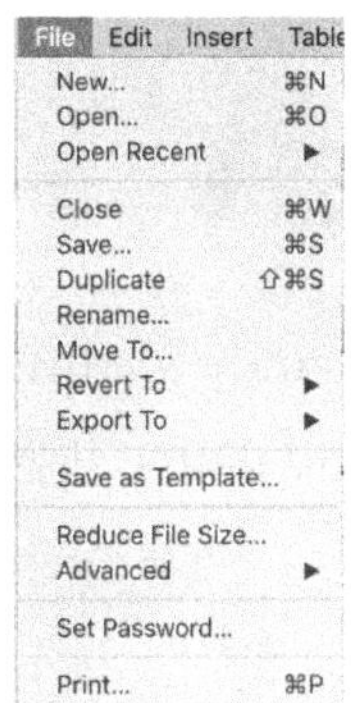

Before we move forward with using other features in Numbers, I want to go over the less straightforward ways to manage documents.

Renaming Documents

Renaming documents is very easy. Like with many things in Numbers, there's more than one way to do it. The easiest way is when your document is open; just click on the name in the top center of the document.

The next way is File > Rename.

The third way is to find it in Finder, click with two fingers, and select Rename.

PRINTING

Printing in Numbers is a little different from other programs. It's in the same place (File > Print), but the print mode looks a bit different.

Since spreadsheets can be quite large, one handy feature in this mode is content scale; this will adjust how large the sheet is so it fits on one or two pages of paper. It will make the content smaller, however.

[2]

PHOTOS FOR NUMBERS

This chapter will cover:

- Insert image
- Arrange / Rotate / Wrap image
- Edit Mask / Alpha
- Image Styling

As much as possible, I'm trying to make learning Numbers fun; there's no better way to make something fun than with photos!

As we go, we'll be learning more about styling tips, but before we get there, we are going to learn about photos—not just about inserting them into the document, but about how to apply more advanced techniques to them.

INSERTING AN IMAGE

Inserting an image can be done several ways. You can copy and paste an image into the spreadsheet, you can drag a photo into the spreadsheet, or you can pick it manually.

To pick it manually, you can go to Insert > Choose, and then find the file location.

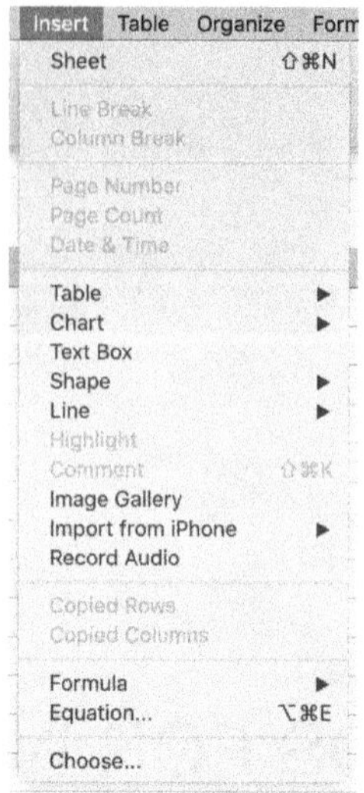

The quicker way to add a photo, however, is from the menu. Click the image button, which shows you all the different media types you can add. You can get photos by clicking on Photos or Image Gallery (if the photos are in your gallery) or by clicking "Choose" to pick where the photo is located.

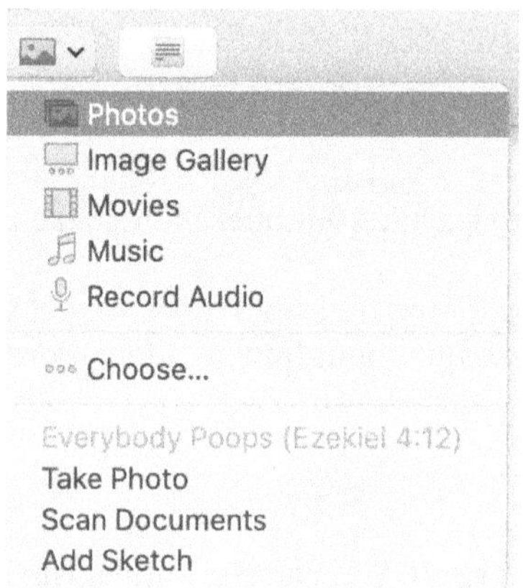

If you pick photos, it's not going to show you all of your photos—just the photos in that photos area of your Mac. You could, for example, have a photo on your USB drive. If that's the case, then you'd want to pick "Choose" from the previous menu instead of photos.

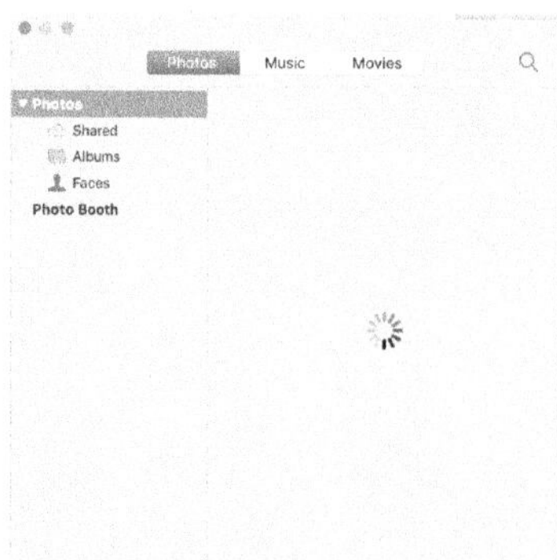

RESIZE AND ROTATE

Once your image is inserted, you can use your mouse to move it, resize it, and rotate it. Resizing is pretty straightforward. Click the image, then move to the corner or side of the image and move the little squares on the edges in and out. To rotate the image you'll do the same thing, but when you get to the corner of the image, press the Command key on your keyboard. This will show you a curved line and also show you the percentage of the rotation as you move the image.

Hint: Looking for images? I often use a website named pexels.com to find public domain (or free to use) images.

There's one more way to rotate an image. When you click on the image, you'll notice that the side panel that you used to format text has changed. It's now a new menu with controls to format an image.

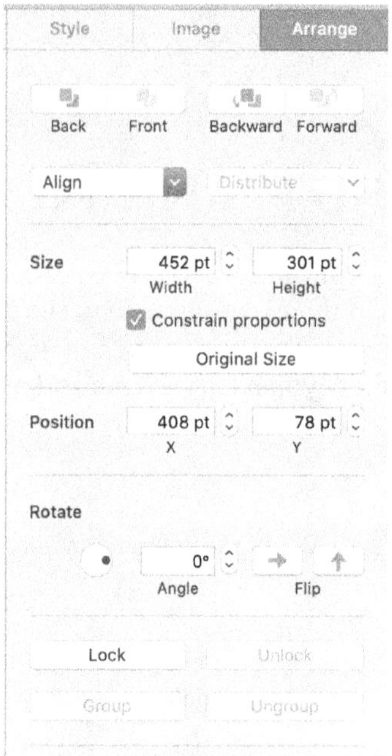

There are three buttons on top of this menu (Style, Image, Arrange); we'll go over the first button in the next section, but for this section, go to Arrange.

On the bottom of this menu, there's a section called Rotate; angle is what you want to use here. The mouse is a quick and easy way to rotate your image, but if you want precision, then this is the best method. Next to the Angle button, you can also vertically and horizontally flip the image using the arrows.

The next set of options let you pick the size of the image; again, you can do this manually with your mouse, but this lets you be a little more precise.

Finally, the last option lets you pick the placement of the image—if you want it in the middle of the page, for example.

Watermark

There's no "official" watermark feature, but you can use the Arrange tab to send a photo behind the spreadsheet (using the back / front, backward / forward buttons)

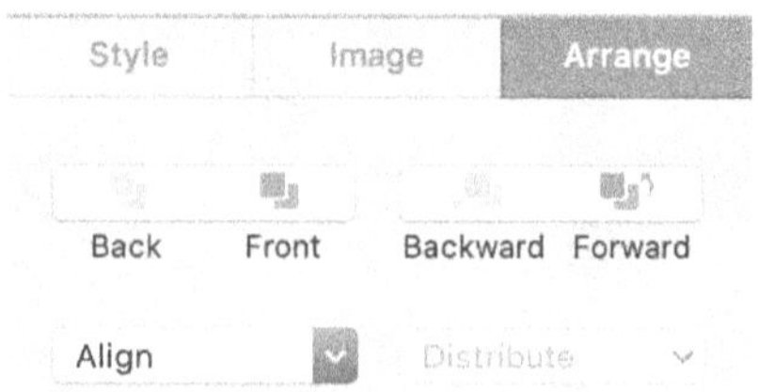

The problem is the photo will probably make the numbers on the sheet difficult to read.

The quick fix is to click the Style menu tab and lower the Opacity.

This makes the image somewhat transparent, which will make text in front of it much easier to see.

IMAGE GROUPING

There's one last section that's greyed out. Grouping. Grouping is greyed out because you need two images to use it.

Add a second image, then click the image, press command on your keyboard, and select the second image; the Group option is no longer greyed out. What grouping does is put two images together, so that when you edit the size, rotation, etc., you are treating the two photos as one image.

If you want to edit just one image, you don't have to ungroup it. You can double click the image to tell Numbers that you want to keep them grouped, but that you want to make changes to one photo while they are grouped.

Edit Mask and Alpha

With your image selected (note: if the images are grouped, you need to double click the image you want to edit—you can't edit both images at the same time), then select the Image button.

This brings up options for image enhancements. At the bottom is the Adjustments section; this section is pretty self-explanatory - the Exposure and Saturation sliders will change the amount of exposure / saturation in the image. The Enhance button will do an auto enhancement based on what the computer thinks the image should look like (the reset button will undo it).

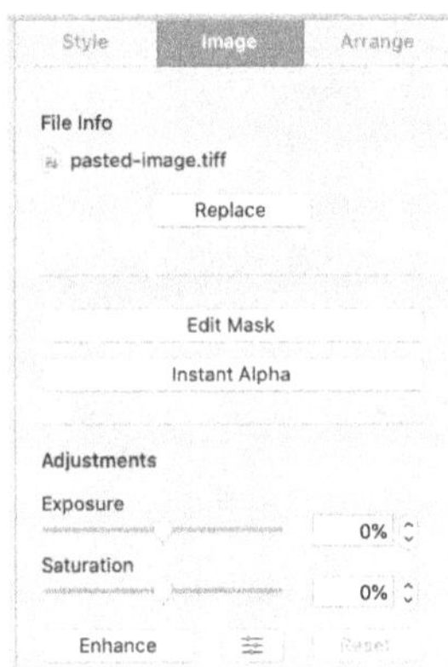

Next to the Enhance button is a control button; this will bring up more adjustment controls.

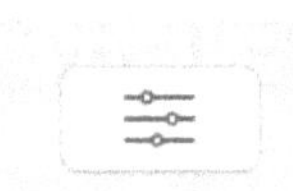

Most people probably won't need this many controls, but it's helpful to know they are there.

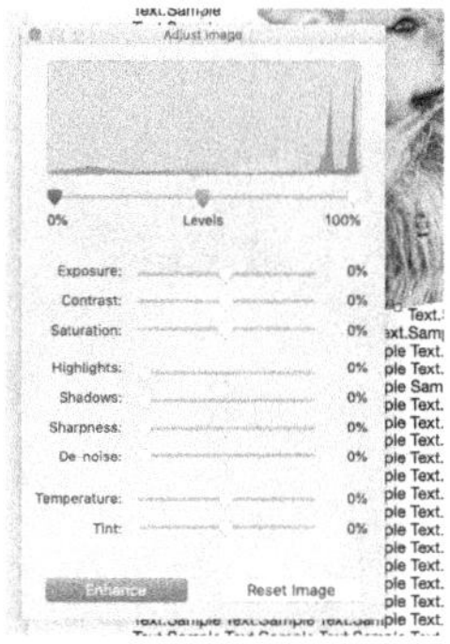

The section that may not be as easy to understand is the top section: Edit Mask and Instant Alpha.

Edit Mask is essentially an image crop. You can use this to cut off parts of the image without resizing it.

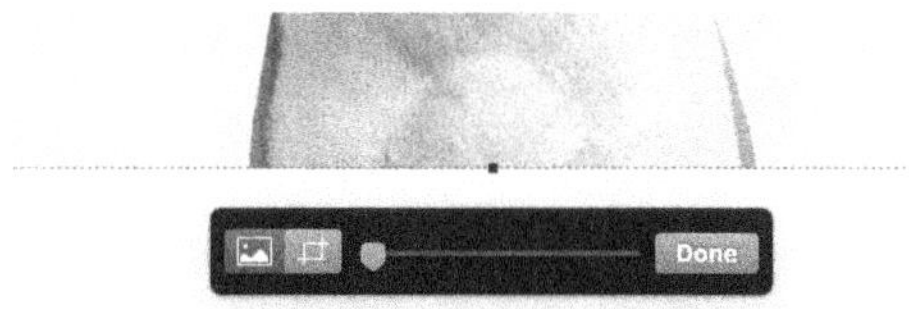

Instant Alpha is one of my personal favorite image editing tools. It removes the background of the image. It's great when your image has a very solid background (you're standing against a solid color wall, for example).

One you click on it, the cursor turns to a square box and you click and drag over the areas you want to take out.

As you click, the sections that are removed will turn a different color to indicate what has been removed. When you're done, let go of the mouse and click the done button.

As you remove the background, it is also autocropping; so if you've removed the background from the top, the image has automatically been cropped to accommodate for it.

Styling Your Image

Now that we know how to move an image around, let's add some style to it.
To style your image, tap the image. Style is the first button on the image edit menu.

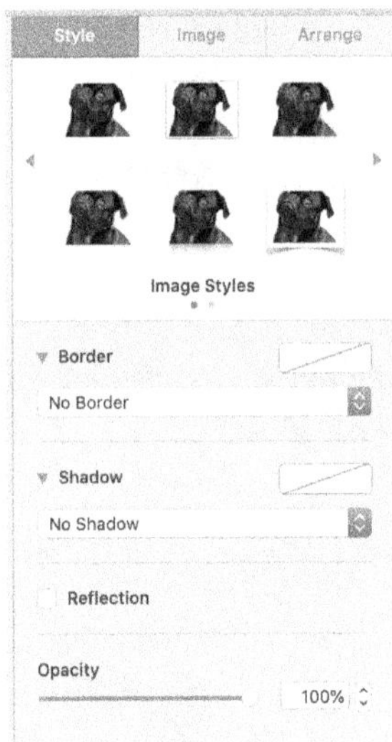

Basic Styles

The top box lets you add quick, pre-defined image styles to your image. For example, if you want your image to have a box around it.

Most people will probably want to do manual editing to the photo, but if you use the arrow in this section, you'll notice a + button. Once you manually make changes to the image (add your transparency, borders, etc.), you can use this button to save these changes, so you can apply them to another photo that you want to have a similar look and feel.

BORDER

The next section is the Border; there is no border on the image by default. If you click the box with the red diagonal line, it will show a dropdown of all the different styles available.

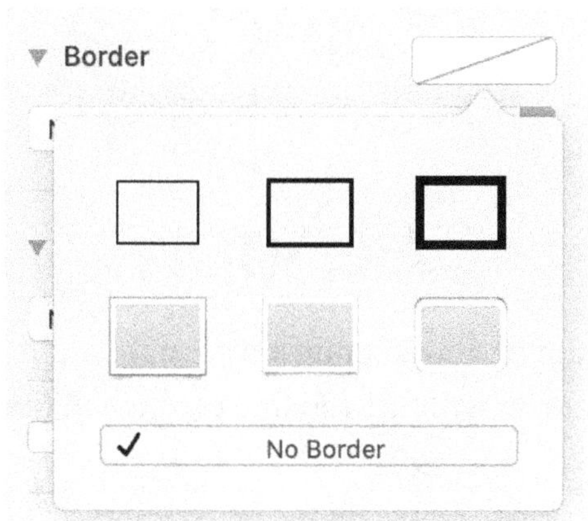

Once you pick your border style, you'll be able to adjust the weight of the border using the slider.

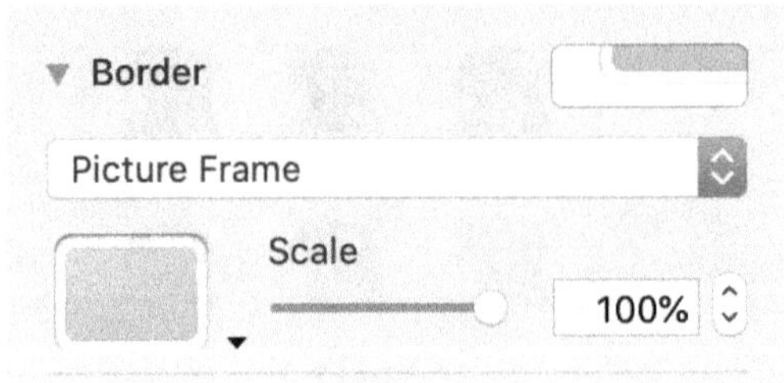

If you click the preview of the border, you will also see all the different border styles available for the style that you have picked. Styles vary depending on the style you are using.

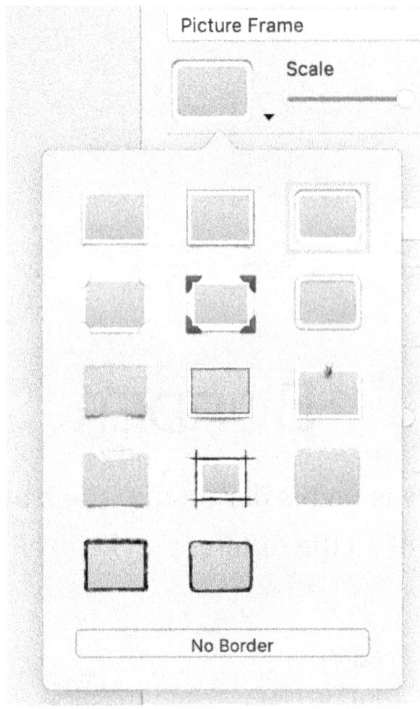

SHADOW

Shadows can add a little more dimension to your photo and help it pop off the page more. It works very similarly to Borders; click the thumbnail with the red line through it, then pick the shadow style.

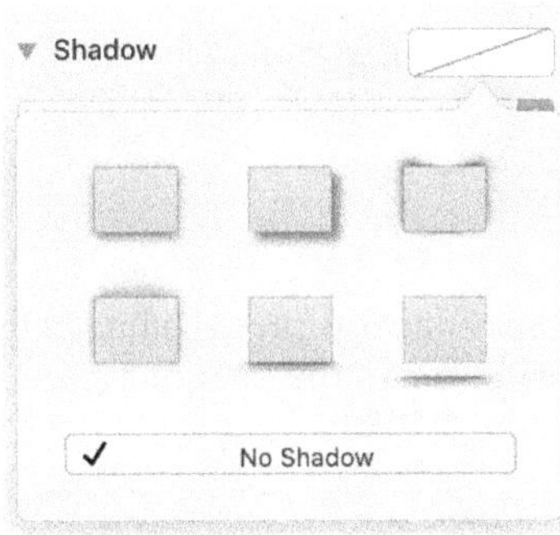

Once you pick the style, you'll get several shadow options to increase or decrease the amount of shadowing used.

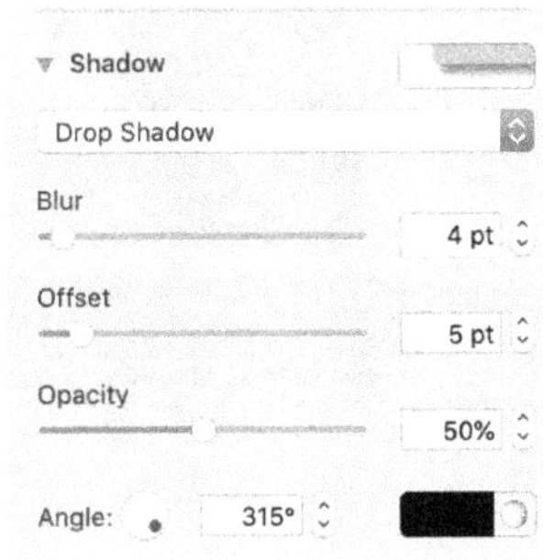

As you make changes, the image will change in real-time, so you immediately see the effects. Notice in the image below how the image has a more 3D look?

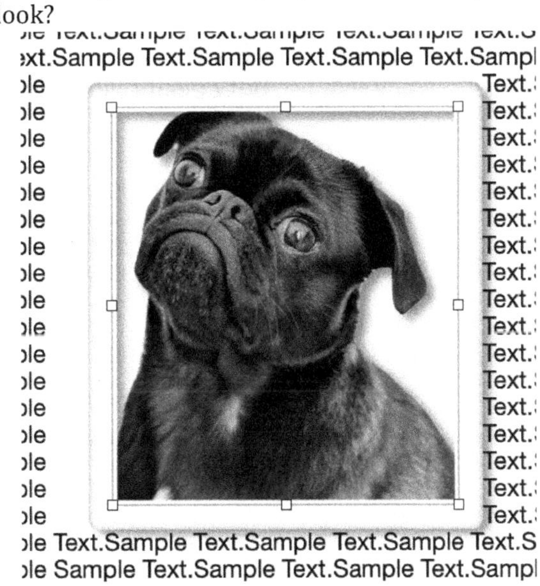

Reflection

Reflection is a simple check / uncheck box; you can use the slider to adjust the amount of reflection used, but that's the only edit available.

You can see in the example below how the reflection gave the image the appearance of an image reflecting on the page (the reflection is the darker area on the bottom of the image).

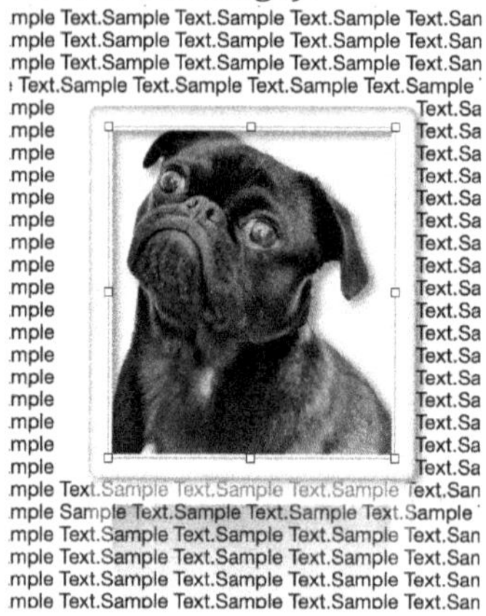

Transparency

The final style change is transparency. Transparency makes an image more see-through (see the example below). This is great for something like a watermark, but doesn't help a lot if you don't have something below the image.

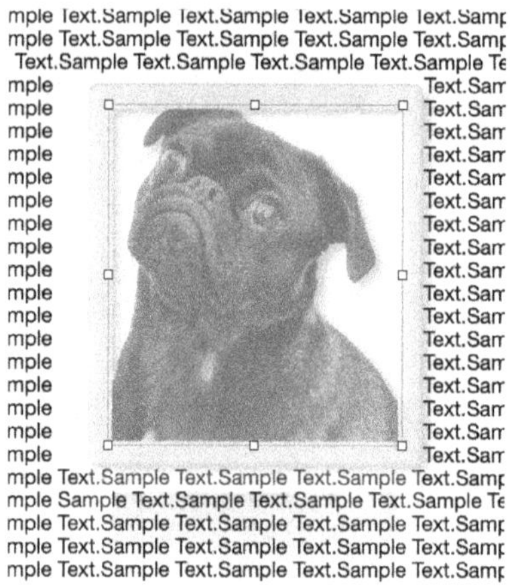

In the below example, I put the transparent image above another photo to illustrate how you can use it on top of another image.

ample Text.Sample Text.Sample Text.Sample Text.Sampl
ample Text.Sample Text.Sample Text.Sample Text.Sampl
ample Text.Sample Text.Sample Text.Sam
ample Sample Text.Sample Text.S
ample Text.Sample Text.Sa
ample Text.Sample
ample Text.Sample
ample Text.Sample
ample Text.Sample
ample Text.Sample
ample Text.Sample T
ample Text.Sample Tex
ample Text.Sample
ample Sample Te
ample Text.Sa
ample Text.S
ample Text.S
ample Text.S
ample Text.
ample Text.
ample Text.
ample Text.Sa
ample Text.Sample Text.Sample
ample Text.Sample Text.Sample Text.Sample Tex
ample Sample Text.Sample Text.Sample Text.Sample Tex

[3]

MANAGING TABLES

This chapter will cover:

- Inserting a table
- Styling a table
- Deleting a table

Numbers is a little different from Excel. You aren't looking at a spreadsheet in Numbers. You're looking at a "table".

What's the difference? At first glance, not a lot. But once you start playing around with tables, you'll notice there are differences. The biggest is that you can have multiple tables in your document. If you wanted to do that in Excel, you'd just open another tab (which you can also do in Numbers).

The below image illustrates two tables in the same workbook (or document). Because they're objects, they can easily be moved around.

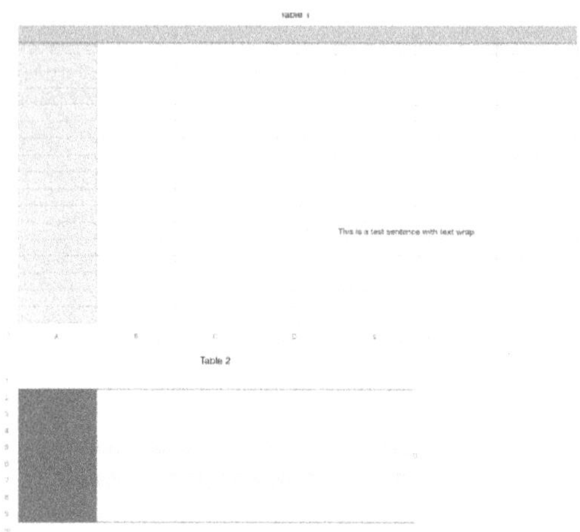

INSERTING A TABLE

If you have ever added a table in Word, then you may be used to picking the size and width before adding the table; in Numbers, you add the table and then adjust it accordingly.

To add a table, tap the Table button from the top menu bar (you can also use Insert > Table from the menu options at the top of MacOS). You'll have several styles to pick from, but again, this is different from Word where you drag it to the number of rows and columns that you want.

Adding Columns and Rows

Your table is now inserted, but chances are it's not the right size.

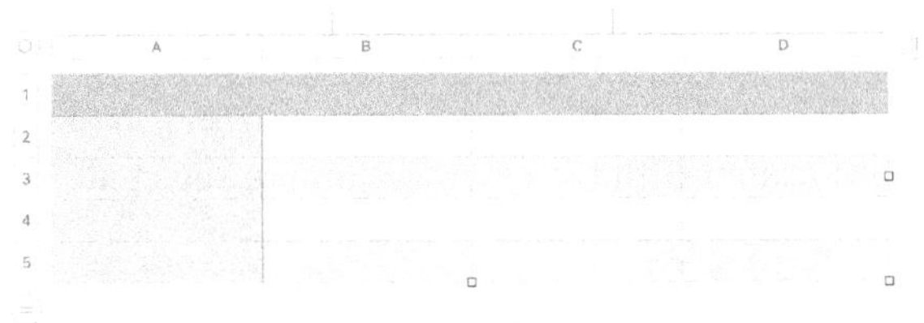

At the bottom of the last row (or the side of the last column) there's a circle with two lines. Click on either of those to adjust the number of columns / rows. You can either use the up / down arrows to pick, or you can click the number and then type the amount you want.

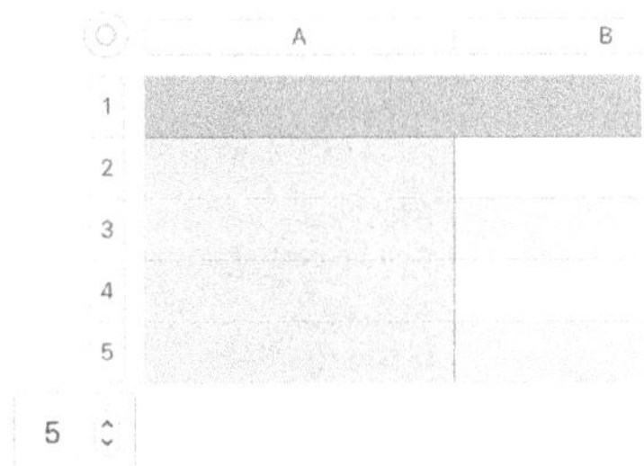

Row / Column Options

If you want to delete or add a row / column, then go to the row or column you want to make changes to, and then click the drop-down arrow. Several options will come up.

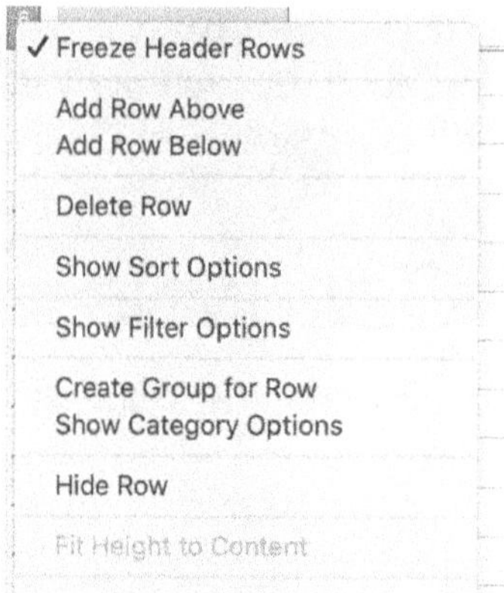

You can also click the number associated with the row / column to select all. This is helpful if you want to copy / paste a row or column.

Table Options

You can see more options by clicking on the Table options in the top menu bar.

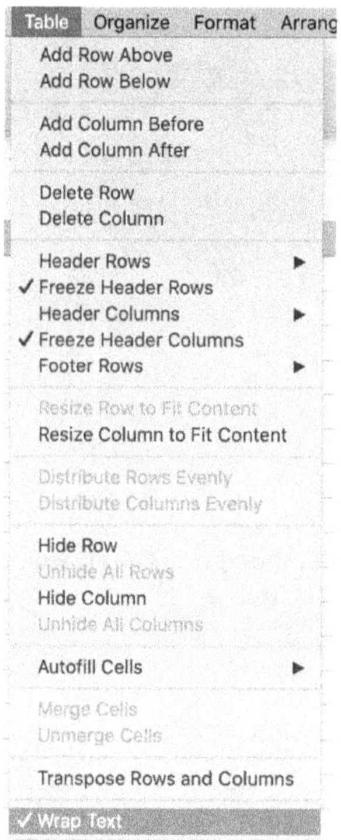

By default, Wrap Text is selected. If you are unfamiliar with text wrap, it means text automatically wraps around the cell like in the example below.

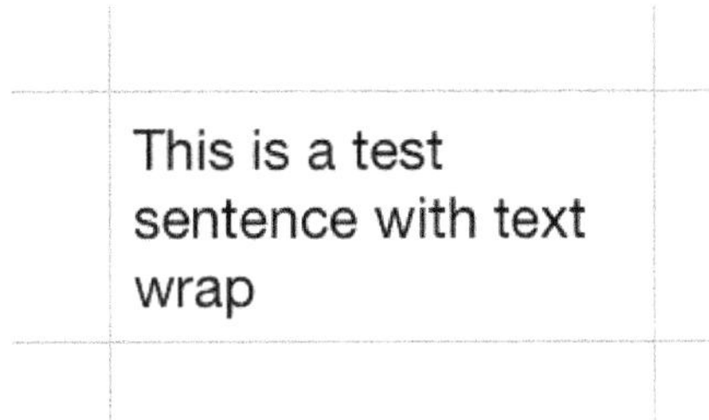

If you turn it off, then it would look like the below example.

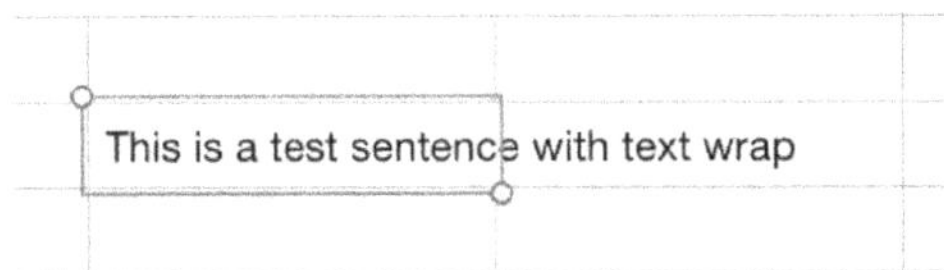

Deleting Tables

Deleting an entire table is a quick process. Click the table. Hit delete.

Importing Tables

Importing a table from somewhere else can be done a few different ways.

The first, and quickest, way is to copy and paste the table. Command V is obviously the easiest way to do this, but go to the Edit menu. Notice there are Paste and Paste and Match Styles options? If you aren't getting the paste results that you want, try this Paste instead.

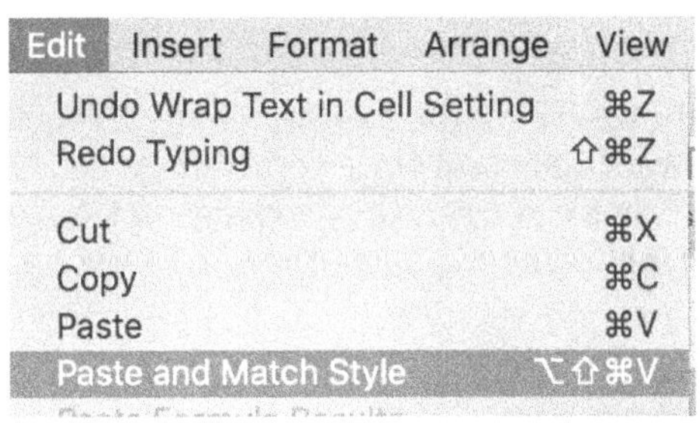

If you don't need to make changes to the table, what a lot of people prefer to do is just make a screenshot of the spreadsheet: Command + Shift + 3 (or Command + Shift + 4 if you want to only select areas of the screen).

[4]

CHARTS

This chapter will cover:

- Inserting a Chart
- Editing Chart Data
- Styling a Chart

Charts can add color and interest to your documents, as well as help you present data more clearly. Numbers includes a powerful Charts feature that allows you to quickly create beautiful, customizable charts that really pop out of the page.

Now that you know how to use Tables, using Charts will be a breeze.

INSERTING A CHART

To insert a chart in Numbers, tap the Insert button, then tap Charts. From here, you'll choose the type of chart (bar, area, line, pie), as well as the style you want. Choose from several different color schemes in 2D, 3D, and interactive. If you change your mind about your chart choice you can always change it later, without losing any data you've entered. Just tap on your favorite chart to insert it into your document.

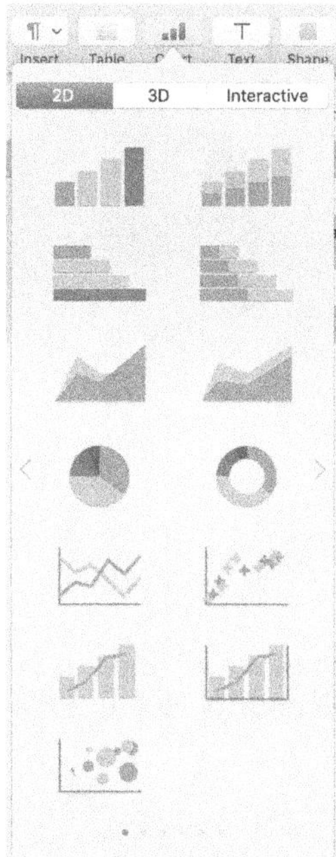

As with almost everything in Numbers, you can also add Charts from the top menu (Insert > Chart).

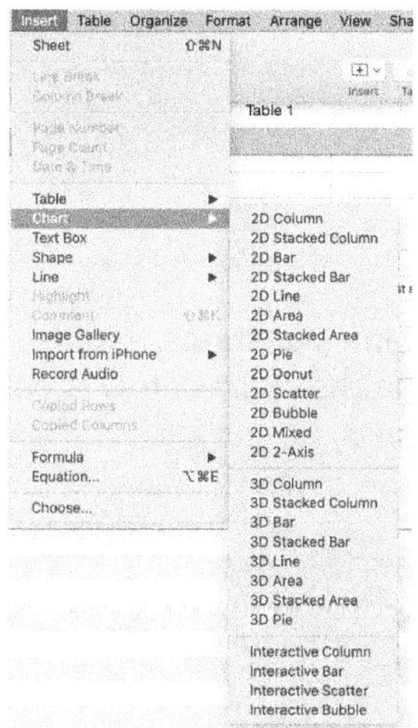

If you want to show a chart of something that's in your table / spreadsheet, then just highlight it before you insert the chart.

Once you have your chart picked, a chart that's already filled out will be added to your document (I'm using a Pie chart in this chapter, but the same features apply to almost all of the charts—they just look a little different).

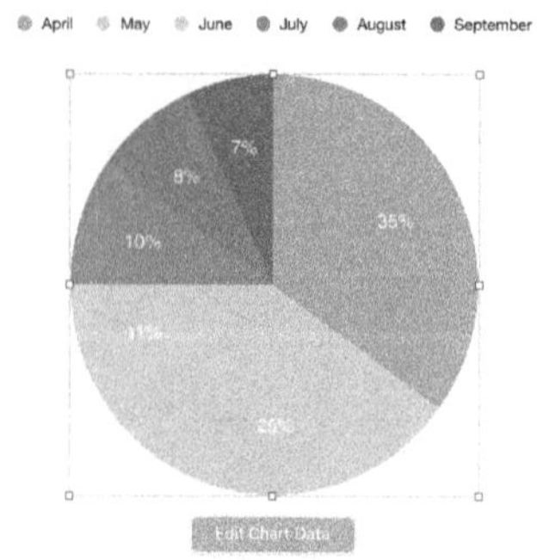

Editing Chart Data

It's so nice for Numbers to put a pretty chart that's all filled out into our document, right? Sure! But wouldn't it be nicer if it had meaningful data? To add your own data, click Edit Chart Data. This brings up a mini table that you can edit with whatever information you want.

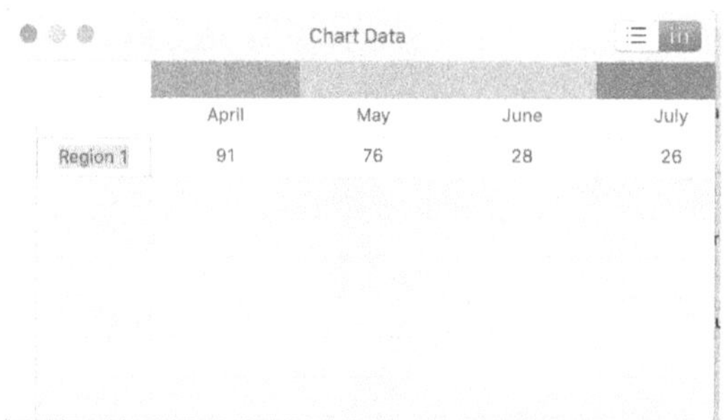

I'm going to replace the months with the names of states, and use an entirely different data range. The chart changes with each change I make in the table. Notice that the chart below is completely different from the one above?

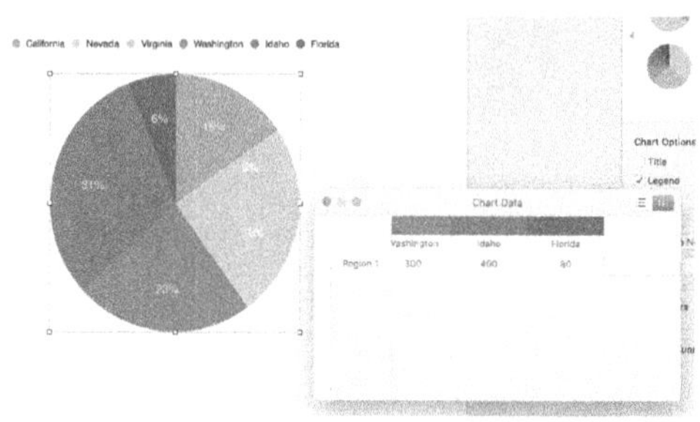

You can enter additional rows if you need to—but this won't work on all charts (like the pie chart).

Styling Your Pie Chart

Now that you have the data you want, it's time to style it.
If you did a pie chart, then you'll see three options on the side (Chart, Wedges, Arrange).

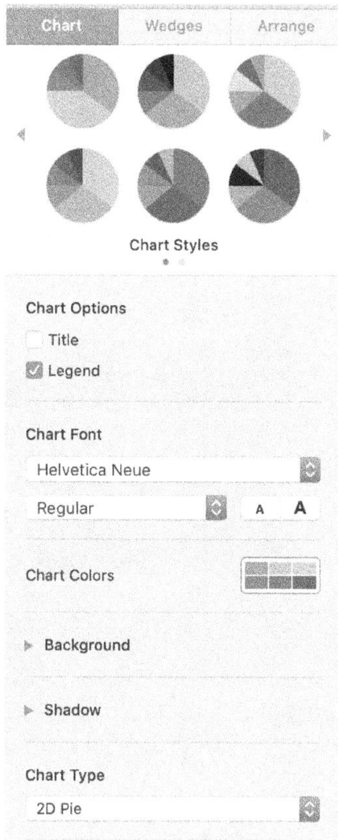

Other charts (like bar charts) have four (Chart, Axis, Series, Arrange).

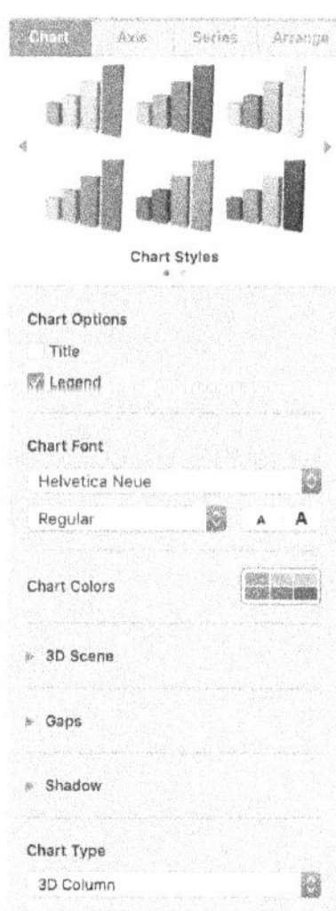

I'll go over the two extra options for a bar chart in the next section.

In the Chart section you can make changes to the entire chart. By default the chart has no title, but if you check off the box, a title (cleverly named "Title") is added to your chart; you'll probably want to name it something else. To do that (and this also applies to renaming pretty much anything in your chart) double click on it and start typing.

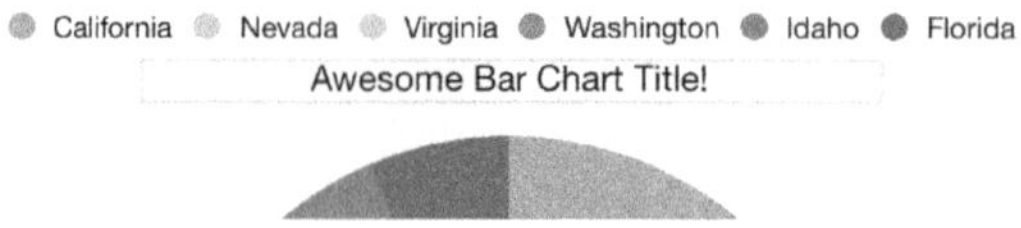

Below the title is where you can change the font, and under that, the chart colors. When you click on the chart colors, it gives you a whole host of pre-defined colors. But what if you want to pick your own?

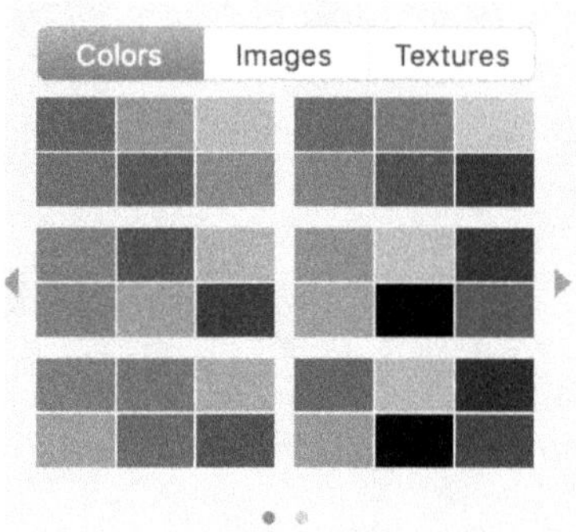

There's one extra small step to picking your own colors. You have to double click on the wedge that you want to change the color of, and then over on the menu options to the right of it, click Style (Style is a new option that's only there if you double click the wedge). From here, you can pick a color under "Fill."

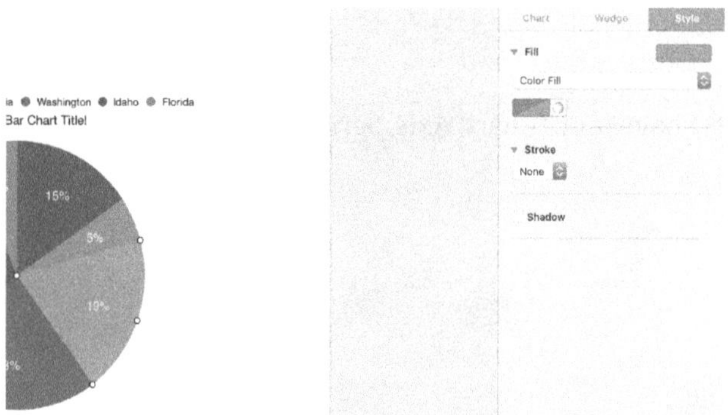

While we are in this section, let's go just under it to Stroke and Shadow. Both of these options help a wedge stand out a little. This is useful if you want to illustrate one area of the chart over others. See in the example below how I added a dotted line (and increased the line weight to 4) and also added a shadow.

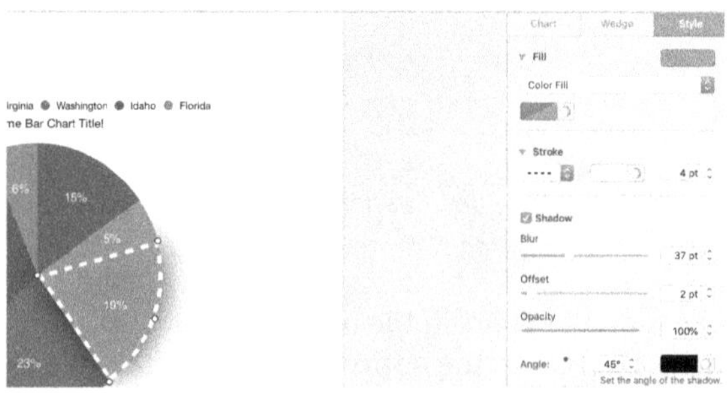

If you really want that wedge to stand out, try pulling it apart from the chart. You can do that by clicking on the Wedge option, and then changing the Wedge Position. Look at the example below; the wedge is now separated in the chart.

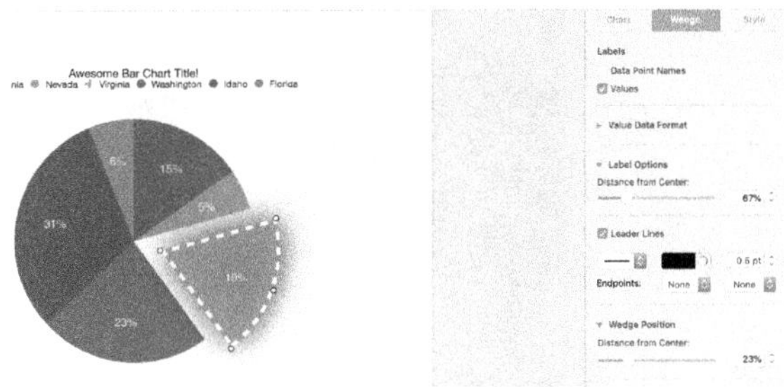

Now let's go back to the chart section and look at the other options we can apply to the entire chart. You can give it a background, add a shadow to it, and finally, change the Chart Type. You can make it a different pie chart or turn it into a line chart (note: this will probably interfere with your data and you may have to redo some of it).

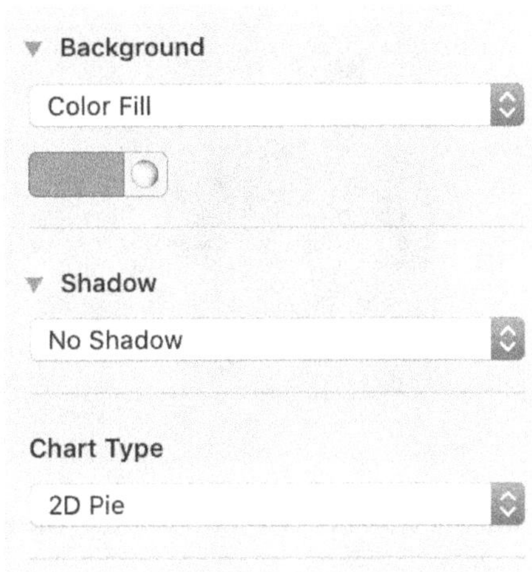

We saw how going to the Wedge section could separate your single wedge from the rest. If you don't double click the wedge and change it, below is what happens.

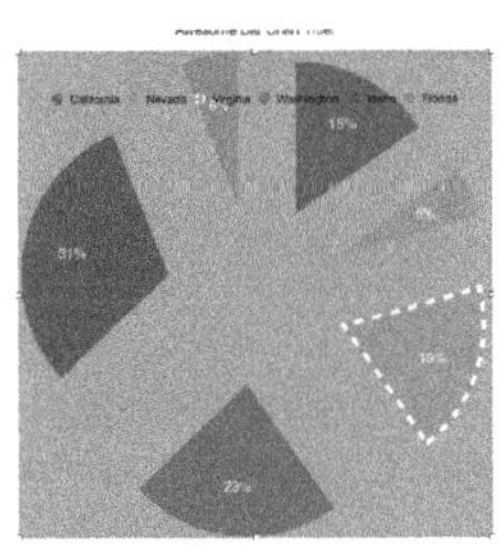

All the wedges separate. If that's what you want, then perfect! If that's not what you want, undo and then double click the wedge you want to separate.

Checking off Data Point Names will put the names of the values in the chart (you can also keep it in the Legend).

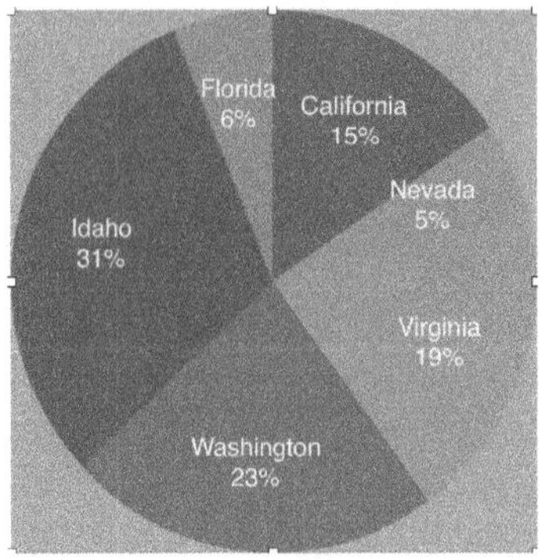

The values on the chart are currently shown as percentages; if you prefer showing them as numbers (or another value type), you can change this under Value Format.

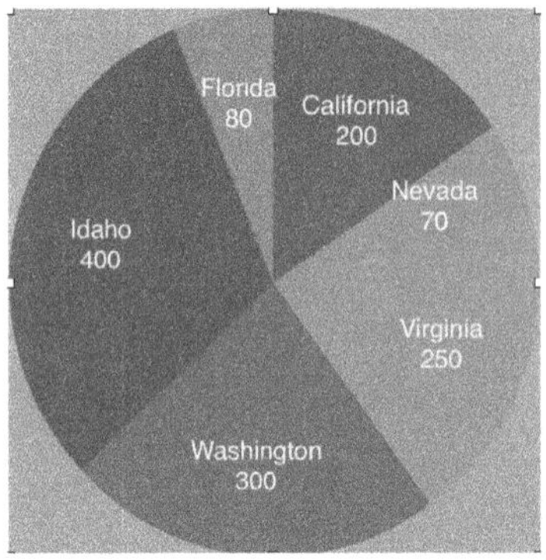

If you check off Lender Lines, you probably won't notice a difference; to see what the lines are, click the Straight drop-down and change it to Angled.

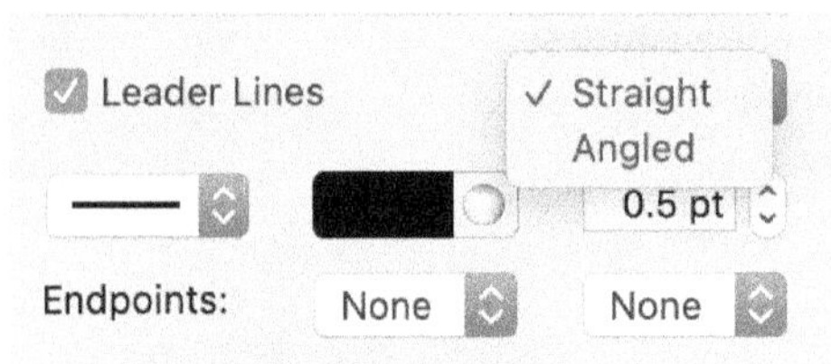

You should now see lines to the sides of the chart.

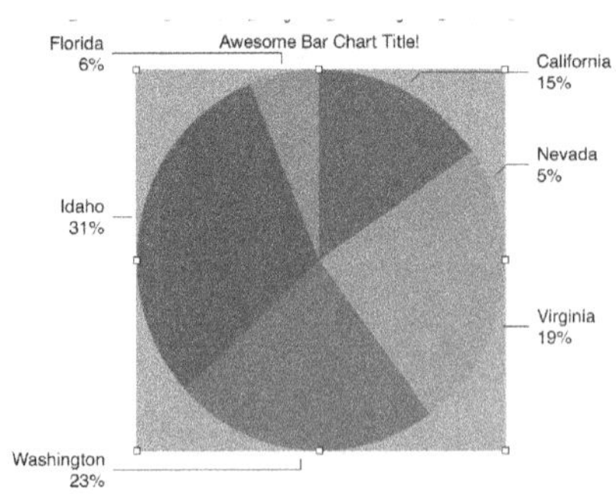

The arrange option should look familiar to you. You've seen it in the Tables section and the Photos section; it's the same features.

Styling Your Bar Chart

Now that you know how to style a Pie Chart, you'll have no problem with the Bar Chart; it's basically the same, but with more options for labels.

In the axis sub-tab, you can turn category labels, series names, gridlines, and titles on and off. Similarly, in the Y-axis or X-axis sub-tab, you can turn value labels, gridlines, and titles on and off. Here you can also specify the number format you'd like to use and adjust the value scale settings. Number formatting includes the option to add prefixes and suffixes, like currency symbols, or suffixes, like %, millions, etc.

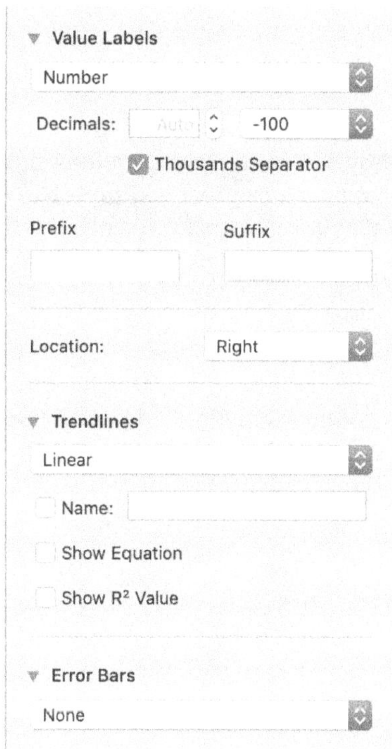

Note: the contents of the sub-tabs change depending on the orientation of your chart. The number formatting option may appear under either the x- or y-axis, depending on the type of chart you've inserted.

[5]

SHAPES

This chapter will cover:

- Inserting a Shape
- Resizing Shapes
- Creating Text Boxes

Pictures are great! They really help your document look snazzy. But there's one more type of graphical illustration you should consider: shapes. Shapes can be great additions to a document – they can be used to draw attention to an area of a document or to illustrate your points graphically. Numbers offers a number of handy pre-made shapes for you to use, and I'll show you how to get the most out of them.

INSERTING A SHAPE

To insert a shape into a document, click the shape button or go to Insert > Shape from the top menu. This will bring up all the shapes available for you. Find the one you like and click it to insert it.

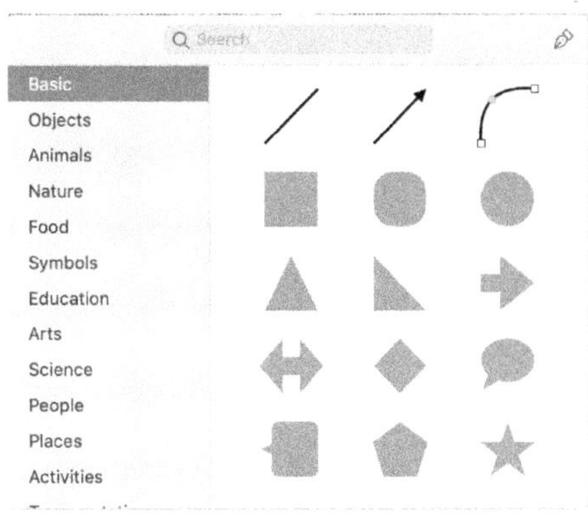

Remember that you can change the color, border and shadow/reflection effects later!

Shapes sounds a little misleading. If you're like me, you're probably thinking square, circle, etc. But shapes in Numbers are kind of like clipart. Yes, basic shapes are there, but so are other things. In the example below I searched for "Dog" and got five results!

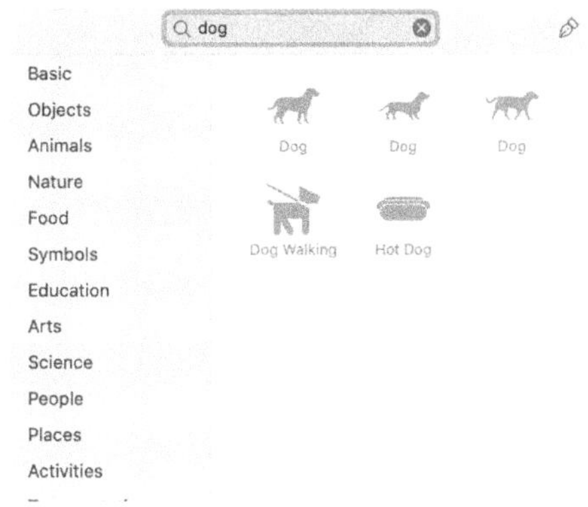

Resizing Shapes and Adjusting Proportions

Shape resizing is just like resizing photos: tap on a corner and drag it to the desired size. However, with Shapes, you can also adjust proportions. What does that mean? It's better shown than explained. Double tap your trackpad on the shape to bring up the shape options. Now click "Make Editable."

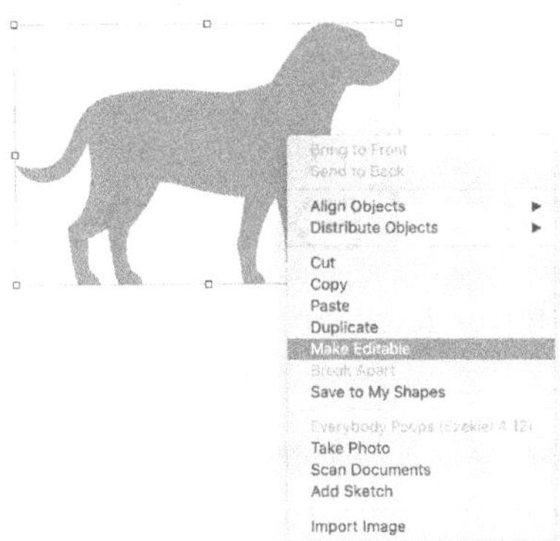

There are now a bunch of dots on the shape. These represent points that you can adjust.

As an example, I moved the point inward from the dog's stomach and look what happened.

By default you make these changes with a curved point, but you can change this by bringing the options up again. Notice the three different points?

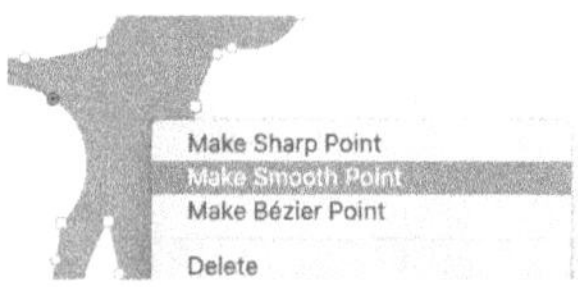

Moving and Rotating Shapes

To move a shape, simply tap on it and drag it to a new location. To rotate a shape, click the image then press the command button—just like you would an image.

Adding Text to a Shape

To add text on top of a shape, double-tap on it to activate its text field. Then just type your text!

Creating Text Boxes

There's one more type of shape, but it's not under shape. It's a Text Box. Text Boxes are exactly what they sound like—floating boxes that have text.

Why use a Text Box instead of typing out the text? Ideally, you want to use them when you are making something like a title—not when you are typing out your epic novel. It's for short text that you want to stand out.

Unlike standard text, Text Boxes are treated in the same way images are, so you can easily move them around and have other things wrap around them.

To get started, click the T in the menu.

You can also do Insert > Text Box.

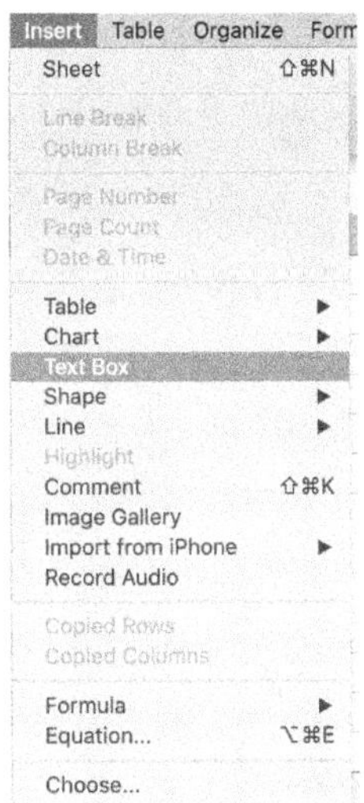

This puts a floating box with generic text in your document.

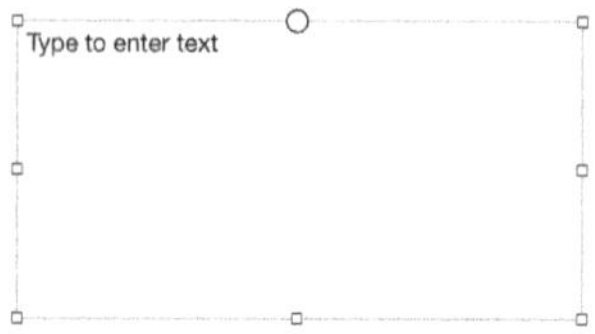

You can change the color of the box and more by clicking on Style; it has all the same types of options that you'd find in the Image or Shape options.

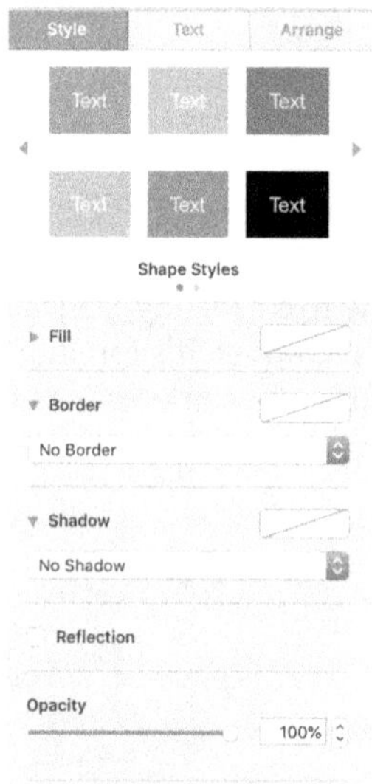

Because it's a Shape, you are able to edit it like you would a shape. In the below example, I curved out the bottom portion of the box.

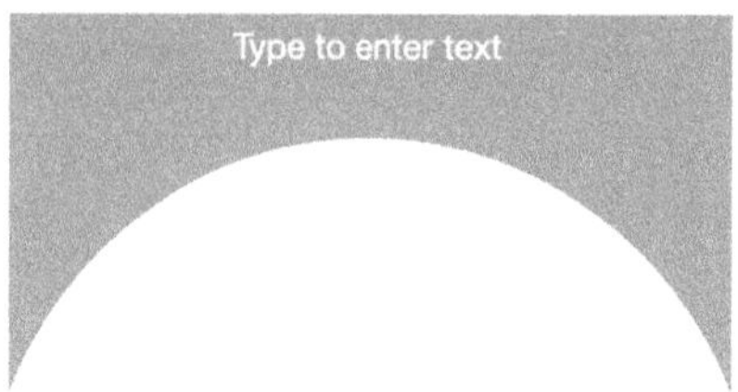

Styling Shapes and Text Boxes

Styling Shapes and Text boxes is the same as styling an image, so I won't repeat myself here. If you are confused about styling, refer to the section in the Photos chapter.

[7]

TEMPLATES

This chapter will cover:

- Using third-party Numbers Templates
- Creating your own Templates

Numbers comes with over two dozen templates in five categories - some for calendars, some for reports and professional use, and others for travel planners.

What exactly is a Template? A Template is a document that's already formatted—complete with text and images. Why would you want that? The idea is you delete the text (and replace the images) to make it your own, but save time on the sometimes complicated formatting aspect of it.

Some templates contain multiple tabs.

Now that you understand most of the formatting options available in Numbers, you can use any of these templates as a starting off point. You can change the images, colors, and layout of each template to suit the needs of your project.

USING THIRD-PARTY NUMBERS TEMPLATES

Two dozen templates is a lot, but if you use Numbers long enough, you probably will want a few more; if you get to that place then there are websites (and even apps) which sell Numbers templates (sometimes they are free). A basic web search for "Numbers templates" or even "free Numbers templates" will show you what I mean.

Word of caution: like anything you download, use at your own risk. If a website looks sketchy, be wary of downloading a template.

To use a template like this, just go to the website, find a template you like, and follow the site's instructions to download it to your computer's hard drive.

After that, Numbers can open the template and you can begin to edit it. It is strongly recommended to make a duplicate of your template document before you begin working on it, so that you will continue to have a blank one for later if you need it.

These third-party templates are great for more variety—for example, if you are looking to give your resume a little more creativity.

Creating Your Own "Templates"

Unfortunately, Numbers currently does not allow you to save templates in the Create New Document screen. However, you can work around this sorely missed feature by setting up your "template" as a regular Numbers document.

Personally, I make a duplicate of the document (i.e. File > Duplicate) and name it something like "Resume Template."

[8]

SHARING AND EXPORTING DOCUMENTS

This chapter will cover:

- Sharing documents
- Exporting documents

In spite of the popularity of iPhones and iPads, Apple users still often find themselves marooned in a Windows-based world. Numbers is a wonderful program, but it's incomprehensible to Microsoft Excel. Fortunately, Numbers offers several methods for sharing and exporting Numbers documents in multiple formats. Numbers also makes moving documents across Apple devices absolutely effortless, thanks to iCloud.

SYNCING DOCUMENTS WITH ICLOUD

If you've enabled iCloud in your Numbers app, your documents will be synced across your devices automatically, with absolutely no work required on your part. You can even access your documents online from any internet connection at www.icloud.com.

EMAILING A DOCUMENT FROM NUMBERS

E-mailing documents is one of the most straightforward methods of sharing your document. Go to Share > Send a Copy.

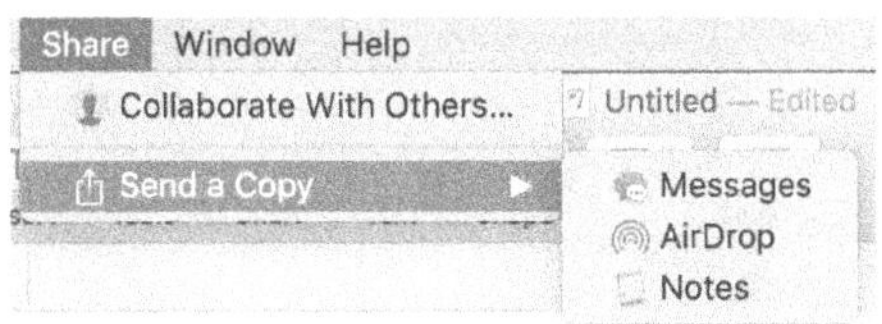

COLLABORATING

You can also collaborate on a document by going to Share > Collaborate With Others.

This brings up an option that asks how you would like to share the document.

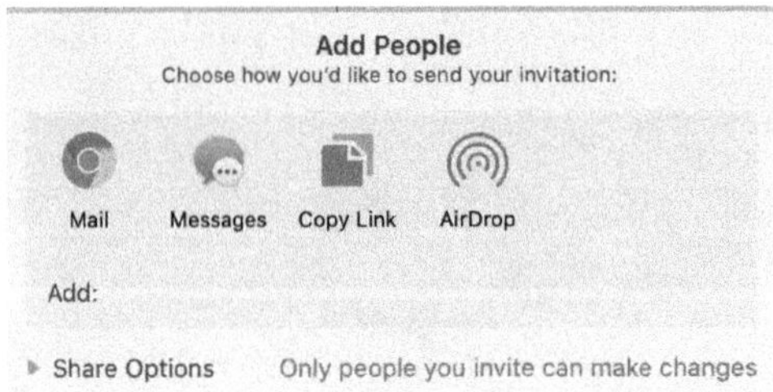

I recommend clicking on the Share Options dropdown to make sure the right permissions are enabled. For example, you can make the document readable to anyone you share it with or anyone who gets the document; you can also give the user permission to make changes.

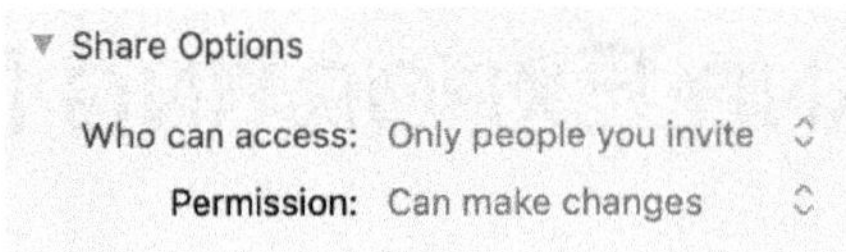

Export a Numbers Document

By default, you'll be saving your file as a Numbers document. That's great if you have Numbers, but if you're sharing it with (or opening it on) a computer that doesn't have pages, or you want to create a universal PDF that anyone can see, then you'll need to export it.

This is pretty straightforward. Go to File > Export.

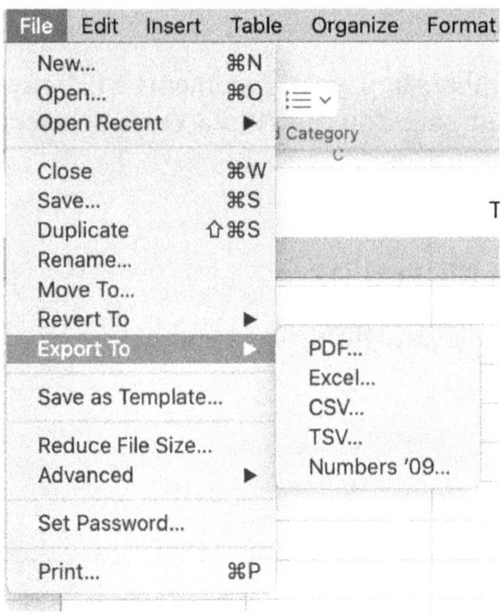

There are five different file types:

- PDF
- Excel
- CSV

- TSV
- Numbers '09

PDF is the best option if you want to preserve all the formatting in the document and make it look exactly as it appears in Numbers.

APPENDIX A: AN EXERCISE IN NUMBERS

By now, you should be familiar with all the basic features of Numbers; before leaving you, I'm going to leave you with a short demonstration of a document to help illustrate some of the things we've learned one more time.

I'm starting with the blank template, but I'm going to go a step further and delete the table in this template. So, I'm starting with something that is completely blank of any tables or objects.

Now I'm going to go to the table button and add in a table that has no formatting.

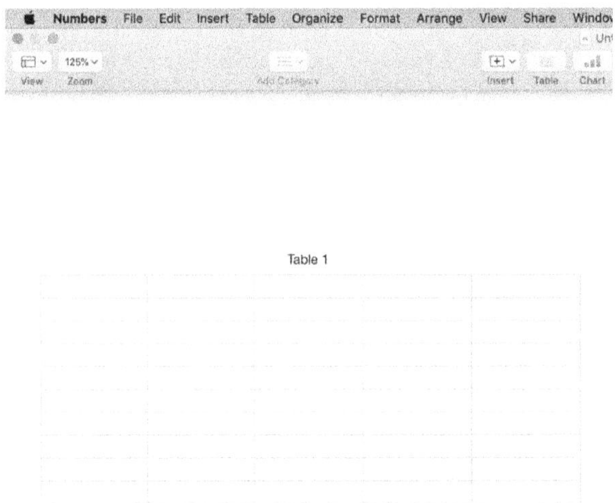

If you look at the example above, you'll notice some white space above the table. That's because I dragged it down a little. You can do the same by clicking and moving down the little circle in the corner of a selected table.

Next, I'm going to stick a logo on top of it. You can add your custom logo if you have an image already; for this example, I'm going to go to the Shapes icon and search for a barn.

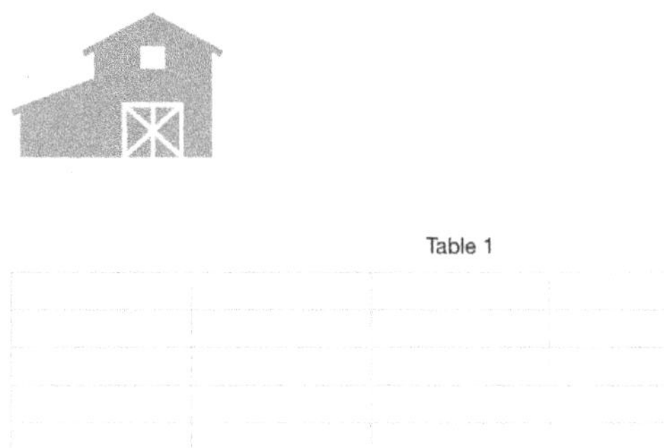

Now I need a title for my little project. I'm going to call it "My Barn Life." I'll move it to the top, and change the font size and color.

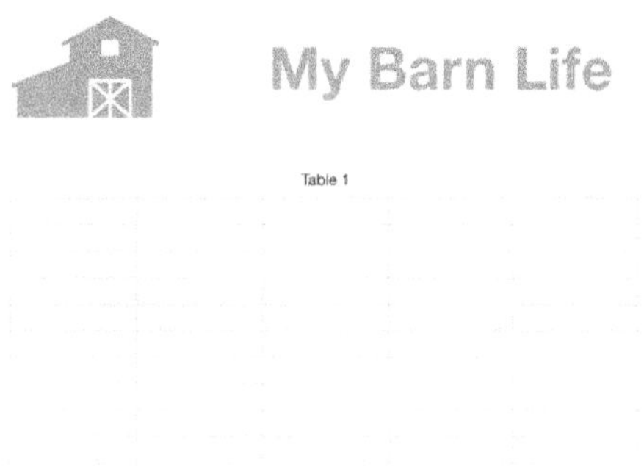

It's starting to come together. Next, I want to show an inventory of all the animals in my imaginary farm. I'm going to change the name of the table to "All My Animals" then create a list of the animal types and the number I have.

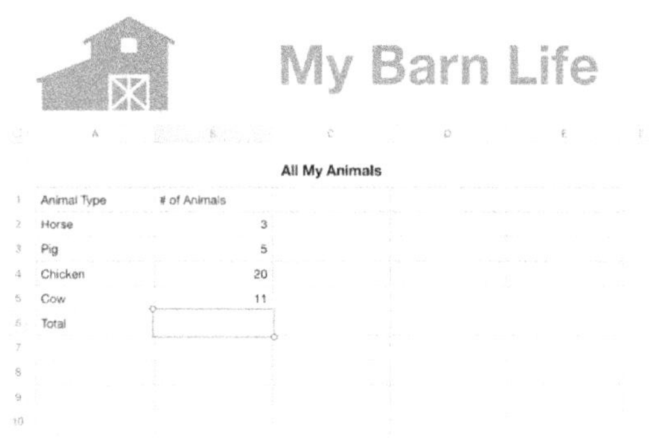

What's an inventory without counting the numbers? I'll do a very simple formula to add them all up by hitting the = key on the keyboard and then highlighting the cells with the number of animals.

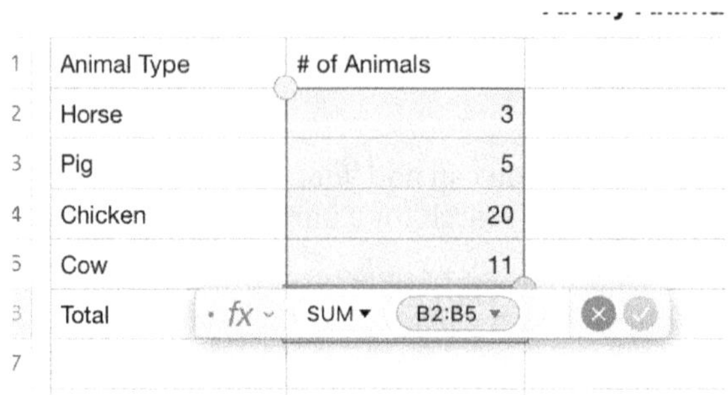

This is all helpful, but what would make it more helpful is if the table had more colors to make the rows pop out. I'm going to highlight cells that I want to change the color of, go to the Cell menu, then select a fill color.

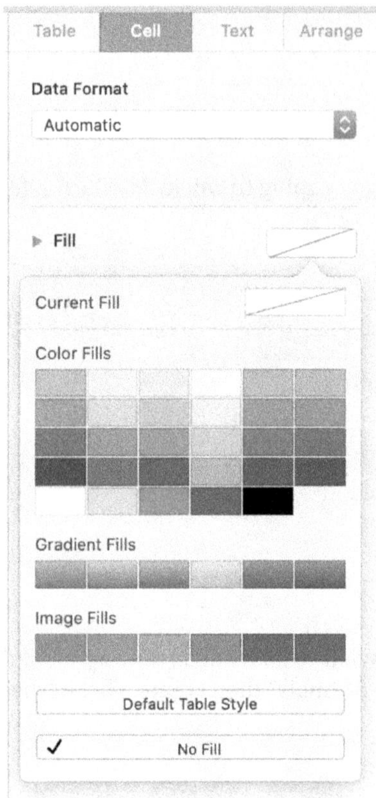

Now my table looks a little more eye-catching.

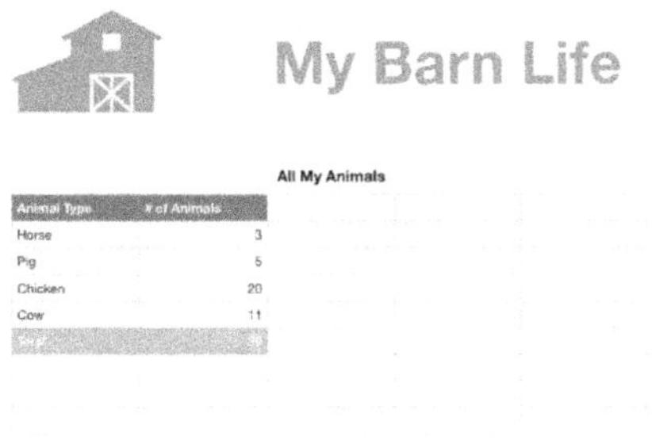

That's better, but there's no need for all of those extra cells. Let's delete them. Highlight the rows you want gone, then right click and select "Delete Selected Columns."

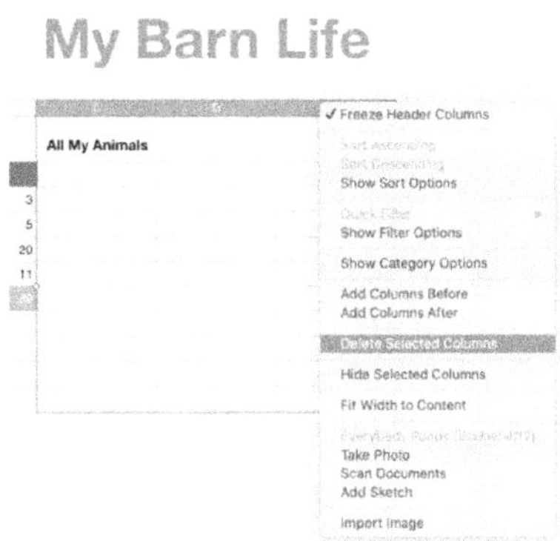

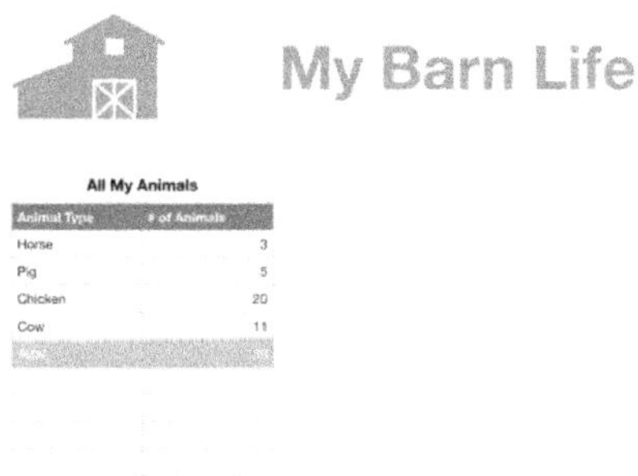

Now do the same for the bottom columns.

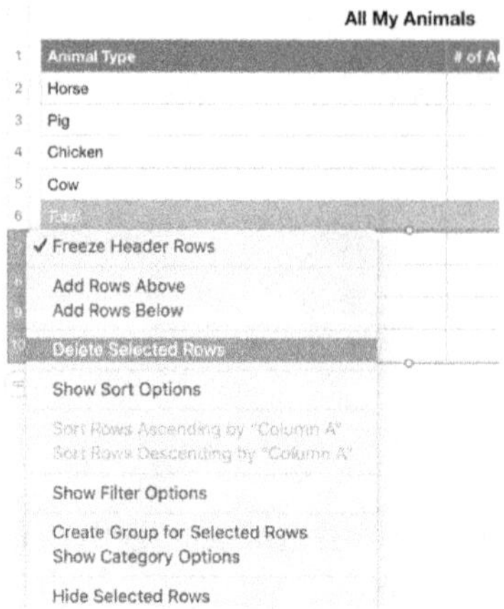

What list of barn animals would be complete without a graph?! Let's make a bar chart of all the animals so you can visually see what types make up the farm. Highlight the columns with numbers in them, then go to the chart button and select a pie chart.

You now have a lovely presentation of your life at the barn.

My Barn Life

All My Animals

Animal Type	# of Animals
Horse	3
Pig	5
Chicken	20
Cow	11
[illegible]	[illegible]

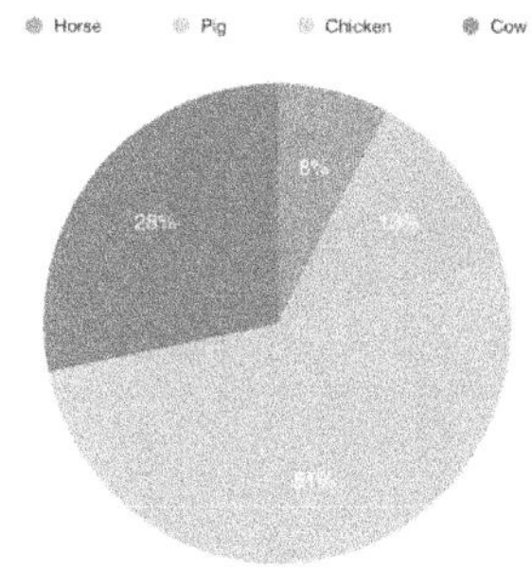

APPENDIX B: KEYBOARD SHORTCUTS

Action	Shortcut
Cmnd-N	Create new spreadsheet
Shft-Cmnd-N	Open Template Chooser
Cmnd-O	Open existing spreadsheet
Cmnd-S	Save
Shft-Cmnd-S	Save as
Cmnd-P	Print selected sheet
Cmnd-?	Open Numbers help
Cmnd-F	Find
Cmnd-G	Find next
Shft-Cmnd-G	Find previous
Cmnd->	Zoom in
Cmnd-<	Zoom out
Cmnd-Q	Quit Numbers
Cmnd-A	Select all text within selected object
Cmnd-T	Show Font panel
Cmnd-B	Make selected text bold
Cmnd-I	Make selected text italic
Cmnd-U	Underline selected text
Cmnd-X	Cut
Cmnd-C	Copy
Cmnd-V	Paste
Optn-Shft-Cmnd-V	Paste and match formatting of destination text
Optn-Space bar	Insert nonbreaking space
Shft-Return or Ctrl-Return	Insert line break (soft return)

KEYNOTE FOR MAC

INTRODUCTION

Showing off your vacation slideshow or photo album used to be boring. With Keynote for Mac, you can create a slideshow or photo album that will be fun to create and which will wow your audience!

Keynote is powerful software, and if you get a Mac, it's free. But let's face it: you've probably spent most of your life using PowerPoint.

For a Mac user, Keynote can make your documents really shine...but first you need to know how to use it. This guide will help!

Instead of spending time on hundreds of Keynote on functions you probably will never use, it shows you what you really want to know: the basics.

In no time, you'll be creating visually stunning presentations!

It will show you the ropes—including how to do all those things you are used to doing in Microsoft PowerPoint - and help you with some of the features you may not even know about.

Ready to get started? Let's go!

[1]

The Basics

This chapter will cover:

- How to get Keynote
- Opening your first document
- Keynote crash course
- Formatting
- Layouts and styles

How To Get Keynote

Depending on how you acquired your Mac, you may or may not have Keynote already. Getting it is easy. And even better: getting it is free! (You can see if you have it by going into the Launchpad from the dock and searching for Keynote).

There's one catch: not all Macs are supported. But most are. MacOS 10.14 is required to run Keynote, which means you must have one of the following computers:

- MacBook: Early 2015 or newer
- MacBook Air: Mid 2012 or newer
- MacBook Pro: Mid 2012 or newer
- Mac Mini: Late 2012 or newer
- iMac: Late 2012 or newer
- iMac Pro
- Mac Pro: Late 2013 or newer; Mid 2010 or Mid 2012 models require a Metal-capable GPU

As long as you have one of those, then you can go to the App Store (it's in your Launchpad). Keynote is a digital download only—you cannot obtain a physical copy of it. The download is a few hundred MB.

From there, type in Keynote in the search bar, and hit the return key.

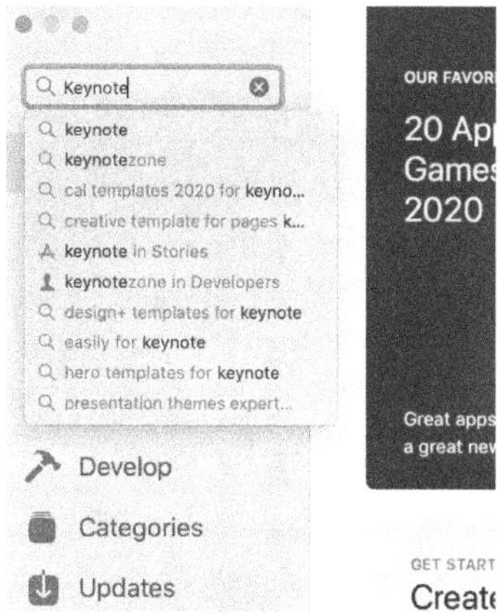

If you have it, the return result will have an Open button; if you don't have it, the result will show a Get button. When you click Get, you'll be prompted to put in your Apple ID and password; if you don't have an Apple ID, then follow the onscreen instructions to get one (it is free).

Running Keynote for the First Time

When you first open Keynote, you'll be asked if you want to use iCloud. I recommend you do; this makes it easy to save and open documents across all devices—if you are creating a presentation on your phone, for instance, you can open that document and continue working on it from your tablet—it's all very seamless and doesn't require anything extra on your part once it's set up.

If you set up iCloud, you can even access and type in documents right in your browser— there is nothing else to install on your computer, which means "technically" you could use Keynote on a Windows computer or even a Chromebook or Android device—I'll show you how at the end of this chapter.

The Keynote Crash Course

The first time you use Keynote, you'll get a brief tutorial. You can either watch it or skip it.

Each time you open Keynote, you'll be greeted with a directory box that asks you if you want to open a document or if you want to create a new one. We'll be working off a new document in this chapter, so click "New Document" in the lower left corner.

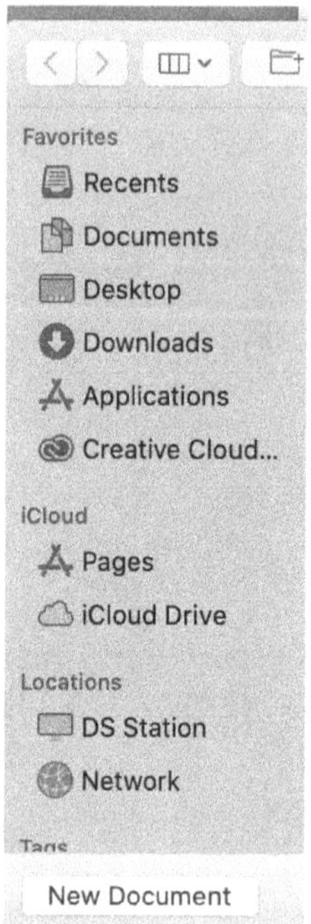

The next box you'll see is all the available templates you can use. A template is a premade document that you can add text into. These have different styles and color choices already assigned.

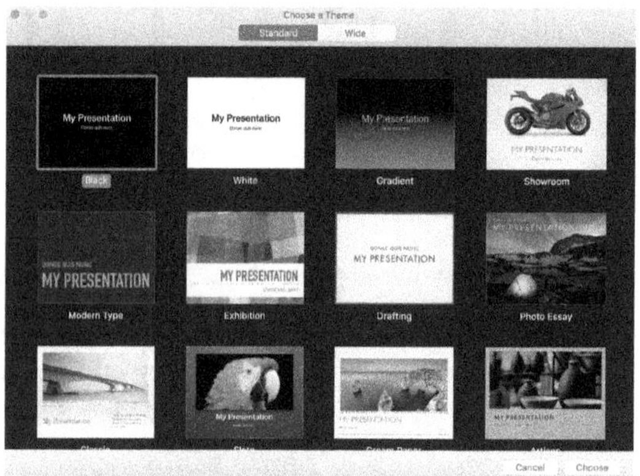

The most barebones styles (meaning you'll be doing most customization of the color / style choices) are Black or White.

Before making your selection, it's important to consider how you will be presenting a presentation. Will you be presenting on a HDTV, for example? Or a projector? The reason this is important is because Keynote has two different dimensions: Standard and Wide. You can see those two dimensions at the top of the template menu.

The styling of the template will stay the same, but the size ratio will be slightly different. Standard is the most universal format and ideal if you don't know how you will be presenting. Wide is best for widescreen TVs—using standard will leave black bars on the sides of the screen. Both will work, but it will fit better if you pick the right ratio prior to presenting.

First time users of Keynote are often a little disappointed the first time they use Keynote; if you've used PowerPoint, then you have ribbons and menus and options everywhere! Keynote looks pretty bare next to that.

Don't worry—looks can be deceiving; there are plenty of options when you know how to find them, and I'll show you each of them in this book.

If you feel overwhelmed already because there are options, you can hide that side panel by clicking on the Format button in the upper right corner. Hint: clicking once on any of these buttons shows it, and clicking on the button again hides it.

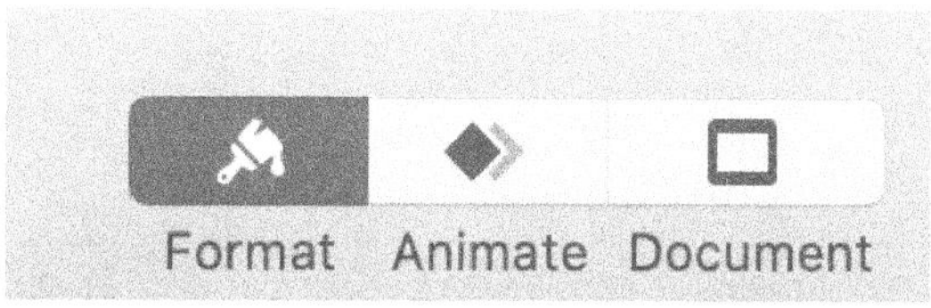

Now that you have a blank screen, let's go over the very basics of Keynote.

SELECT ALL SLIDES

Select All selects everything in your document. It's a very powerful command! It brings up the same options as Select, but any changes you make will be applied to the entire document.

To Select All, use Command + A on your keyboard.

SELECT OPTIONS

Once you have some content on your slide, how do you do stuff to it? If you click with two fingers on your trackpad or mouse, then the options box comes up. We'll go over what these options are as we continue in the book.

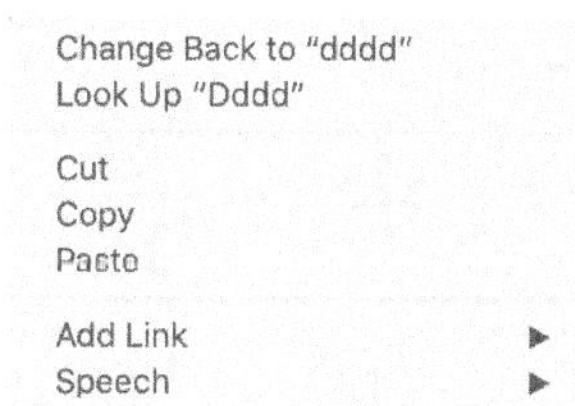

CUT, COPY AND PASTE

To copy and paste words (and images, tables and charts) quicker, you can use keyboard shortcuts. Selecting content and hitting COMMAND + C will copy it.
Selecting content and hitting COMMAND + X will cut it.
And hitting COMMAND + V will copy the content anywhere you want it in the document.

FIND AND REPLACE

Find and Replace is a handy little feature in Keynote that allows you to replace your selection with alternatives.

Let's say you just created 50 slides for your big presentation on why men are mean. But once you are done, you realize the topic is not men being mean, but pigs being mean! You can change 'men' to 'pigs' in seconds!

Go to edit from your menu bar, and select Find > Find.

From here you can find all the uses of the word you want to find, but you can also click the down arrow on the left side and select Find & Replace. This lets you search for a word (top line) and replace the word once it finds it (bottom line); when you have both the find and replace word added, then you can click Replace & Find.

DEFINE

Keynote has a handy little dictionary built in. You can select any word, tap the trackpad twice to bring up the options menu, and tap Look Up to see the definition of any word.

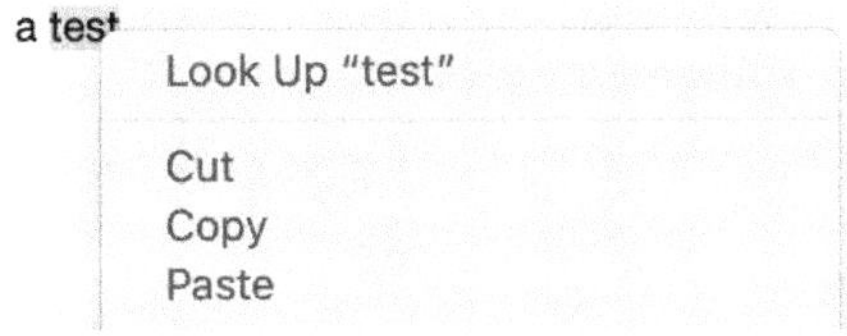

The dictionary will give you multiple definitions (and a thesaurus); even more, you can select options on the bottom to see movies related to the word, Siri Knowledge (which is encyclopedic information), apps related to it, and more!

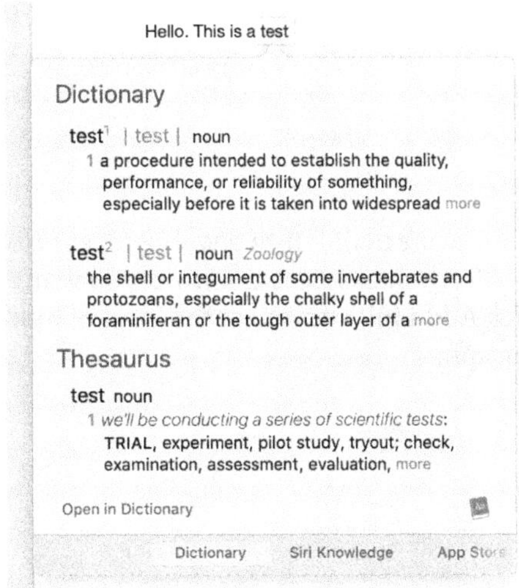

Copy Style

The Copy Style command lets you copy and paste styles, like the Microsoft Word format painter feature. If you ever want to make a piece of text look like another, just select the text with the format you'd like to copy, click Format > Copy Style; then select the text you want to alter and click Format > Paste Style. This can be a major time saver!

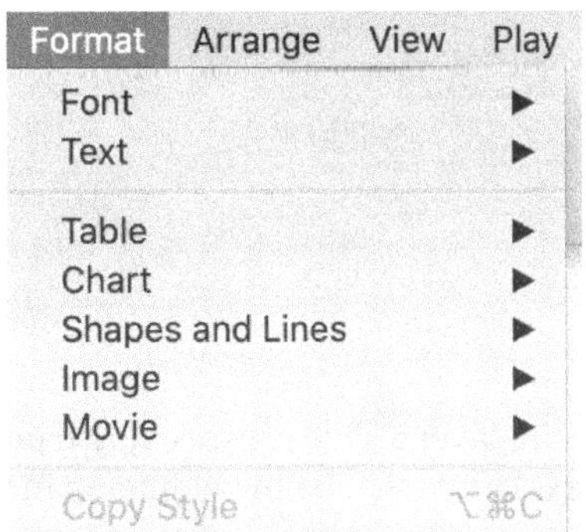

Inserting Hyperlinks

If you want to insert a hyperlink to an internet resource, just type out the link. Keynote automatically detects hyperlinks and will insert the link for you. To edit the link or to change the displayed text, just click the link and then tap Link Settings. Here you can edit the link itself, change the text displayed, or remove the link altogether.

If you aren't typing a web address, but want to link it to a web address (for example, you are typing: "I go to UCLA" and you want to provide a hyperlink to UCLA), then select the word you want to hyperlink and click with two fingers to bring up the options. From here, just click Add Link and select the kind of link you want to add. You can edit and remove it the same way as in the previous paragraph.

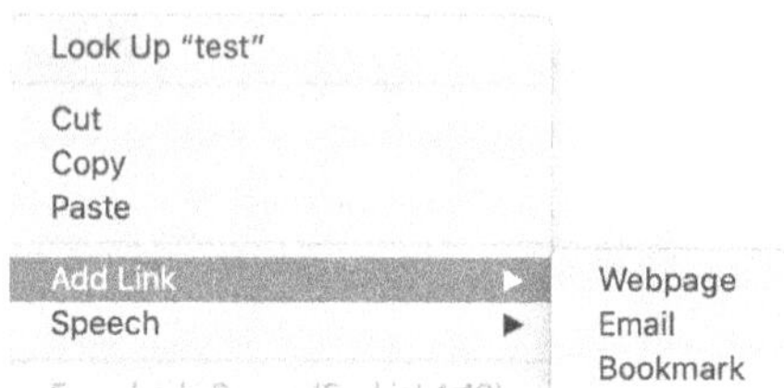

Undo/Redo

If you mess up (for example you delete a paragraph that you shouldn't have deleted) you can Undo it by going to Edit > Undo; you can also redo it under the same menu.

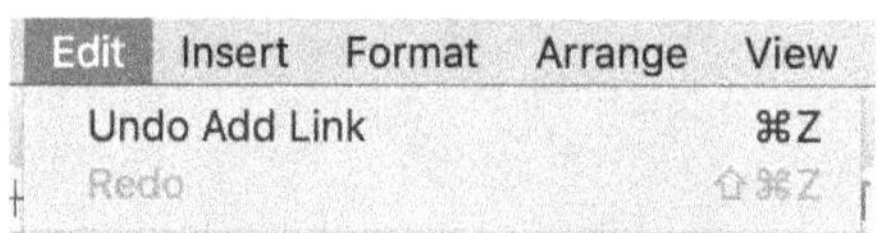

Menus

The best way to think about Keynote is in layers. This is especially true when you are working with menus.

The first layer is the slide itself; the next layers will be the elements in that slide (i.e. text boxes, graphics, bullet points, etc.).

When you take a look at the right side of your screen, you'll see three menu option icons: Format, Animate, and Document.

When I click format, I'll see a menu that looks like the graphic below.

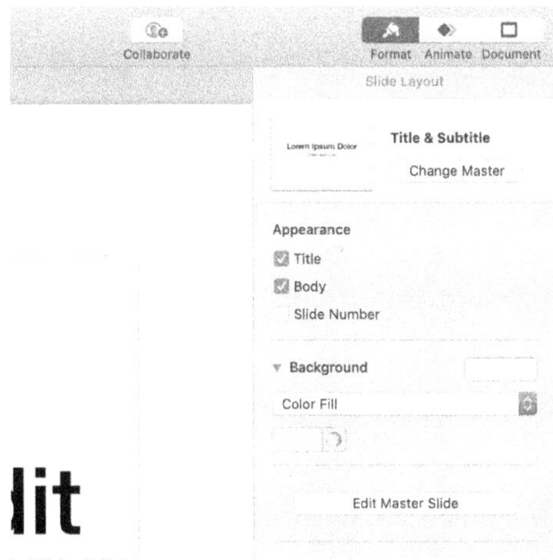

It has nothing about style or fonts, as you might expect in a format menu; that's because I haven't clicked anything. It's assuming I want to format the slide itself and not the text.

If I click the textbox inside this slide, however, the formatting menu will immediately change to something that lets me adjust the style.

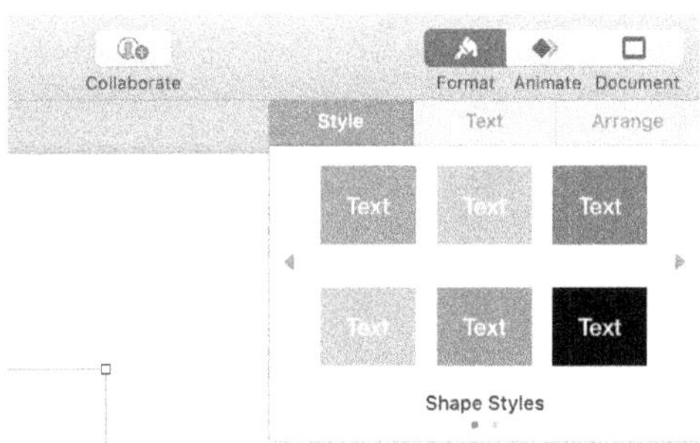

Slide Menus

Now that you understand the difference between formatting slides and formatting elements or layers within those slides, let's take a look at the Slide Menus.

The first menu is found by clicking the Format icon; this menu lets you adjust the layout of the slide. Personally, I usually prefer to work with a completely blank slide and add in all my own elements; if that sounds like you then uncheck the Title and Body boxes (which are always checked off by default).

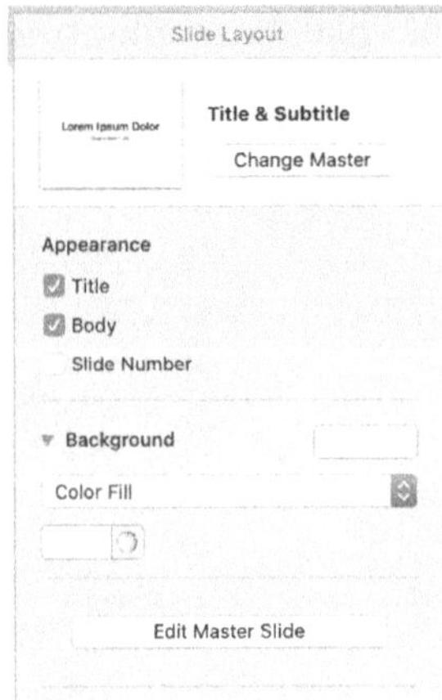

At the top of the menu is an option that says Change Master. What's that about? By default, you'll start with a title slide—in other words, a slide that lets you put the name and subtitle of your presentation. When you click Change Master, then you'll see all the possible types of slides. So, for example, you want to have a bulleted slide or a slide with a photo and bullets.

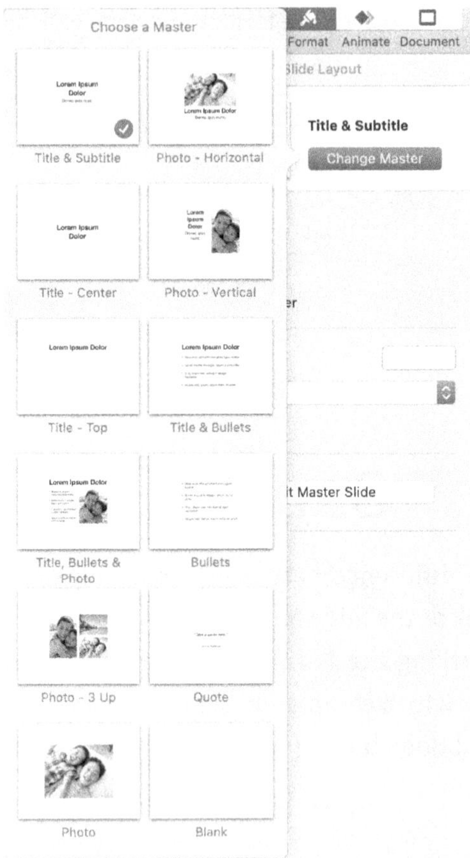

This is a more advanced topic that I won't cover in depth in this book because most people will not use it, but you can make changes to the Master Slides. At the bottom of the menu, there's a button that says Edit Master Slides. This brings up all your slide masters. You can click on any of those and add elements. Once you add them, then hit done near the bottom right corner of the screen to return to the main menu. Once the element is added, any time you change a slide to that master slide, the element will be there. It can be a major time saver if you find you are using the same type of slide over and over again.

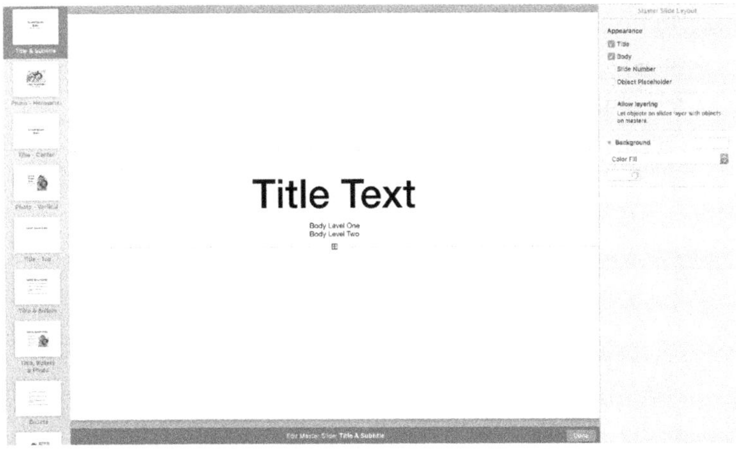

Also in the Format menu is the option to change the background; if, for example, you want to use a different color (or you want an image as the background), then you can add it in here.

The next menu is Animate. Animate is a transition to the slide; so, for example, the slide will give the appearance of falling onto the screen when it appears (or leaves). You choose for this to happen "On Click", which means it happens as soon as you click your mouse, or you can add a timed delay—which means it happens on a timer after a set amount of seconds / minutes. For most people, on click will be the way to go; using the timed feature would be ideal if you were turning your slide into a short movie (which I'll cover later).

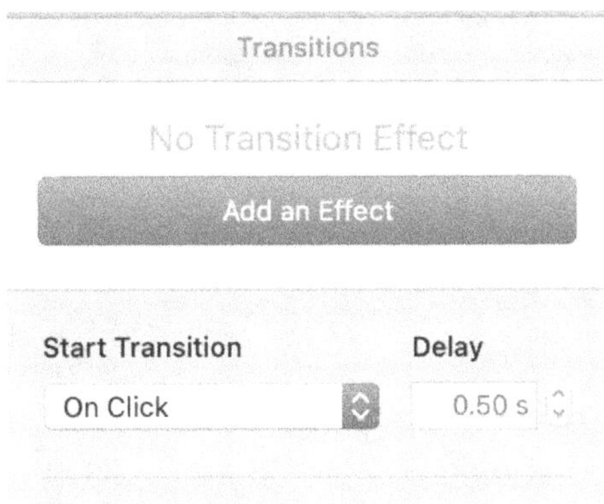

There are dozens of different animation to try. You can preview them by hovering your mouse over the name and then selecting preview.

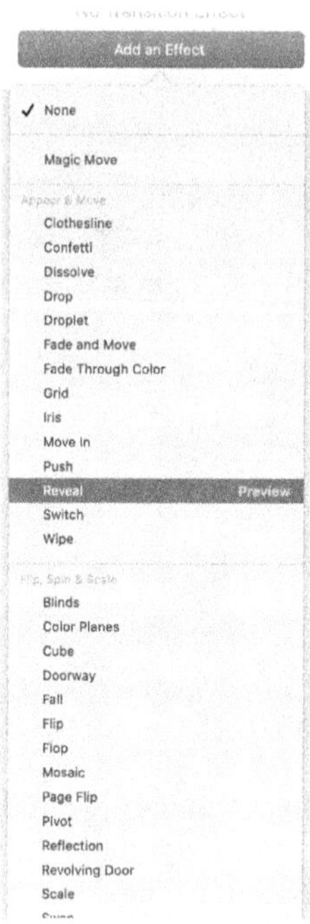

Once you make your selection, a new menu will appear with options for that animation. The options will change depending on the type of animation that's been chosen. Most will only give the option to change the direction of the animation and how the animation is started (i.e. On Click). You can also change and preview the transition at the top.

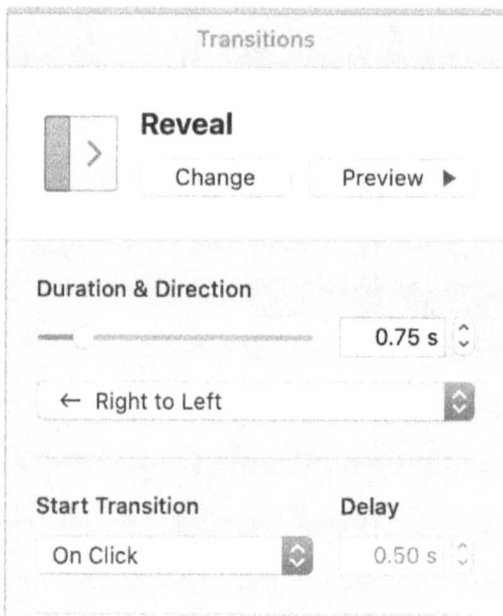

The last menu option for the slide is Document. There are two important things to note here: you can change the theme (if you chose the wrong one when you started), and, at the bottom, you can pick a different size. For example, let's say you did the presentation in 4:3, but on the day of the presentation, you found out it is going to be on a widescreen display. 4:3 will still work, but there will be black bars on the sides. So you can change the size here to fit better. Keep in mind, however, if you change the size, then it might make adjustments to the slide—moving text boxes and images over. It's always a good idea to go through your presentation one more time when changing the size.

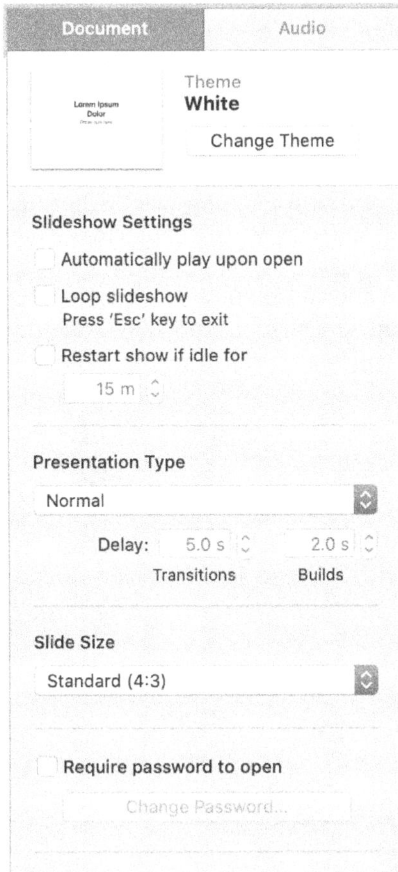

There's a second menu tab for audio in the Document menu. Most people won't use this feature. This is an excellent tool, however, if you are creating a movie from your slide so someone on the web can watch it later.

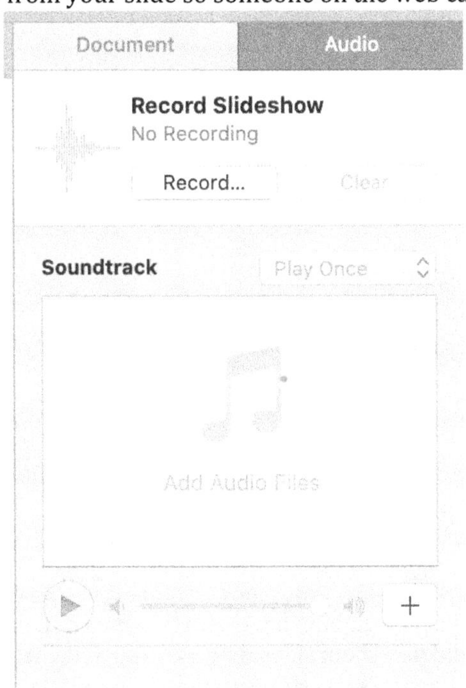

Elements Menu

The elements menus aren't very different from the slide menus; in fact, many of them are the same.

The biggest difference between them will be when you click the Format menu.

There are three tabs when you edit an element: Style, Text, Arrange (some elements, such as Images, will look slightly different and not have the Text tab).

Under style, you can add a border, fill, and add shadow to the element; what I find most useful is the Opacity option. This option adds transparency to the element, which can be useful if you are using an image behind text.

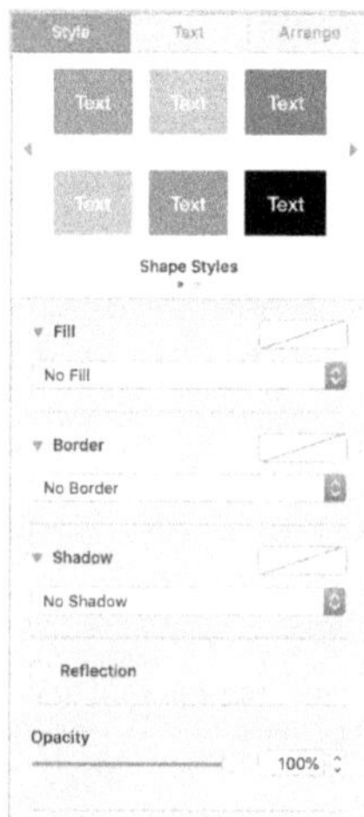

Under Text, you can change the type of text it is (a subtitle, title, or body, for example).

When you click it, you'll see several options. "Body" is normal text in a document—the text you are reading right here would be considered Body Text; but documents have several types of paragraph text. For example, each section of this chapter has a "Heading"—you could just change the font size and make it "look" like a heading, but using a Paragraph Style tells Keynote what kind of text it is so it can put together a table of contents later.

Some of the styles will not be very common, "Label Dark" for example.

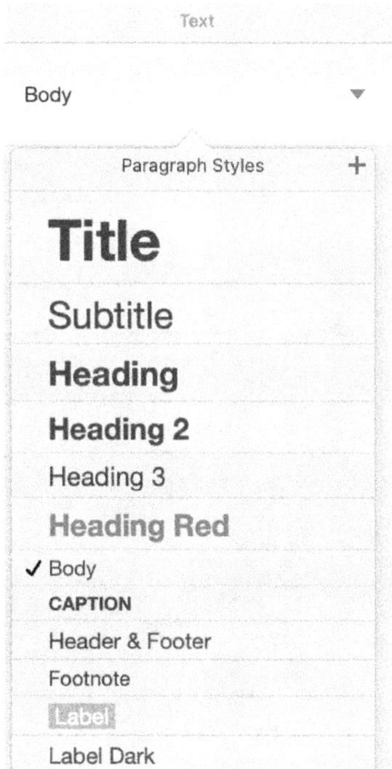

Under this are options for Style, Layout, and More. Let's stay on Style for now, so the next option is Font.

It says 11pt Helvetica; this is the font. If you tap on it, you'll be able to select a new font and adjust the size. Keynote offers a healthy font selection, including perennial favorites like Arial, Times New Roman, and Helvetica. Some notable absences include Comic Sans (and yet Papyrus still made the cut), Calibri, and Cambria.

The "regular" drop down shows you all the style choices for that font (some fonts have different options).

The next three buttons are fairly standard. If you're not familiar with computerized word processing, though, remember B for Bold, I for Italic, and U for underline. The S with a line through it puts a strike across any text you type.

Below this are your alignment buttons. Tap them for options to align your text left, center or right, or justify it. Justified text is text that fills one line exactly. Try it out to see how it works.

The next two buttons are indent buttons. Use them to indent, or to move backwards through indents.
Finally, below this is where you can add bulleted lists and line spacing (if you want to double space, for example).
The final tab is Arrange.

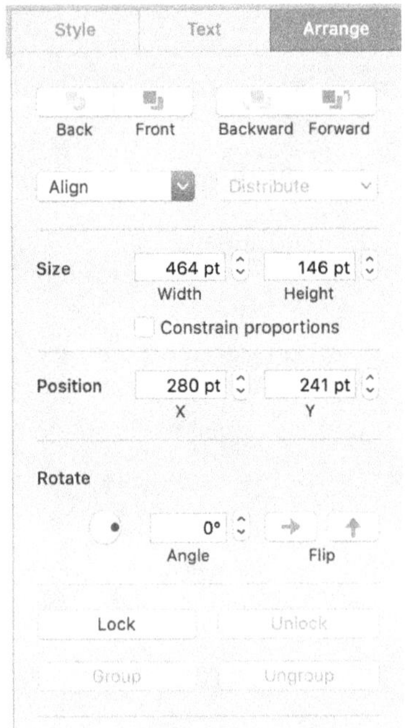

I first said to think of Keynote in terms of layers; I could have just as easily said Elements (and I have in this section); an element is a layer. The reason I use the word "layer" is because layer helps illustrate what an element can do—they can move in front and behind different elements. That's what the Arrange menu is all about. For example, let's say you want to put an image behind a text box. You can add an image to your slide and move it in front of the text box, then go here, and click the "Back" icon to send it behind the Text Box. You can also lock it in place so it can't be moved accidently.

Top Menus

At the top of Keynote are a few menus that you should understand; other menus will come up as you continue to read this book.

Slide Menu

The slide menu is pretty bare; it's helpful if you have dozens of slides and need to find it quickly, or if you want to add slide numbers. For the average presentation, however, you probably won't refer to it very often.

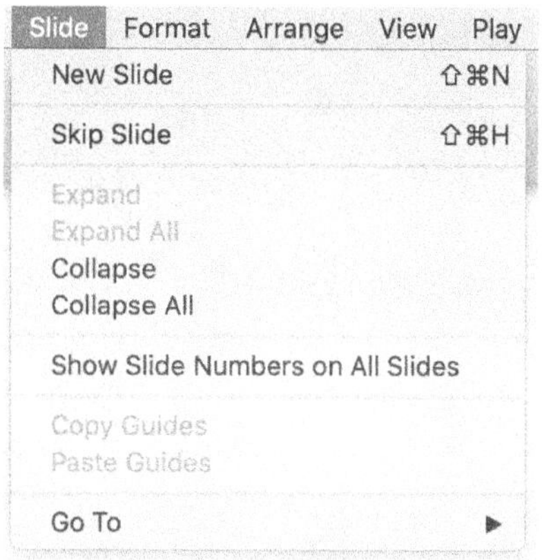

There is something worth talking more about in this menu, however: collapse. What exactly are you going to collapse? This is an organizational feature. You can have main slides and sub slides within those slides. Think of a main slide like a chapter and the sub slide like a subtopic within that chapter.

To create a sub-slide, add a slide (you can add a slide by clicking on the slide in front of it and hitting enter, or by right clicking a slide and click New Slide. Once it's added, move the new slide to the right with your mouse. It will now be indented over from the main slide.

You can do this to as many slides as you want; notice that there's now an arrow on the main slide? Click that and it will collapse it.

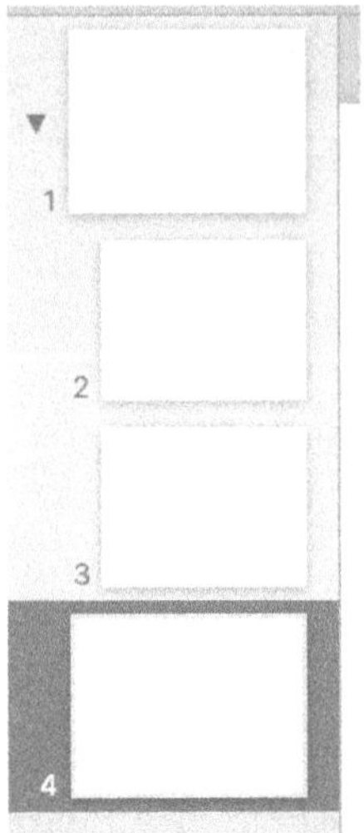

Play Menu

The Play menu is also a little bare, but unlike the slide menu, you'll want to pay close attention to the features if you'll be presenting this presentation somewhere. There are three main features here:

- Play Slideshow – Play will turn your computer into a screen. This is useful if you are presenting from your computer; if you are presenting on a TV or projector, it will look different (which I'll show you below).
- Record Slideshow – Record puts it into presenter mode, so you can narrate the presentation.
- Rehearse Slideshow – Rehearse looks the same as record, but nothing is being recorded; it's in present mode, but it's for practicing only.

Present view looks like the image below; the idea is your presentation will show up as you intend on the TV screen, but on your computer it will look like the presenter's view; here you can preview your next slides, see notes, a timer, etc.—but this is all viewable to you only.

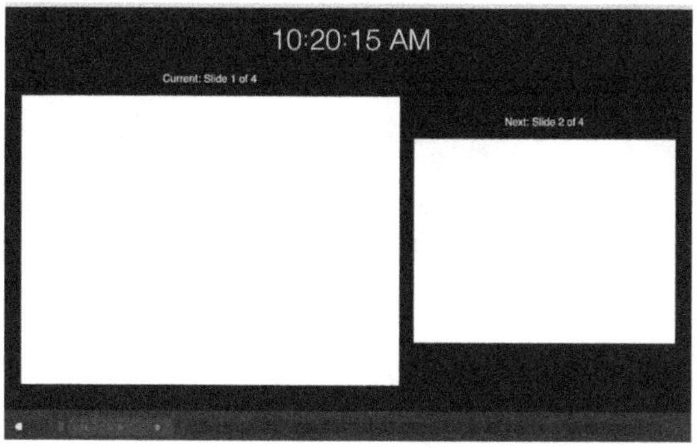

If you go to customize presenter display, you'll see several options for what shows up when you are in this mode.

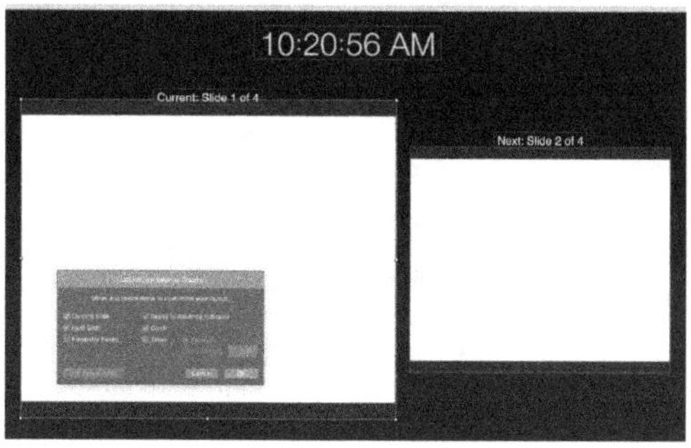

View Menu

The View Menu is where you show and hide menus; we've covered most of the menus, but there's one to note here: Presenter Notes.

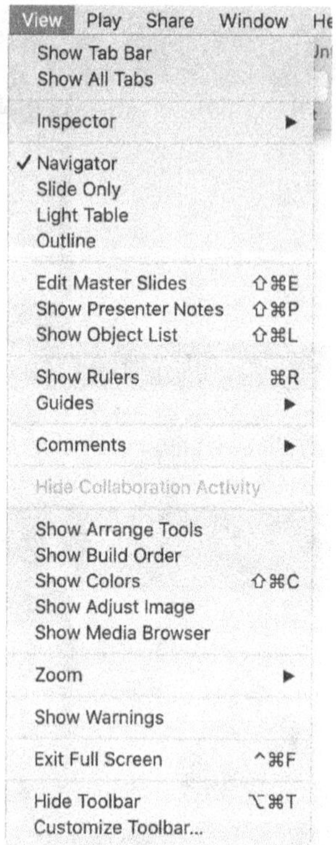

Presenter Notes is where you can add your own comments—such as an outline or even the script for what you intended to say on this slide.

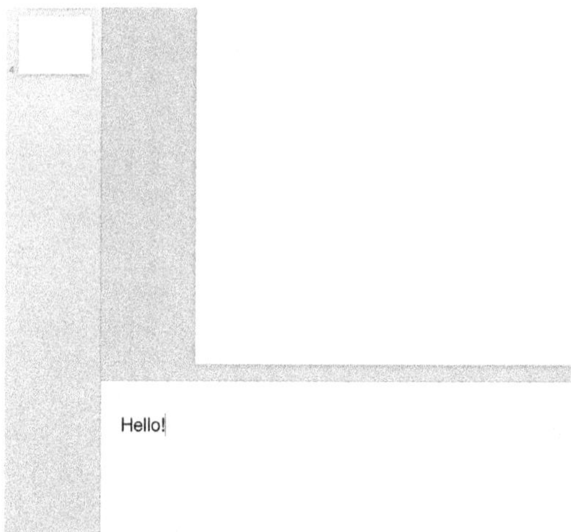

When you present this on a TV, it won't be present to your audience, but you can add it into your presenter mode display.

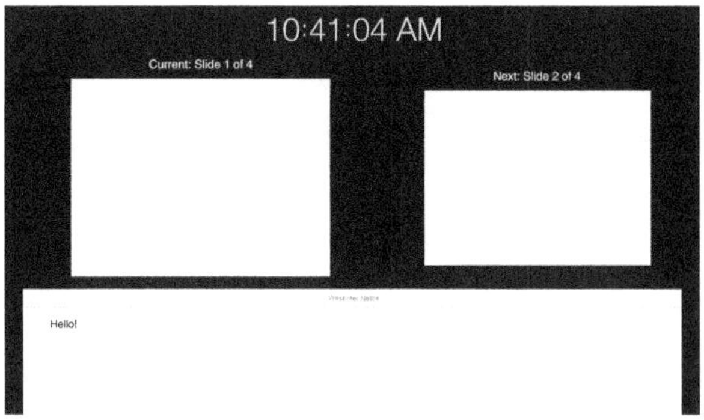

Opening Keynote From iCloud

Keynote can be run right from your browser; it's great for editing, but for intensive design work, the best solution will be your computer.

To access it from your browser, head to iCloud.com and sign in with your Apple ID.

The first screen you'll see will show you all the things you can do from the cloud; one of them is Keynote. Click it once to open it.

As long as you've been saving your work to the cloud, then any recent docs will show up here, and you can click on their thumbnail once to open them.

You can additionally start a new Doc by clicking on the + button in the upper right corner. This will open up Keynote for iCloud. All the features covered in this book can be found in Keynote for iCloud as well.

Managing Documents

Saving in Keynote is pretty straightforward—especially if you've used Windows before. It's under File > Save.

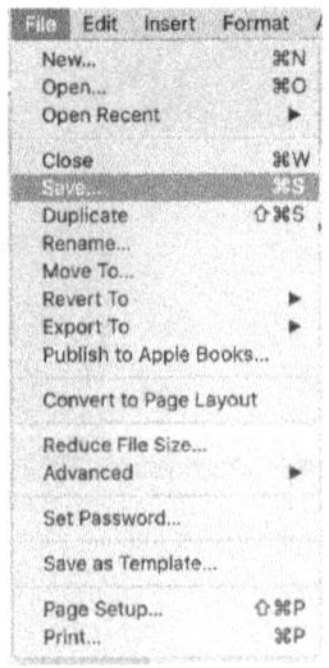

Before we move forward with using other features in Keynote, I want to go over the less straightforward ways to manage documents.

Renaming Documents

Renaming documents is very easy. Like many things in Keynote, there's more than one way to do it.
The easiest way is when your document is open; just click on the name in the top center of the document.

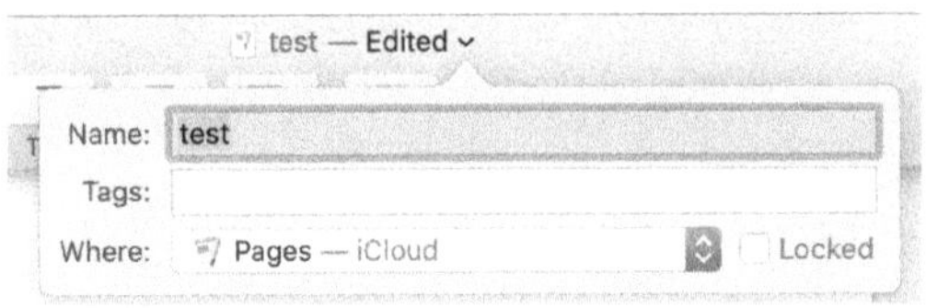

The next way is File > Rename.

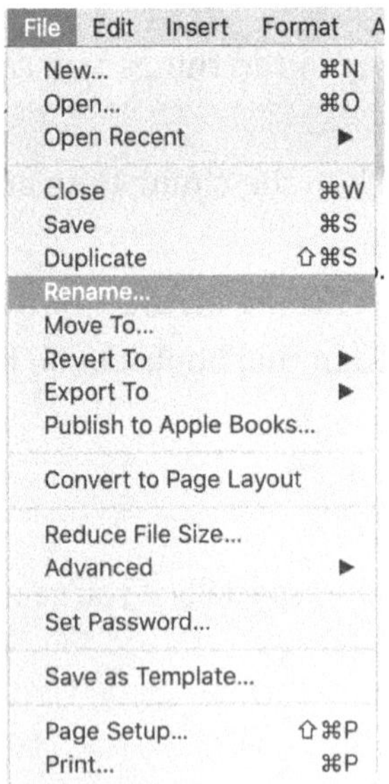

The third way is to find it in Finder, click with two fingers, and select Rename.

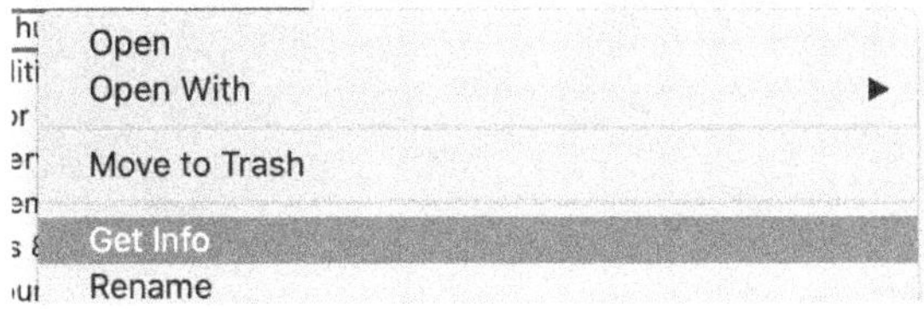
Open
Open With
Move to Trash
Get Info
Rename

[2]

PHOTOS FOR KEYNOTE

This chapter will cover:

- Insert image
- Arrange / Rotate / Wrap image
- Edit Mask / Alpha
- Image Styling

As much as possible, I'm trying to make learning Keynote fun; there's no better way to make something fun than with photos!

As we go, we'll be learning more about styling tips, but before we get there, we are going to learn about photos—not just about inserting them into the document, but about how to apply more advanced techniques to them.

INSERTING AN IMAGE

Inserting an image can be done several ways. You can copy and paste an image into the document; you can drag a photo into the document; or you can pick it manually.

To pick it manually, you can go to Insert > Choose, and then find the file location.

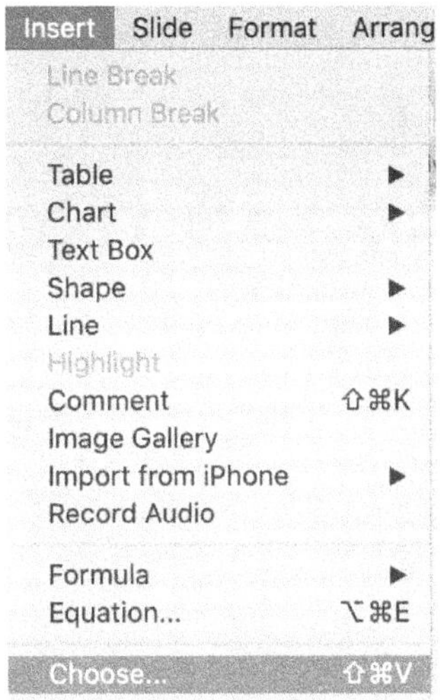

The quicker way to add a photo, however, is from the menu. Click the image button, which shows you all the different types of media types you can add. You can get photos by clicking on Photos or Image Gallery (if the photos are in your gallery) or by clicking "Choose" to pick where the photo is located.

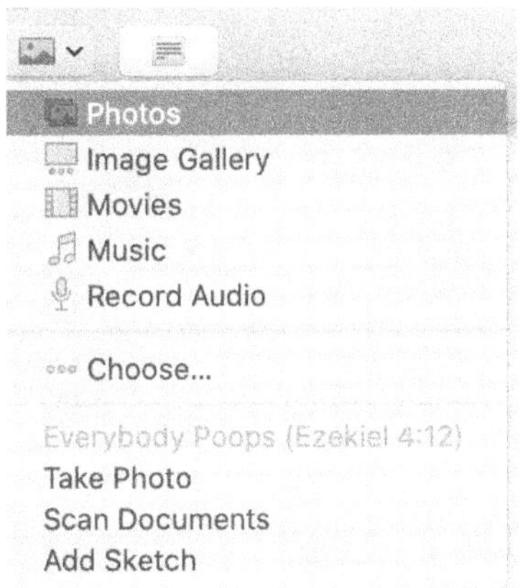

If you pick photos, it's not going to show you all your photos—just the photos in that photos area of your Mac. You could, for example, have a photo on your USB drive. If that's the case, then you'd want to pick "Choose" from the previous menu instead of photos.

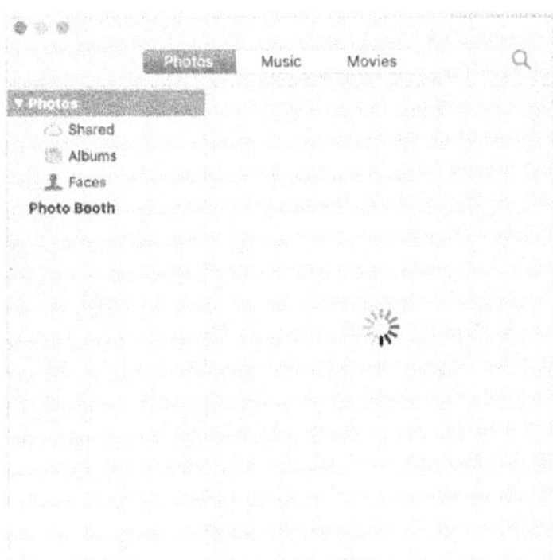

ARRANGING IMAGES

RESIZE AND ROTATE

Once your image is inserted, you can use your mouse to move it, resize it, and rotate it. Resizing is pretty straightforward. Click the image, then move to the corner or side of the image and move the little squares on the edges in and out. To rotate the image you'll do the same thing, but when you get to the corner of the image, press the Command key on your keyboard. This will show you a curved line and also show you the percentage of the rotation as you move the image.

Hint: Looking for images? I often use a website named pexels.com to find public domain (or free to use) images.

There's one more way to rotate an image. When you click on the image, you'll notice that the side panel that you used to format text has changed. It's now a new menu with controls to format an image.

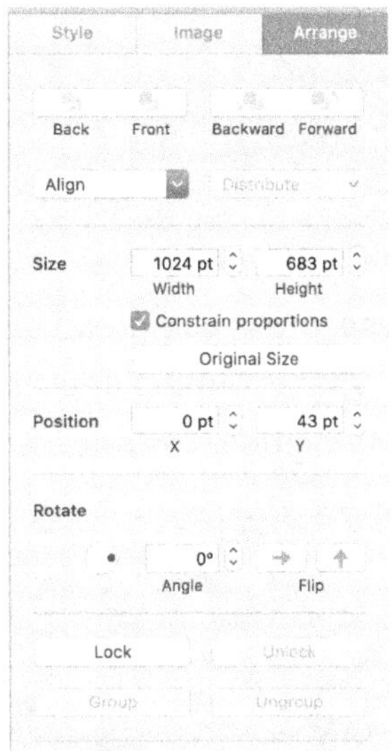

There are three buttons on top of this menu (Style, Image, Arrange); we'll go over the first button in the next section, but for this section, go to Arrange.

On the bottom of this menu, there's a section called Rotate; angle is what you want to use. The mouse is a quick and easy way to rotate your image, but if you want precision, then this is the best method. Next to the Angle, you can also vertically and horizontally flip the image using the arrows.

Placement

Because a photo is essentially just a layer in your slide, you can position it behind or in front of other layers.

If you go to the Arrange menu, you'll notice a bar with icons that say Back / Front.

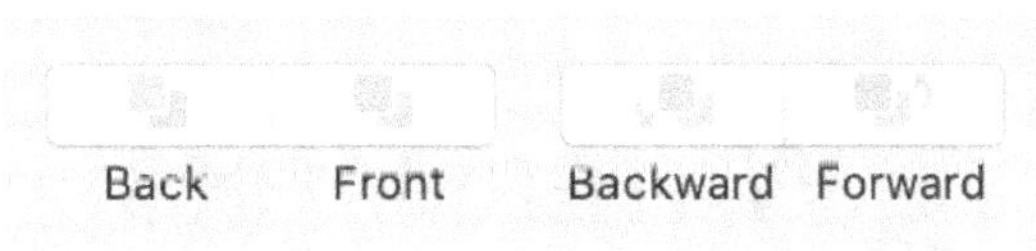

This is where you go to move the image behind or in front of other images.

Image Grouping

There's one last section that's greyed out in Arrange: Grouping. Grouping is greyed out because you need two images to use it.

Add a second image, then click one image, press command on your keyboard and select the second image; the Group option is no longer greyed out. What grouping does is put two images together; so when you edit the size, rotation, etc. you are treating the two photos as one image.

If you want to edit just one image, you don't have to ungroup it. You can double click the image to tell Keynote that you want to keep them grouped, but you want to make changes to one photo while they are grouped.

WATERMARKS

There are a few ways to create a Watermark in Keynote; the easiest way is to move the image behind everything and make it a little bit transparent in the Style menu.

What if you want that same image on every slide, however? You can do that by changing the master slides, which I mentioned in the previous chapter.

EDIT MASK AND ALPHA

With your image selected (note: if the images are grouped, you need to double click the image you want to edit—you can't edit both images at the same time), select the Image button.

This brings up options for image enhancements. At the bottom is the Adjustments section; this section is pretty self-explanatory- the Exposure and Saturation sliders will change the amount of exposure / saturation in the image. The

Enhance button will do an auto enhancement based on what the computer thinks the image should look like (the reset button will undo it).

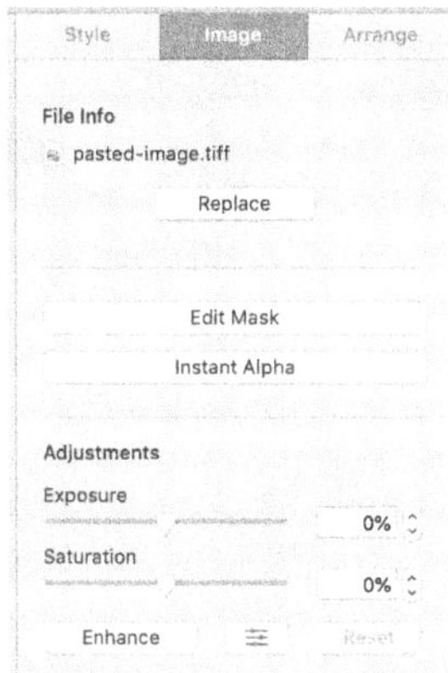

Next to the Enhance button is a control button; this will bring up more adjustment controls.

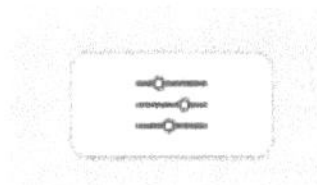

Most people probably won't need this many controls, but it's helpful to know they are there.

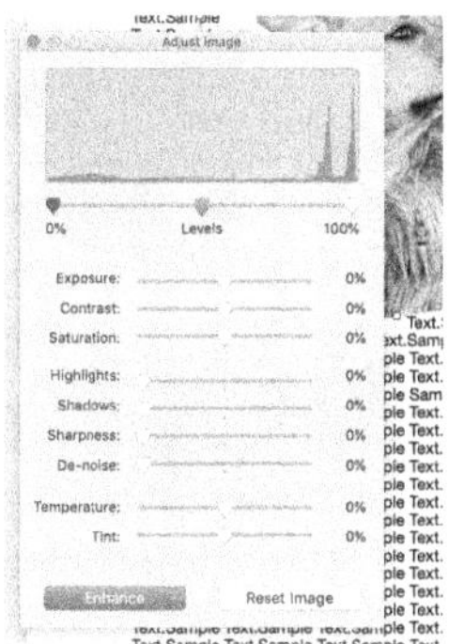

The section that may not be as easy to understand is the top section: Edit Mask and Instant Alpha.
Edit Mask is essentially an image crop. You can use this to cut off parts of the image without resizing it.

Instant Alpha is one of my personal favorite image editing tools. It removes the background of the image. It's great when your image has a very solid background (you're standing against a solid color wall, for example).

One you click on it, the cursor turns to a square box and you can click and drag over the areas you want to take out.

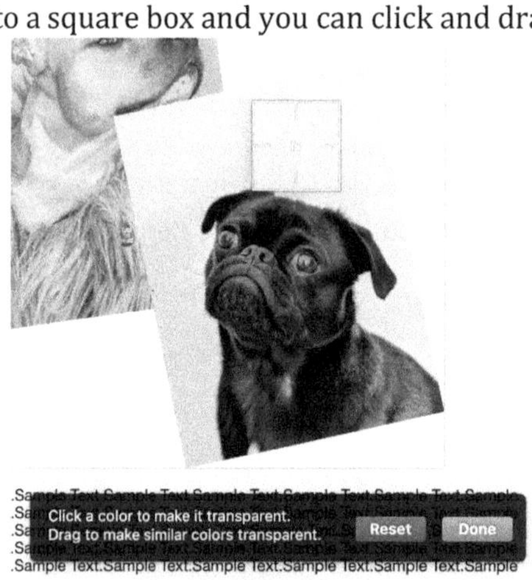

As you click, the sections that are removed will turn a different color to indicate what has been removed. When you're done, let go of the mouse and click the done button.

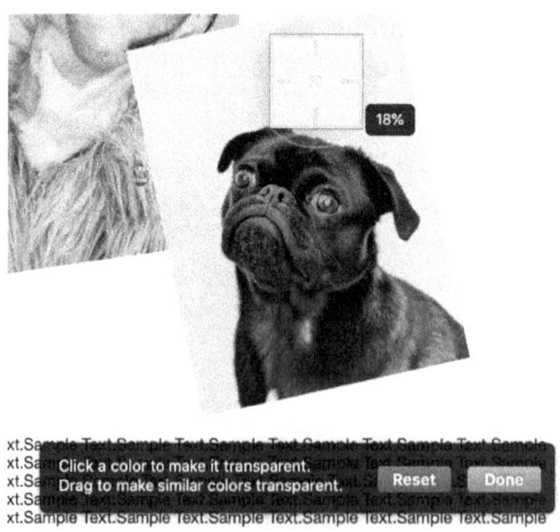

As you remove the background, it is also autocropping; so if you've removed the background from the top, the image has automatically been cropped to accommodate for it.

STYLING YOUR IMAGE

Now that we know how to move an image around, let's add some style to it.
To style your image, tap the image. Style is the first button on the image edit menu.

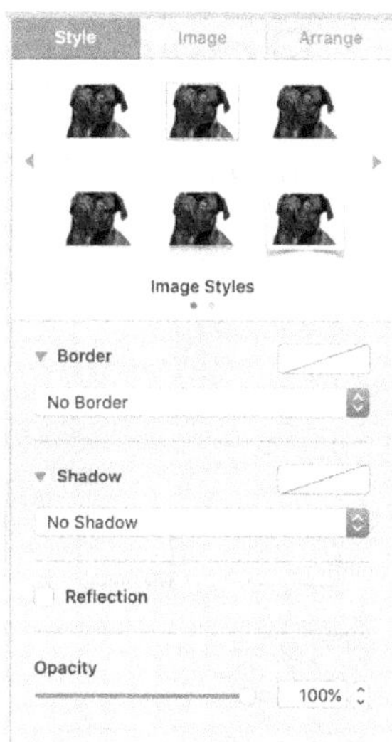

BASIC STYLES

The top box lets you add quick, pre-defined image styles to your image. For example, if you want your image to have a box around it.

Most people will probably want to do manual editing to the photo, but if you use the arrow in this section, you'll notice a + button. Once you manually make changes to the image (add your transparency, borders, etc.), you can use this button to save these changes so you can apply them to another photo that you want to have a similar look and feel.

Border

The next section is the Border; there is no border on the image by default. If you click the box with the red diagonal line, it will show a drop down of all the different styles.

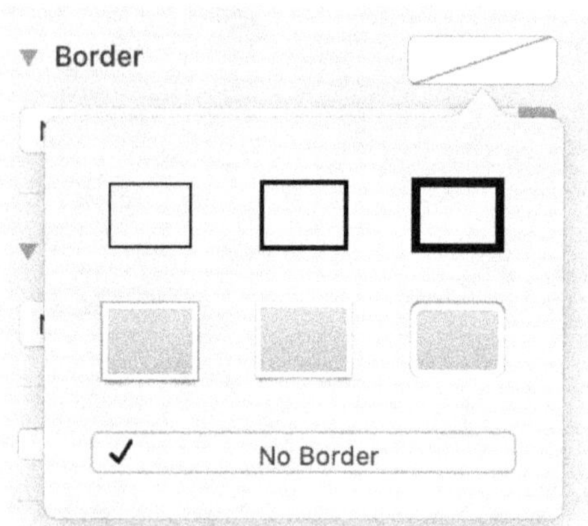

Once you pick your border style, you be able to adjust weight of the border using the slider.

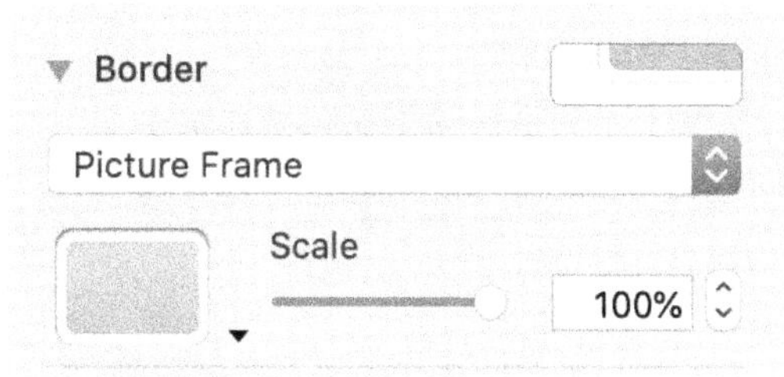

If you click the preview of the border, you will also see all the different border styles for the style that you have picked. Styles vary depending on the style you are using.

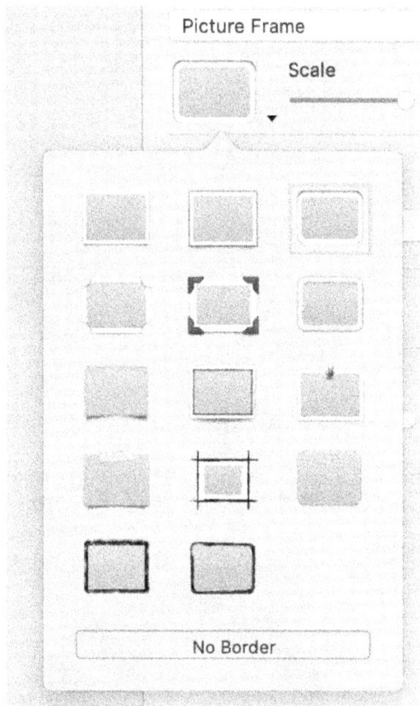

Shadow

Shadows can add a little more dimension to your photo and help it pop off the page more. It works very similar to Borders; click the thumbnail with the red line through it, then pick the shadow style.

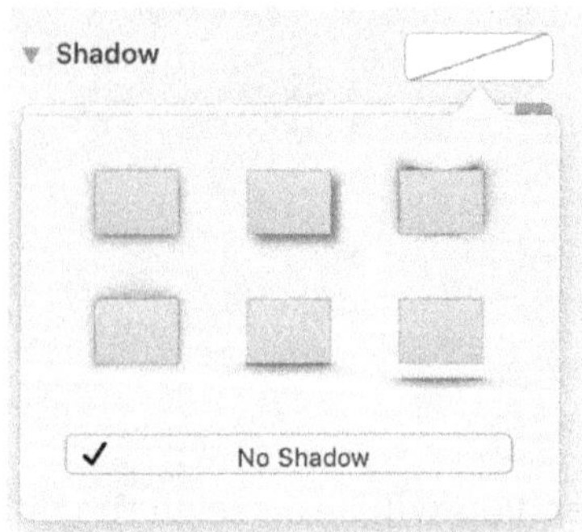

Once you pick the style, you'll get several shadow options to increase or decrease the amount of shadowing used.

As you make changes, the image will change in real-time, so you will immediately see the effects. Notice in the image below how the image has a more 3D look?

Reflection

Reflection is a simple check / uncheck box; you can use the slider to adjust the amount of reflection used, but that's the only edit available.

You can see in the example below how the reflection gave the image the appearance of an image reflecting on the page (the reflection is the darken area on the bottom of the image).

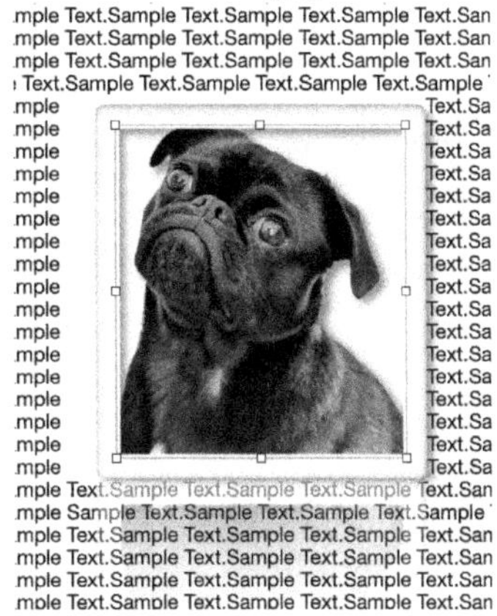

TRANSPARENCY

The final style change is transparency. Transparency makes an image more see-through (see the example below). This is great for something like a watermark, but doesn't help a lot if you don't have something below the image.

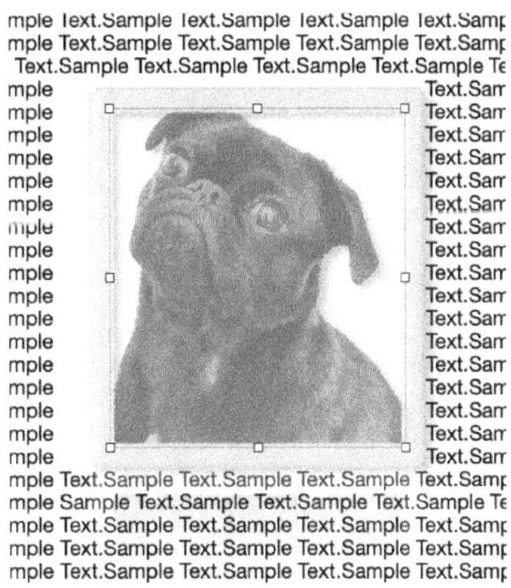

In the below example, I put the transparent image above another photo to illustrate how you can use it on top of another image.

[3]

TABLES

This chapter will cover:

- Inserting a table
- Styling a table
- Deleting a table
- Importing a table

Keynote works seamlessly with other iWork apps like Numbers and Pages; this is especially true with tables. You can insert tables into your document manually, but you can also import tables from Numbers into it. This section will show you how and will also serve as a brief introduction to Numbers for the iPad.

INSERTING A TABLE

If you have ever added a table in Word, then you may be used to picking the size and width before adding the table; in Keynote, you add the table and then adjust it accordingly.

To add a table, tap the Table button from the top menu bar (you can also use Insert > Table from the menu options at the top of MacOS). You'll have several styles to pick from, but, again, this is different from Word where you drag to the number of rows and columns that you want.

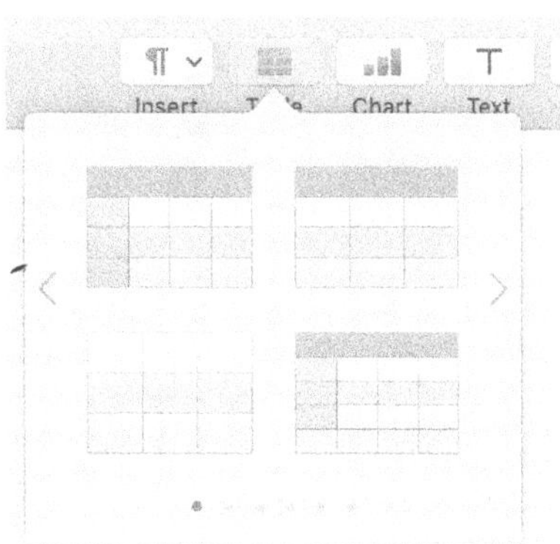

ADDING COLUMNS AND ROWS

Your table is now inserted, but chances are it's not the right size.

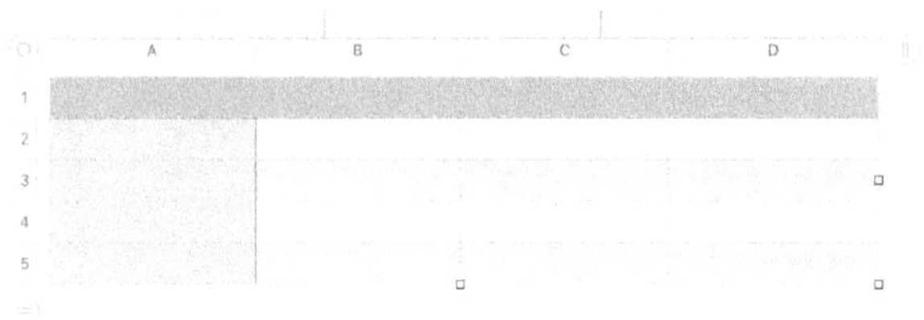

At the bottom of the last row (or side of the last column) there's a circle with two lines. Click on either of those to adjust the number of columns / rows. You can either use the up / down arrows to pick, or you can click the number and then type the amount you want.

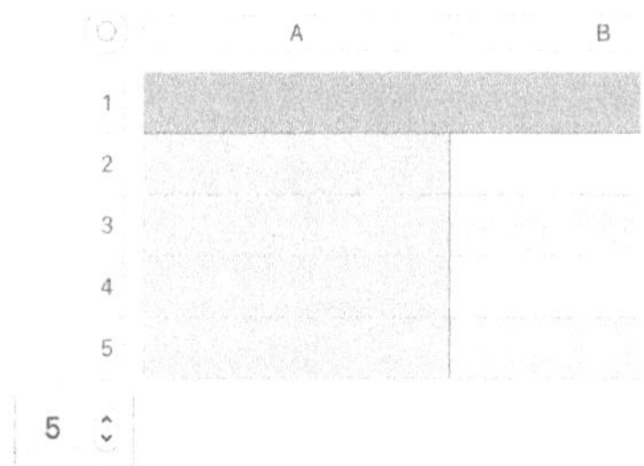

INTERACTING WITH TABLES

It can be a little tricky to work with a table in Keynote at first. Double clicking a cell will bring up the keyboard, but single clicking it will select the entire cell (Microsoft Excel users should have an easier time with this concept).

If there's no text you can single click and start typing, but if you want to edit the text that's already there, there you need to double click.

ROW / COLUMN OPTIONS

If you want to delete or add a row / column, then go to the row or column you want to make changes to, and then click the drop-down arrow. Several options will come up.

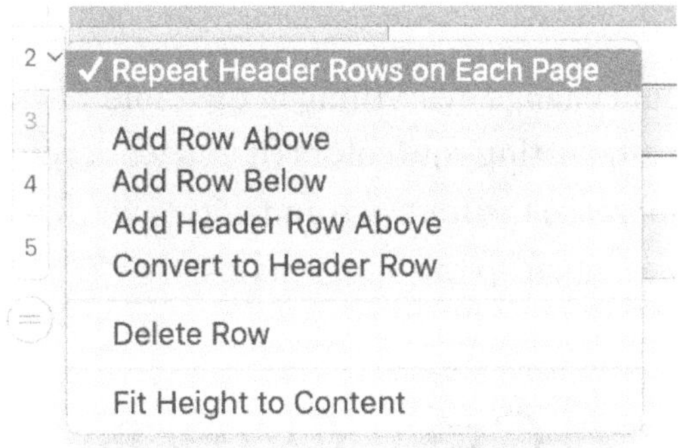

You can also click the number associated with the row / column to select all. This is helpful if you want to copy / paste a row or column.

STYLING TABLES

Apple's predefined tables look great, but if you've got a specific color scheme or style in mind, it's easy to customize your tables to match that. Just select your table (or certain cells in your table) and look to the right-side menu, which has changed to a table-style menu.

TABLE OPTIONS

The first set of options is for the entire table.

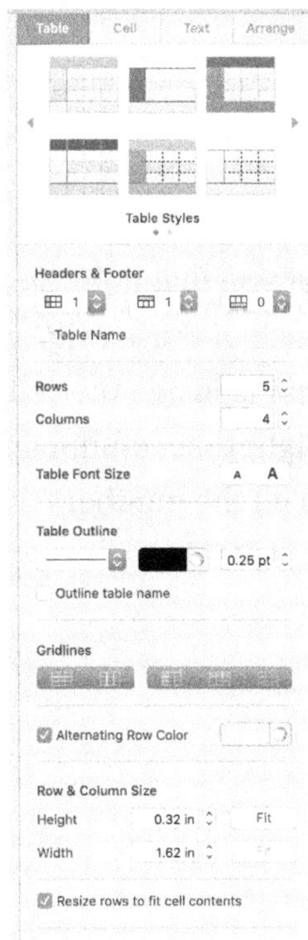

These are all options that would change everything in the table. Such as the table outline, for example if you want, you can see grids and alternating row colors (if you want row 1 white, row 2 black, row 3 white, row 4 black, etc.). You can also increase the font size and add new rows and columns.

The Table Styles at the top are similar to the image styles; they're predefined styles.

Cell Options

The table options are great if you want to change everything about the table. But what if you just want to change a cell, column, or row? That's where the Cell Option tab comes into play.

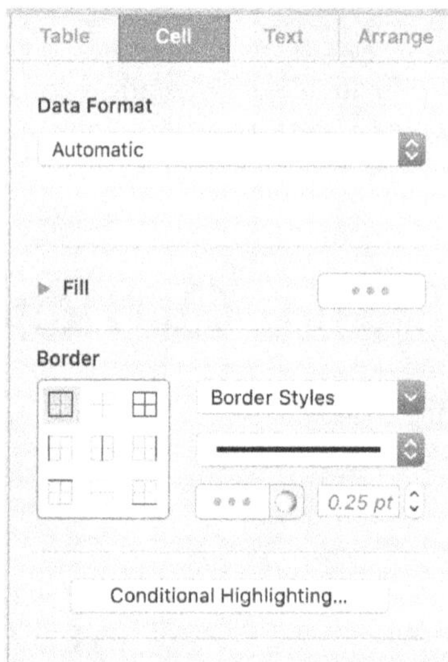

It says "Cell" but Cell here is anything that you highlight. So if you highlight one cell, then it's just that cell; but if you highlight multiple cells, then it's each of those cells.

Data Format is where you can change what is inside the cell; what does that mean? Let's say one of your columns had only currency; you could highlight that column and then say that everything in those cells was currency, so a dollar sign would be added to all the numbers in the cells.

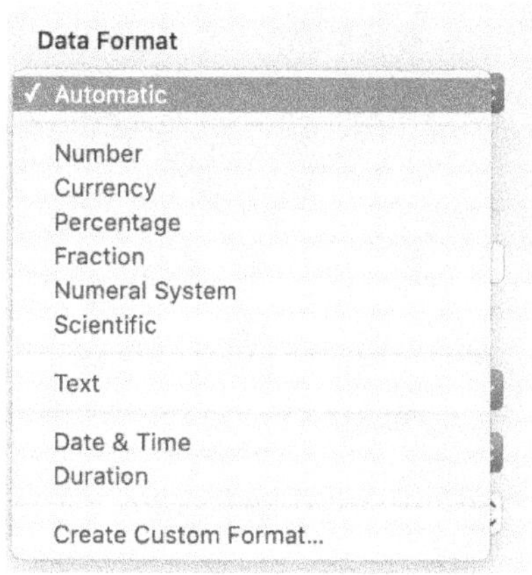

You can change the color of the cell under Fill; you can change the border style, border color, and border weight under Border.

Conditional Highlighting is a little less obvious that those first couple of options.

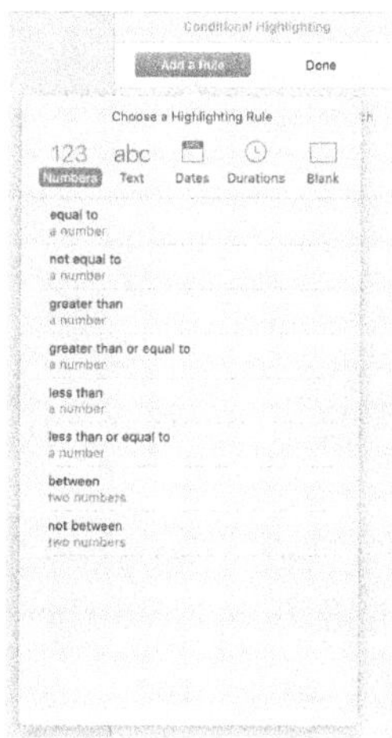

This lets you create rules; for example anytime you have a cell with the number 2, the cell text turns Bold.

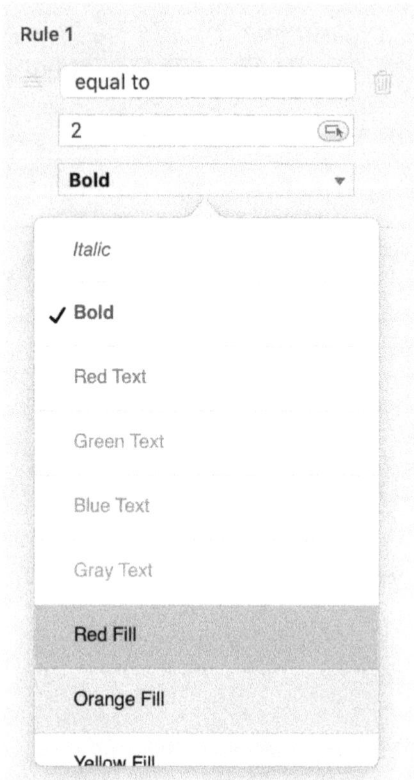

Text Options

By now you should understand how to format text. It's no different when you are doing a table. The same rules as before apply—any cell you highlight will have the text changed—so if you have the entire row highlighted, then all the text in those cells changes.

There is one box worth noting: Wrap text in cell. It's just a check / uncheck box, but it's important because if you have a long string of text and you want it to fit within a cell without going into the next cell, then you need it to wrap.

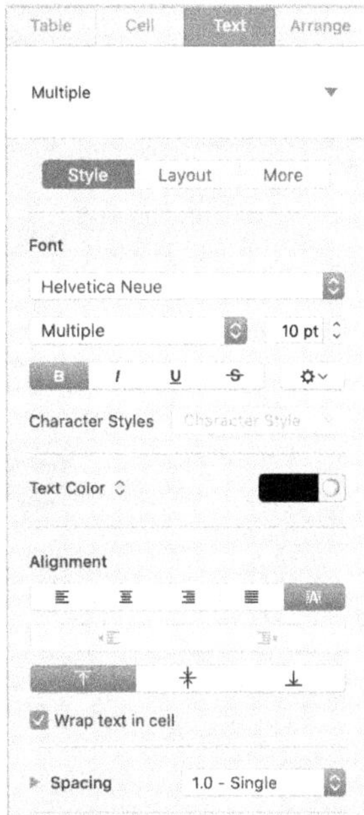

Here's an example of wrapping off.

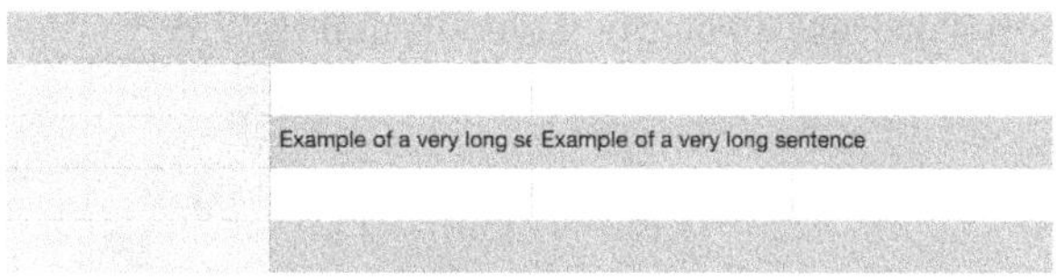

And here's what it looks like on.

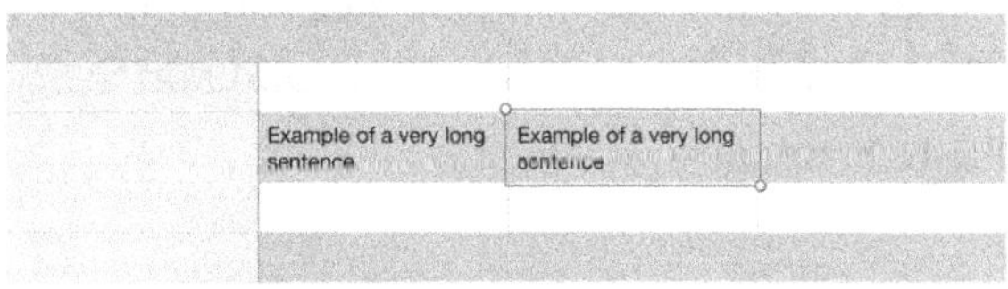

ARRANGE OPTIONS

Just like text options are the same as formatting options outside of the table, Arrange Options are almost identical that the options covered in Photo Arrangement options.

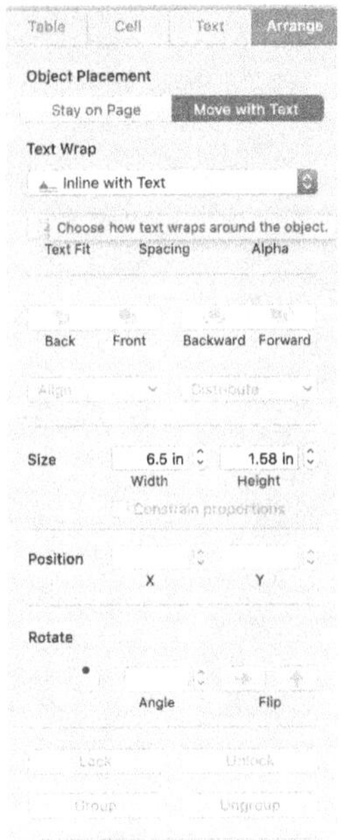

Deleting Tables

Deleting an entire table is a quick process. Click the table. Hit delete.

Importing Tables

Importing a table from somewhere else can be done a few different ways.

The first, and quickest, way is to copy and paste the table. Command V is obviously the easiest way to do this, but go to the Edit menu. Notice there's a Paste and a Paste and Match Styles? If you aren't getting the paste results that you want, try this Paste instead.

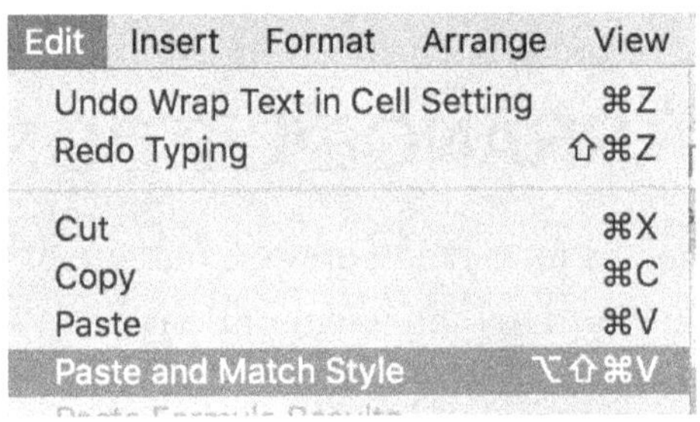

If you don't need to make changes to the table, what a lot of people prefer to do is just make a screenshot of the spreadsheet: Command + Shift + 3 (or Command + Shift + 4 if you want to do only select areas of the screen).

[4]

CHARTS

This chapter will cover:

- Inserting a Chart
- Editing Chart Data
- Styling a Chart

Charts can add color and interest to your documents, as well as help you present data more clearly. Keynote includes a powerful Charts feature that allows you to quickly create beautiful, customizable charts that really pop out of the page.

Now that you know how to use Tables, using Charts will be a breeze.

INSERTING A CHART

To insert a chart in Keynote, tap the Insert button, then tap Charts. From here, you'll choose the type of chart (bar, area, line, pie), as well as the style you want. Choose from several different color schemes in 2D, 3D, and interactive. If you change your mind about your chart choice, you can always change it later, without losing any data you've entered. Just tap on your favorite chart to insert it into your document.

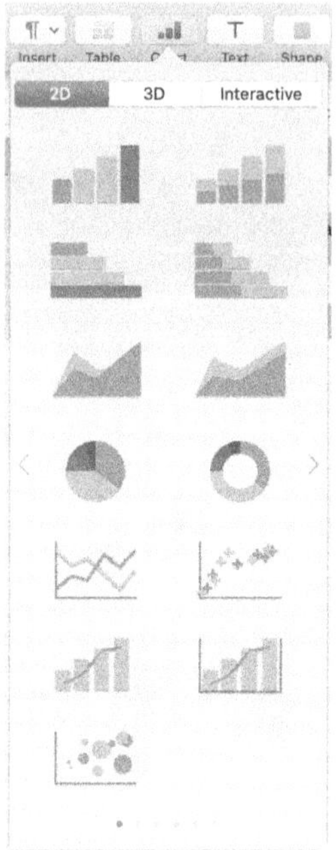

As with almost everything in Keynote, you can also add Charts from the top menu (Insert > Chart).

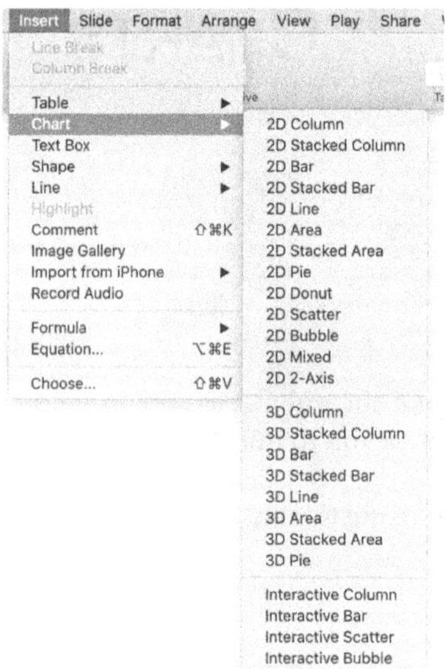

Once you have your chart picked, a chart that's already filled out will be added to your document (I'm using a Pie chart in this chapter, but the same features apply to almost all of the charts—they just look a little different).

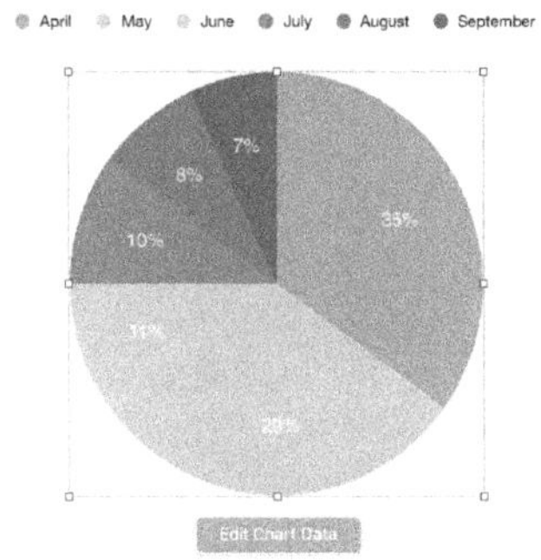

EDITING CHART DATA

It's so nice for Keynote to put a pretty chart that's all filled out into our document, right? Sure! But wouldn't it be nicer if it had meaningful data? To add your own data, click Edit Chart Data. This brings up a mini table that you can edit with whatever information you want.

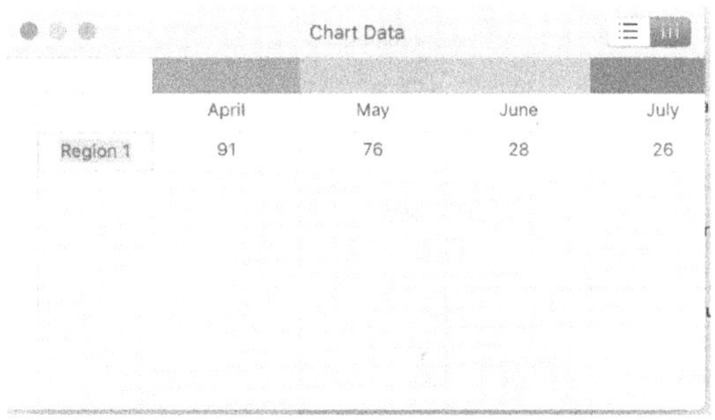

I'm going to replace the months with the names of states, and use an entirely different data range. The chart changes with each change I make in the table. Notice the chart below is completely different from the one above?

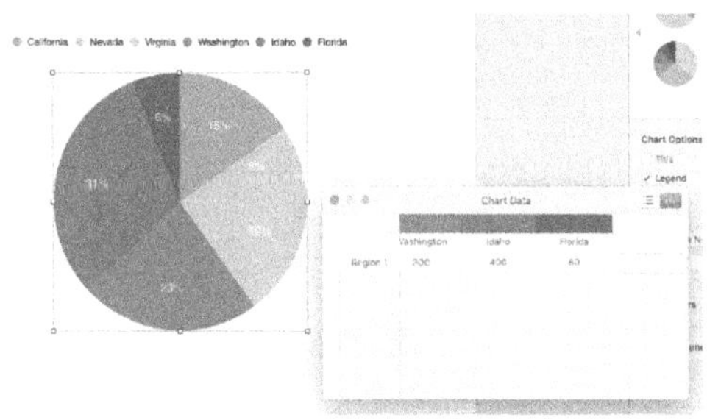

You can enter additional rows if you need to—but this won't work on all charts (like the pie chart).

STYLING YOUR PIE CHART

Now that you have the data you want, it's time to style it.
If you did a pie chart, then you'll see three options on the side (Chart, Wedges, Arrange).

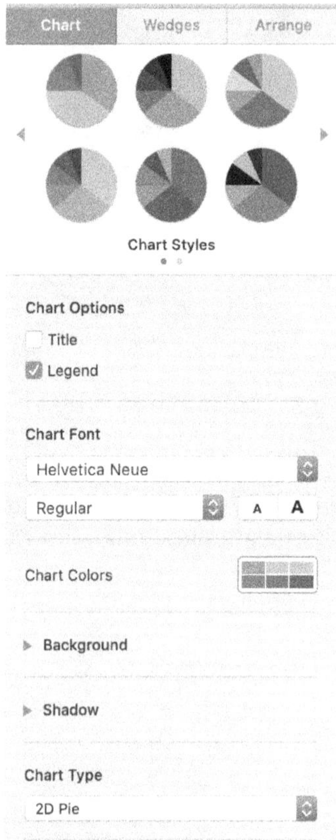

Other charts (like bar charts) have four (Chart, Axis, Series, Arrange).

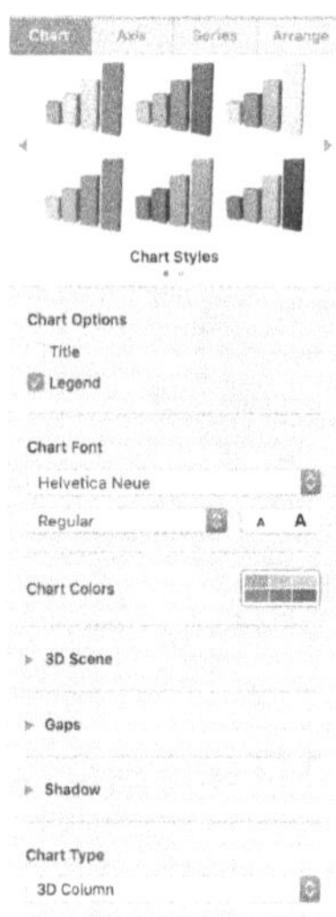

I'll go over the two extra options for a bar chart in the next section.

In the Chart section you can make changes to the entire chart. By default the chart has no title, but if you check off the box, a title (cleverly named "Title") is added to your chart; you'll probably want to name it something else. To do that (and this also applies to renaming pretty much anything in your chart) double click on it and start typing.

Below the title is where you can change the font; and under that, the chart colors. When you click on the chart colors, it gives you a whole host of pre-defined colors. But what if you want to pick your own?

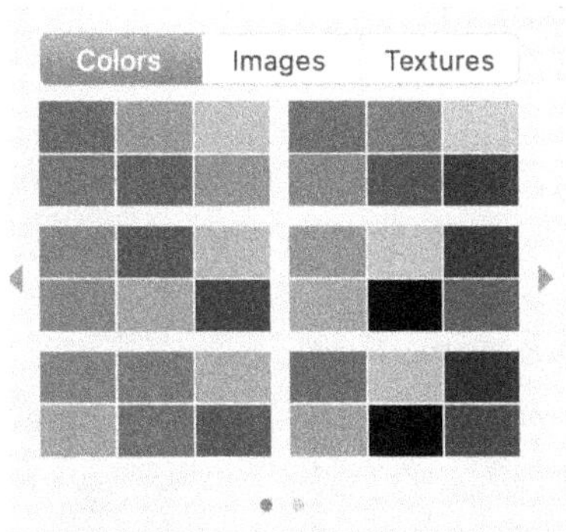

There's one extra small step to pick your own colors. You have to double click on the wedge that you want to change the color of, and then over on the menu options to the right of it, click Style (Style is a new option that's only there if you double click the wedge). From here, you can pick a color under "Fill."

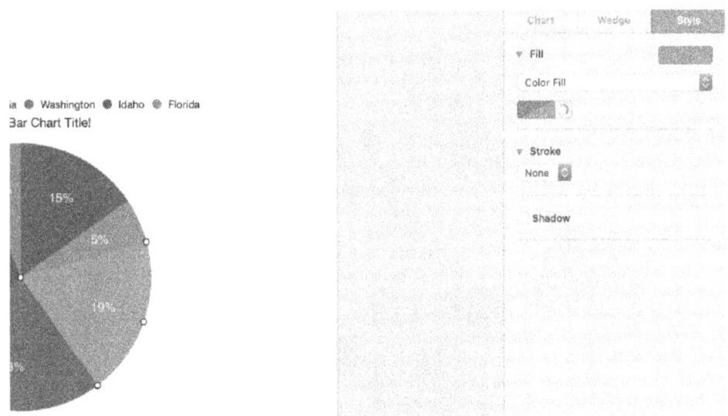

While we are in this section, let's go just under it to Stroke and Shadow. Both of these options help a wedge stand out a little. This is useful if you want to illustrate one area of the chart of others. See in the example below how I added a dotted line (and increased the line weight to 4) and also added a shadow.

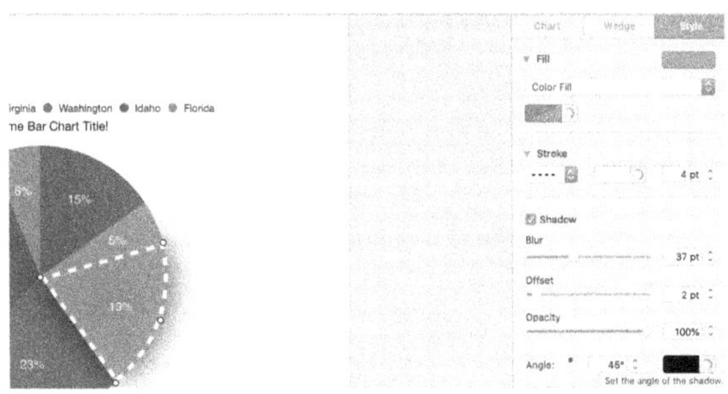

If you really want that wedge to stand out, try pulling it apart from the chart. You can do that by clicking on the Wedge option, and then changing the Wedge Position. Look at the example below; the wedge is now separated in the chart.

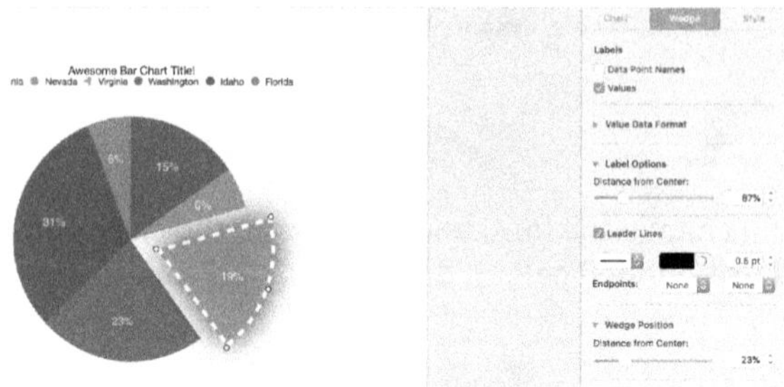

Now let's go back to the chart section and look at the other options we can apply to the entire chart. You can give it a background, add a shadow to it, and finally, change the Chart Type. You can make it a different Pie chart or turn it into a line chart (note: this will probably interfere with your data and you may have to redo some of it).

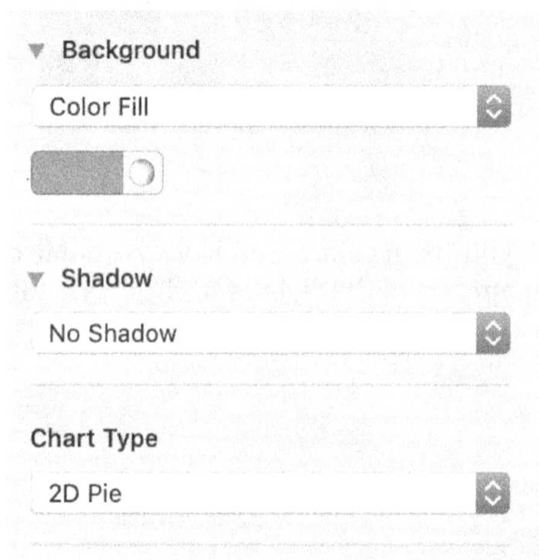

We saw how going to the Wedge section could separate your single wedge from the rest. If you don't double click the wedge and change it, below is what happens.

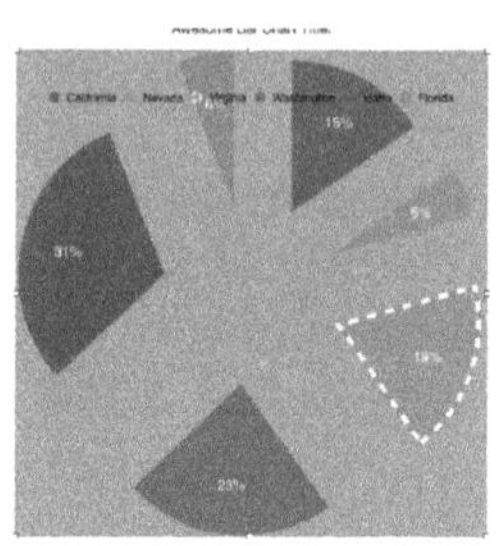

All the wedges separate. If that's what you want, then perfect! If that's not what you want, undo and then double click the wedge you want to separate.

Checking off Data Point Names will put the names of the value in the chart (you can also keep it in the Legend).

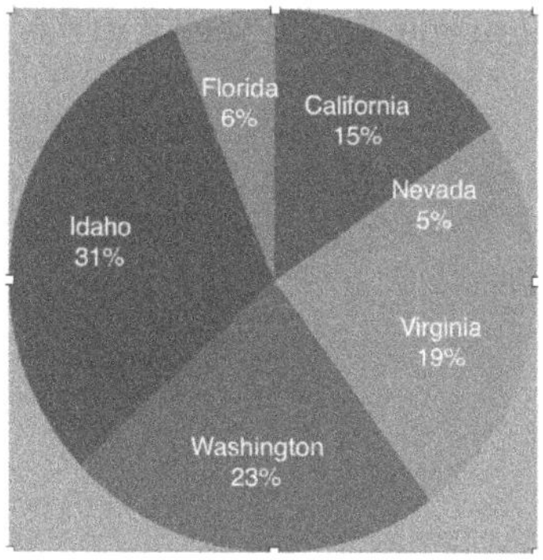

The values on the chart are currently showing as a percentage; if you prefer showing them as a number (or another value type), you can change this under Value Format.

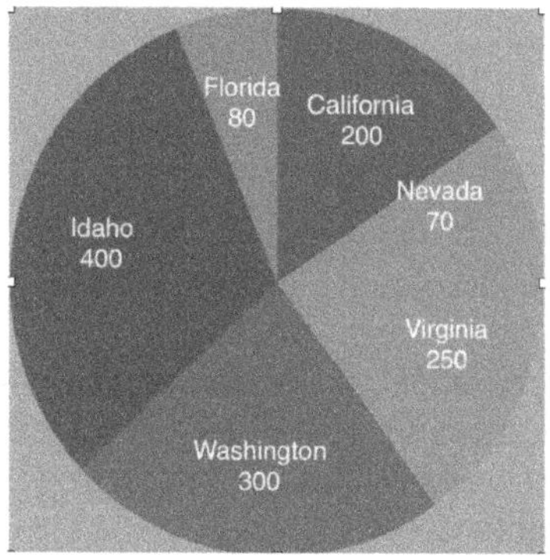

If you check off Lender Lines, you probably won't notice a difference; to see what the lines are, click the Straight drop-down and change it to Angled.

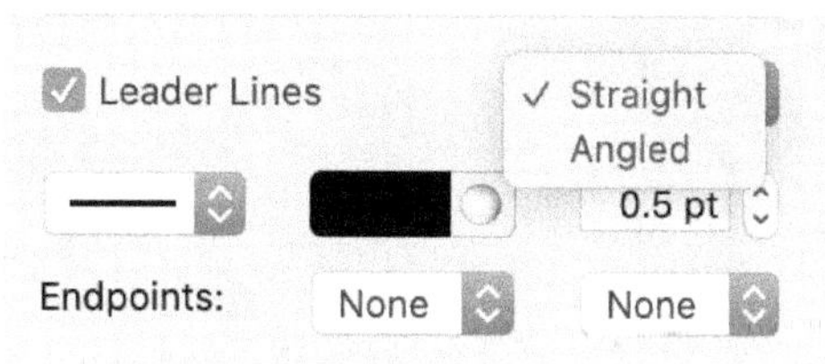

You should now see lines to the side of the chart.

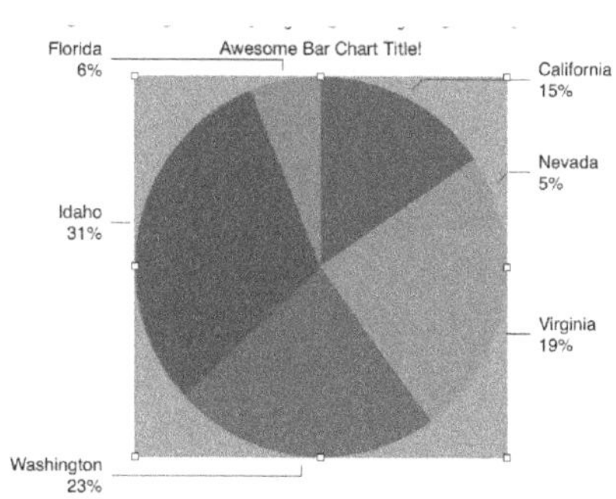

The arrange option should look familiar to you. You've seen it in the Tables section and the Photos section; it's the same features.

Styling Your Bar Chart

Now that you know how to style a Pie Chart, you'll have no problem with the Bar Chart; it's basically the same, but with more options for labels.

In the axis sub-tab, you can turn category labels, series names, gridlines and titles on and off. Similarly, in the Y-axis or X-axis sub-tab, you can turn value labels, gridlines and titles on and off. Here you can also specify the number format you'd like to use and adjust the value scale settings. Number formatting includes the option to add prefixes and suffixes, like currency symbols or suffixes like %, millions, etc.

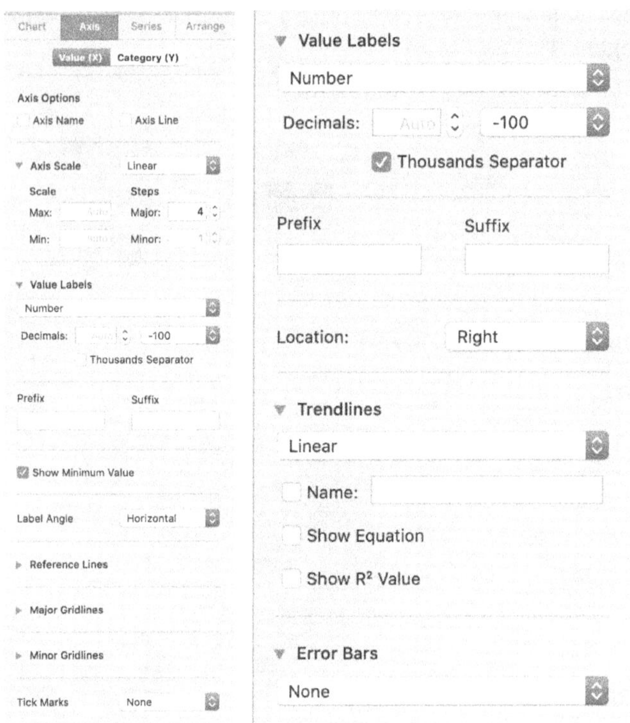

Note: the contents of the sub-tabs change depending on the orientation of your chart. The number formatting option may appear under either the x- or y-axis, depending on the type of chart you've inserted.

[5]

Shapes

This chapter will cover:

- Inserting a Shape
- Resizing Shapes
- Creating Text Boxes

Pictures are great! They really help your document look snazzy. But there's one more type of graphical illustration you should consider: shapes. Shapes can be great additions to a document – they can be used to draw attention to an area of a document or to illustrate your points graphically. Keynote offers a number of handy pre-made shapes for you to use, and I'll show you how to get the most out of them.

Inserting a Shape

To insert a shape into a document, click the shape button or go to Insert > Shape from the top menu. This will bring up all of the shapes available for you. Find the one you like and click it to insert it.

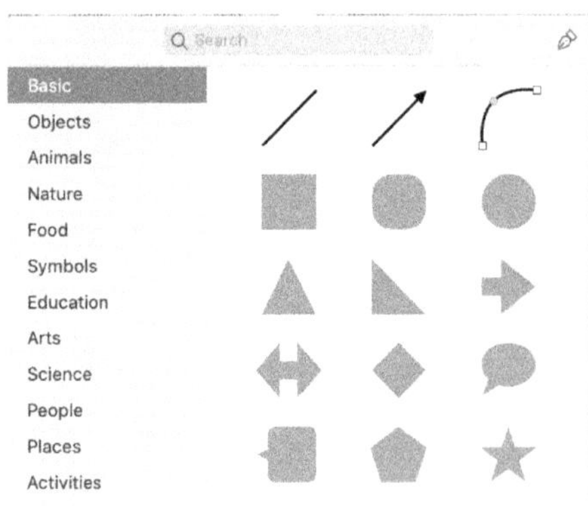

Remember that you can change the color, border and shadow/reflection effects later!

Shapes sounds a little misleading. If you're like me, you're probably thinking square, circle, etc. But shapes in Keynote are kind of like clipart. Yes, basic shapes are there, but so are other things. In the example below I searched for "Dog" and got five results.

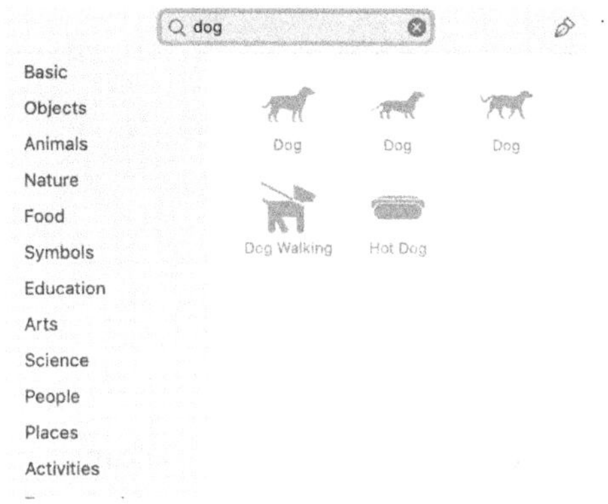

Resizing Shapes and Adjusting Proportions

Shape resizing is just like resizing photos: tap on a corner and drag it to the desired size. However, with Shapes, you can also adjust proportions. What does that mean? It's better shown than explained. Double tap your trackpad on the shape to bring up the shape options. Now click "Make Editable."

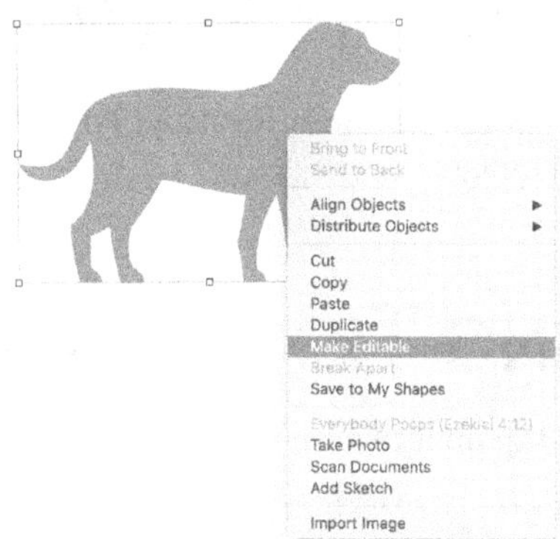

There are now a bunch of dots on the shape. These represent points that you can adjust.

As an example, I moved the point inward from the dog's stomach and look what happened.

By default, you make these changes with a curved point, but you can change this by bringing the options up again. Notice the three different points?

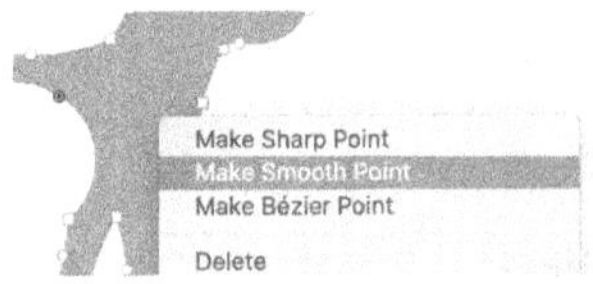

Moving and Rotating Shapes

To move a shape, simply tap on it and drag it to a new location. To rotate a shape, click image then press the command button—just like you would an image.

Adding Text to a Shape

To add text on top of a shape, double-tap on it to activate its text field. Then just type your text!

Creating Text Boxes

There's one more type of shape, but it's not under shape. It's a Text Box. Text Boxes are exactly what they sound like—floating boxes that have text.

Why use Text Box instead of typing out the text? Ideally, you want to use them when you are making something like a title—not when you are typing out your epic novel. It's for short text that you want to stand out.

Unlike standard text, Text Boxes are treated in the same way images are, so you can easily move them around and have other things wrap around them.

To get started, click the T in the menu.

You can also do Insert > Text Box.

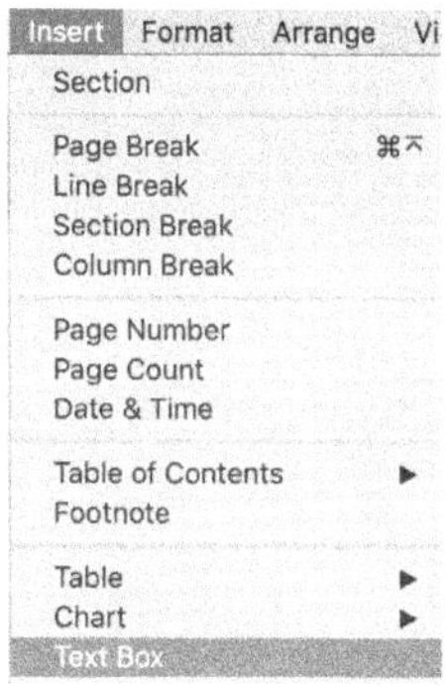

This puts a floating box with generic text in your document.

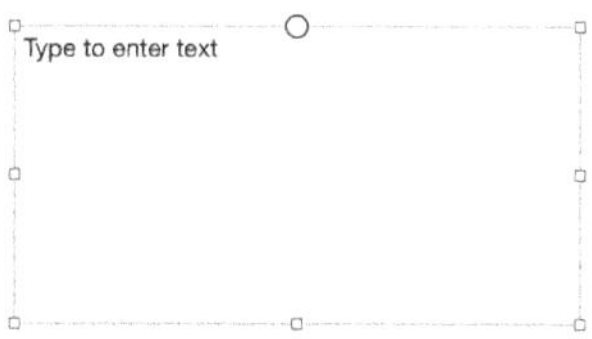

You can change the color of the box and more by clicking on Style; it has all the same types of options that you'd find in the Image or Shape options.

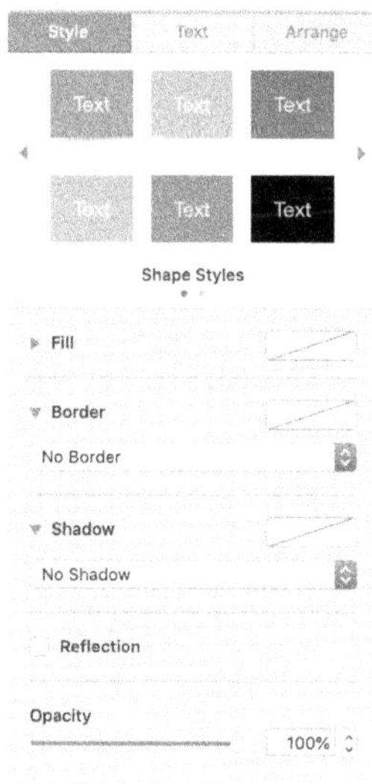

Because it's a Shape, you are able to edit it like you would a shape. In the below example, I curved out the bottom portion of the box.

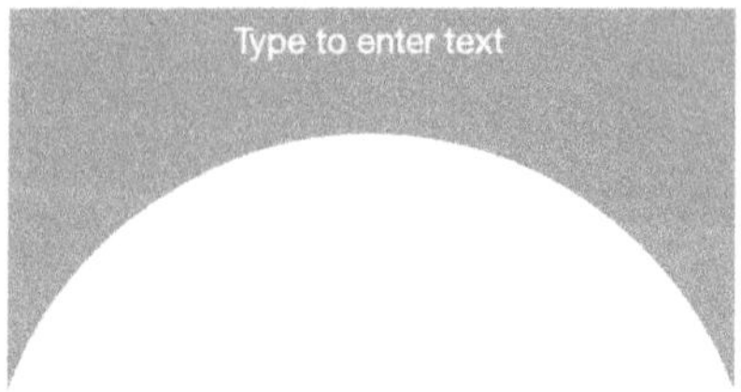

Styling Shapes and Text Boxes

Styling Shapes and Text boxes is the same as styling an image, so I won't repeat myself here. If you are confused about styling, refer to the section in the Photos chapter.

[6]

TEMPLATES

This chapter will cover:

- Using third-part Keynote Templates
- Creating your own Templates

Keynote comes with several templates. What exactly is a Template? A Template is a document that's already formatted—complete with text and images. Why would you want that? The idea is you delete the text (and replace the images) to make it your own, but save time on the sometimes complicated formatting aspect of it.

USING THIRD-PARTY KEYNOTE TEMPLATES

The templates in Keynote are nice, but if you use it long enough, you probably will want a few more; if you get to that place, there are websites (and even apps), which sell Keynote templates (sometimes they are free). A basically web search for "Keynote templates" or even "free Keynote templates" will show you what I mean.

Word of caution: like anything you download, use at your own risk. If a website looks sketchy, be wary of downloading a template.

To use a template like this, just go to the website, find a template you like, follow the site's instructions to download it to your computer's hard drive, and then sync it with your iPad as if it were any other Keynote document, using the iTunes File Sharing syncing process discussed in "Basic Features."

After that, Keynote can open the template and you can begin to edit it. It is strongly recommended to make a duplicate of your template document before you begin working on it, so that you will continue to have a blank one for later if you need it.

These third party templates are great for more variety—for example, if you are looking to give your resume a little more creativity.

CREATING YOUR OWN "TEMPLATES"

Unfortunately, Keynote currently does not allow you to save templates in the Create New Document screen. However, you can work around this sorely missed feature by setting up your "template" as a regular Keynote document.

Personally, I make a duplicate of the document (i.e. File > Duplicate) and name it something like "Resume Template."

[7]

SHARING AND EXPORTING DOCUMENT

This chapter will cover:

- Sharing your presentation

In spite of the popularity of iPhones and iPads, Apple users still often find themselves marooned in a Windows-based world. Keynote is a wonderful program, but it's incomprehensible to Microsoft PowerPoint. Fortunately, Keynote offers several methods for sharing and exporting Keynote documents in multiple formats. Keynote also makes moving documents across Apple devices absolutely effortless, thanks to iCloud.

SYNCING DOCUMENTS WITH ICLOUD

If you've enabled iCloud in your Keynote app, your documents will be synced across your devices automatically with absolutely no work required on your part. You can even access your documents online from any internet connection at www.icloud.com.

EMAILING A DOCUMENT FROM KEYNOTE

E-mailing documents is one of the most straightforward methods of sharing your document. Go to Share > Send a Copy.

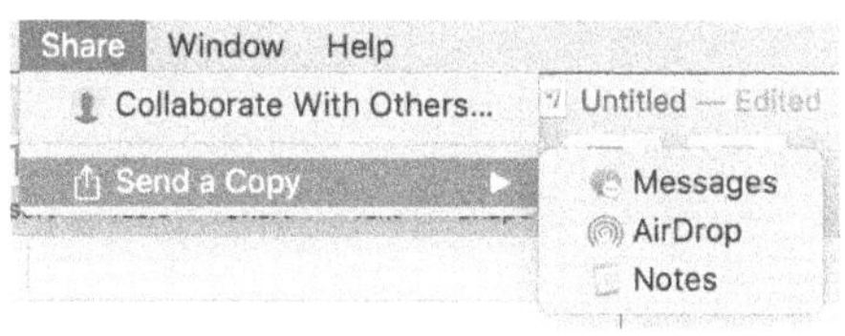

COLLABORATING

You can also collaborate on a document by going to Share > Collaborate With Others.

This brings up an option that asks how you would like the share the document.

I recommend clicking on the Share Options drop down to make sure the right permissions are enabled. For example, you can make the document readable to anyone you share it with or anyone who gets the document; you can also give the user permission to make changes.

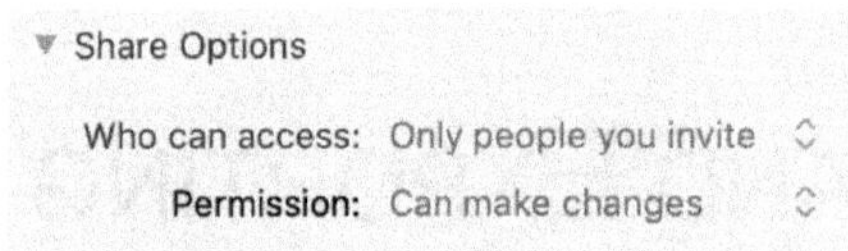

Export a Keynote Document

By default, you'll be saving your file as a .Keynote document. That's great if you have Keynote, but if you're sharing it (or opening it) on a computer that doesn't have Keynote—or you want to create a universal PDF that anyone can see- then you'll need to export it.

This is pretty straightforward. Go to File > Export.

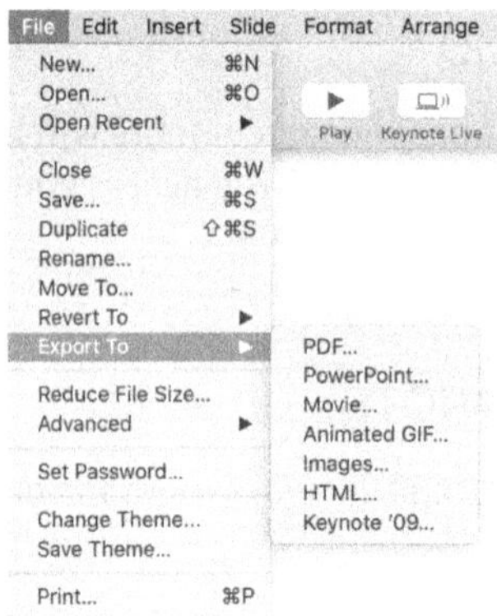

There are seven different file types:

- PDF
- PowerPoint
- Movie
- Animated GIF
- Images
- HTML
- Keynote '09

PDF is the best option if you want to preserve all the formatting in the document and make it look exactly as it appears in Keynote.

Movie and Animated GIF are good if you are sticking it somewhere like a website and you are letting it present itself—in other words, the slides progress without you clicking. Images will export each slide as an Image. And HTML turns your presentation into a website of sorts.

EXPORTING A MOVIE

Why would you want to make a movie out of your presentation? There are a number of reasons people do this; the obvious is to deliver presentations without a speaker. Exporting a movie, however, can be used for digital signage, webpages and lots more.

There are two types of moving presentations that you can export: movie and animated GIF. An animated GIF is typically shorter, smaller in size (and resolution), doesn't have sound; that makes it great for websites.

Depending on what you export, you'll have a couple of different options.

For movies, it will ask if it will play automatically, what slides will be in it (All slides is the default), and how long between slides and builds (i.e. the elements you have added - like images and text boxes—assuming you have transitions applied to them); the last option is the resolution.

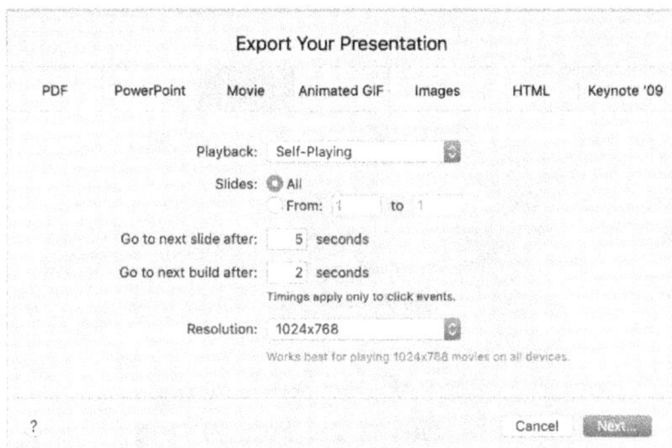

For animated GIFs it will ask what slides, the resolution, and the Frame rate (more frame rate will typically increase your file size).

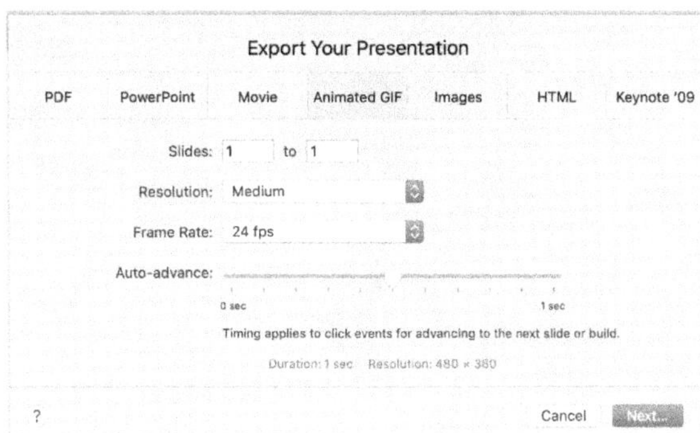

PRINTING

To print a document, go to File > Print.

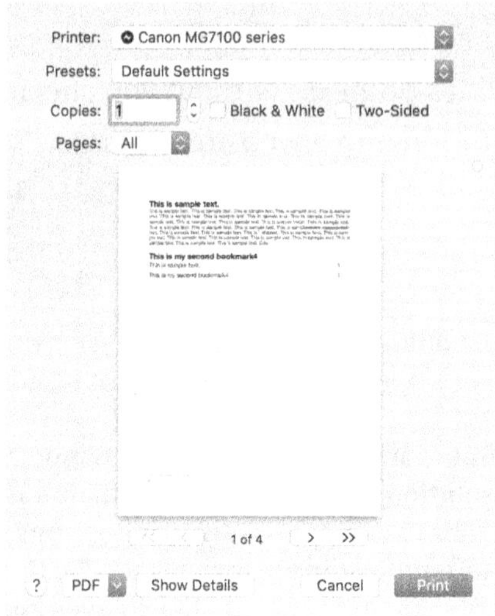

At the bottom of the print menu, there's also an option to save as a PDF. It's Keynote's version of Print to File.

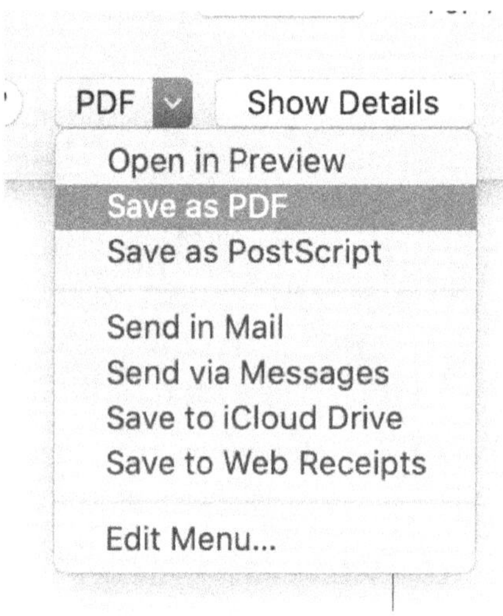

[8]

Understanding Accessibility On the Mac

This chapter will cover:

- Sharing documents
- Exporting documents

Accessibility helps you adjust the computer if you have any kind of impairment or disability. It lets you change things like making the display larger, having a voiceover that describes what's on your screen, and put captions on videos when available. This might be helpful for you in Pages.

To open Accessibility, click System Settings and Accessibility. On the left side of the box that comes up will be all the various things you can change. Clicking on each one will create more options.

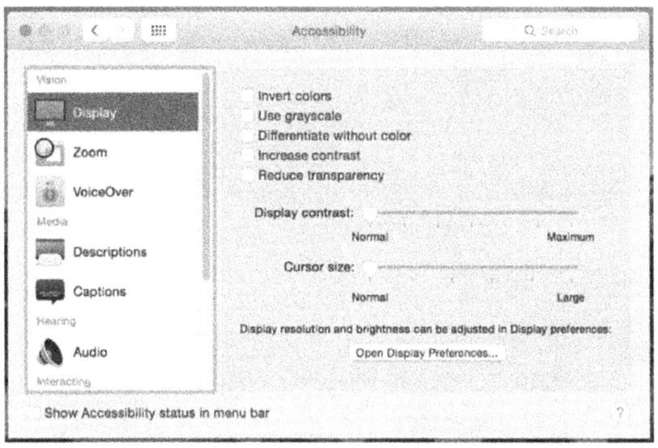

Vision

Under Display, you can make the screen grayscale, invert colors, decrease the contrast, etc. Zoom allows you to create a zoom effect over smaller areas of the screen when you hit a keyboard shortcut. VoiceOver reads back any text that's on the screen.

Media

The Media section includes a few different settings for audio and video playback. Click on Descriptions to enable spoken descriptions for videos.

Captions will apply subtitles and captions to videos.

HEARING

The Sound tab provides options for the hearing disabled. You can choose to set up a visual flash of the screen each time an alert sound is played, and also decide if you'd like to play stereo audio as mono instead.

INTERACTING

Keyboard includes settings for Sticky Keys and Slow Keys. Sticky Keys allows certain buttons to remain activated without you having to hold down the key. For example, if you have Sticky Keys turned on and want to copy some text, instead of holding down Command-C at the same time, you could press the Command button first, followed by the C key. When enabled, you'll hear a lock sound, and any time you use a modifier key like Command, a large icon will appear in the top right corner of the screen indicating that a Sticky Key combination has been started. Slow Keys increases the amount of time between a button press and activation, so if you press Enter, it will take a little longer to actually process.

Mouse & Trackpad features settings like Mouse Keys, which lets you move the mouse around using the number pad on your keyboard, double-click speed, and the option to ignore the built-in Trackpad (on MacBooks) if there is a separate mouse or Trackpad connected to the computer.

Switch Control requires you to enter your administrator password before making any changes, because it's a powerful function that allows you to control the computer using one or more switches that you designate. You can also modify other settings like what to do while navigating, determine pointer precision, and change the size for the Switch Control cursor.

The Dictation tab does exactly what it sounds like—it lets you dictate commands and write or edit text using only your voice. To enable dictation, you first need to click on the bottom button that says Open Dictation & Speech Preferences and selecting the On radio button.

VOICE CONTROL

Voice Control lets you control your computer with your voice.

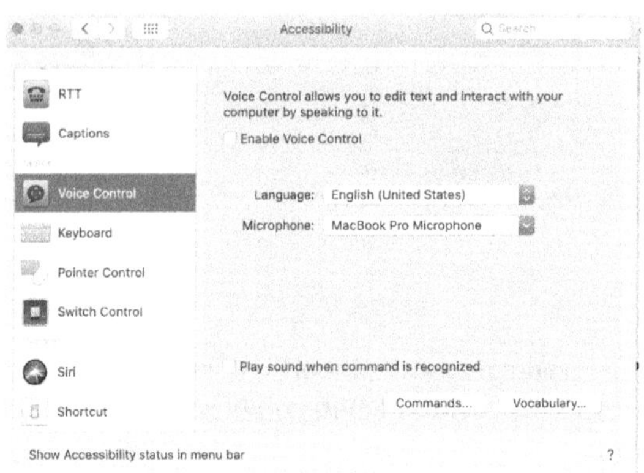

APPENDIX: KEYBOARD SHORTCUTS

GENERAL KEYBOARD SHORTCUTS

Action	Shortcut
Close a window	Command-W
Close all windows	Option-Command-W
Duplicate a document	Shift-Command-S
Enter full-screen view	Control-Command-F
Hide or show sidebars on the right side of the Keynote window	Option-Command-I
Hide or show the toolbar	Option-Command-T
Hide Keynote	Command-H
Hide windows of other applications	Option-Command-H
Minimize a window	Command-M
Minimize all windows	Option-Command-M
Open a new document	Command-N
Open an existing document	Command-O
Open the Page Setup window	Shift-Command-P
Print a document	Command-P
Quit Keynote	Command-Q
Quit Keynote and keep windows open	Option-Command-Q
Rearrange an item in the toolbar	Command-drag
Redo the last action	Shift-Command-Z

Remove an item from the toolbar	Command-drag away from the toolbar
Return to actual size	Command-0
Save a document	Command-S
Save As	Option-Shift-Command-S
Show or hide layout boundaries	Shift-Command-L
Show or hide the ruler	Command-R
Show or hide the tab bar	Shift-Command-T
Show page thumbnails	Option-Command-P
Show the Colors window	Shift-Command-C
Start dictation	Press Fn twice
Undo the last action	Command-Z
Zoom in	Command-Right Angle Bracket (>)
Zoom out	Command-Left Angle Bracket (<)
Zoom to selection	Shift-Command-0

Formatting Keyboard Shortcuts

Action	Shortcut
Show the Fonts window	Command-T
Show the Colors window	Shift-Command-C
Apply boldface to selected text	Command-B
Apply italic to selected text	Command-I
Apply underline to selected text	Command-U
Make the font size bigger	Command-Plus Sign (+)
Make the font size smaller	Command-Minus Sign (-)
Make the text superscript	Control-Shift-Command-Plus Sign (+)

Make the text subscript	Control-Command-Minus Sign (-)
Insert an equation	Option-Command-E
Decrease the indent level of a list item	Shift-Tab
Increase the indent level of a list item	Tab
Turn text into a link	Command-K
Add a bookmark	Option-Command-B
Cut the selection	Command-X
Copy the selection	Command-C
Copy the paragraph style	Option-Command-C
Paste the selection	Command-V
Paste the paragraph style	Option-Command-V
Paste and match the style of the destination text	Option-Shift-Command-V
Copy the graphic style of text	Option-Command-C
Paste the graphic style of text	Option-Command-V
Add a range to (or remove it from) the selection	Shift-drag
Insert a nonbreaking space	Option-Space bar
Insert a line break (soft return)	Shift-Return
Insert a paragraph break	Return
Insert a new line after the insertion point	Control-O
Insert a page break	Fn-Command-Return
Enter special characters	Control-Command-Space bar
Transpose the characters on either side of the insertion point	Control-T

Add an EndNote bibliography	Shift-Option-Command-E

About the Author

Scott La Counte is a librarian and writer. His first book, *Quiet, Please: Dispatches from a Public Librarian* (Da Capo 2008) was the editor's choice for the Chicago Tribune and a Discovery title for the Los Angeles Times; in 2011, he published the YA book The N00b Warriors, which became a #1 Amazon bestseller; his most recent book is *#OrganicJesus: Finding Your Way to an Unprocessed, GMO-Free Christianity* (Kregel 2016).

He has written dozens of best-selling how-to guides on tech products.

You can connect with him at ScottDouglas.org.

CPSIA information can be obtained
at www.ICGtesting.com
Printed in the USA
BVHW011149280720
584857BV00011B/157

9 781629 175171